Science Fiction in India: Parallel Worlds and Postcolonial Paradigms is possibly the first anthology of scholarship to focus exclusively on Indian science fiction. The chapters collected in this volume address not only established authors and works now considered 'classics' of Indian science fiction, but also works less known to the outside world, works that are new, and works both in English and other Indian languages. The editors expertly bind these myriad perspectives together through their nuanced introductions to each chapter. Foregrounding new critical voices and fresh perspectives on existing debates, this book is an important addition to the growing field of scholarship on Indian science fiction.

—Suparno Banerjee, Associate Professor of English, Texas State University and author of *Indian Science Fiction: Patterns, History and Hybridity*

Shweta Khilnani and Ritwick Bhattacharjee's *Science Fiction in India: Parallel Worlds and Postcolonial Paradigms* is a valuable addition to the growing corpus of critical writing on Indian science fiction. At a time when a minor renaissance of the genre is taking shape, the editors' and essayists' engagement with major critical questions regarding science fiction produced in India since the genre's inception is timely and pertinent, especially in the light of a paucity of adequate assessments of its significance, only begun to be remedied recently. The varied perspectives brought to bear here on a wide range of texts, from historical SF in the Indian languages to contemporary SF narratives in various subgenres in both English and regional languages, are fresh and analytically rigorous and will certainly stimulate further debate.

—Tarun K. Saint, Editor of the series *The Gollancz Book of South Asian Science Fiction* (vols. 1 and 2)

This excellent collection of chapters does the much needed and much awaited task of spotlighting the long history and complex traditions of Indian science-fiction writing. Science fiction scholarship predominantly privileges the West-European writers and literary theorists. This book, by contrast, draws our attention to the non-West—alternative political contexts, vernacular imaginations and the rigours of social change and scientific developments all of which contributed to the making of the Indian science fiction. At a time when the improbable seems routine, and science fiction dominates our global cultural landscape and collective imaginations, this book is a valuable and timely contribution for those interested in expanding their knowledge of the genre beyond Europe.

—Gautam Basu Thakur, Associate Professor of English,
Boise State University

A much-needed, brilliantly edited collection [alt. anthology] of pioneering studies in Indian science fiction and fantasy. Rich in original conceptual frameworks and open problems, this work will be of great use for scholars interested in the genre.

—Anil Menon, Author of *Half of What I Say*

SCIENCE FICTION IN INDIA

SCIENCE FICTION IN INDIA

Parallel Worlds and Postcolonial Paradigms

Edited by

Shweta Khilnani and Ritwick Bhattacharjee

BLOOMSBURY
NEW DELHI • LONDON • OXFORD • NEW YORK • SYDNEY

BLOOMSBURY INDIA
Bloomsbury Publishing India Pvt. Ltd
Second Floor, LSC Building No. 4, DDA Complex, Pocket C – 6 & 7,
Vasant Kunj, New Delhi, 110070

BLOOMSBURY, BLOOMSBURY INDIA and the Diana logo
are trademarks of Bloomsbury Publishing Plc

First published in India 2022
This edition published 2022

Bloomsbury Academic
An imprint of Bloomsbury Publishing Plc

ISBN: HB: 978-93-54353-37-6 ; eBook: 978-93-54353-43-7
2 4 6 8 10 9 7 5 3 1

Typeset in Minion Pro by Manipal Technologies Limited
Printed and bound in India by Replika Press Pvt. Ltd.

To both Science and Fiction

CONTENTS

ACKNOWLEDGEMENTS

The first and, perhaps, most important gratitude that the editors wish to show is to Sri Guru Tegh Bahadur Khalsa College, University of Delhi, and its principal, Professor Jaswinder Singh, for hosting the workshop that ultimately allowed this book to see the light of day. The project would not have been possible without the constant support of our principal at whatever level necessary. We would also like to take this moment and thank Prof. Angelie Multani (IIT Delhi), Dr Gautam Basu Thakur (Boise State University) and Dr Sachita Kaushal (Delhi University), Prof. Shaswati Mazumdar (Retd. Delhi University), Dr Suparno Banerjee (Texas State University), Dr Tarun Saint for their guidance and help. We would also like to thank Saikat Ghosh for overseeing and helping out with the organisation of the said workshop. We are also indebted to our friend Sakshi Dogra for helping us in the initial stages of conceptualisation of this collection.

This book is a result of a lot of minds working together for the success of the project. Therefore, a special acknowledgement goes out to all those who answered our call for papers. While we could not include all the papers that were sent to us, the sheer number of entries was, if nothing else, quite encouraging.

Finally, our heartfelt gratitude to the people at Bloomsbury who made this book possible, particularly in such a challenging time as now.

INTRODUCTION

Shweta Khilnani and Ritwick Bhattacharjee

Indian science-fiction (SF) narratives may have been around for quite some time, but it is only fairly recently that academia has begun to take a serious interest in them. (The relatively new resurgence of Jagadish Chandra Bose's 1896 story 'Runaway Cyclone'[1] within academic circles immediately comes to mind). Western SF narratives, on the other hand, have not only captured the critical imagination of literary theorists, both Western and Indian, but have also found prominence, and, often, seminal positions within academia. This is proven by the inclusion of such narratives and theorists in university syllabi across the globe. For a long time, thus, any mainstream academic exploration of SF as a form has always found itself talking about the stalwarts: the most prominent being Arthur Clarke, Isaac Asimov, Ursula K. Le Guin and Philip K. Dick. It is only with the publication, in the last half-decade, of books like Tarun K. Saint's *The Gollancz Book of South Asian Science Fiction* (2019), Suparno Banerjee's *Indian Science Fiction: Patterns, History and Hybridity* (2020), Sakshi Dogra and Shweta Khilnani's *Imagining Worlds, Mapping Possibilities: Select Science Fiction Stories* (2020) and Sami Ahmad Khan's *Star Warriors of the Modern Raj: Materiality, Mythology and Technology of Indian Science Fiction* (2021) that there has been an earnest effort towards filling up this academic gap and bringing *Indian* SF into the academic discourses of the world.

On the face of it, this complaint—of the absence of a critical engagement with Indian SF in light of the 'Indianness' and, thus, 'national-isation'[2] of SF—may seem somewhat frivolous. It is, however, acknowledgement of not only the kind of sociopolitical[3] insight that SF as a form holds but also of the novel possibilities of comprehending the imagination of the Indian nation; for this imagination, in itself, is a pivotal moment in the construction of the political entity of the nation. In fact, as Benedict Anderson writes in *Imagined Communities*, 'all communities larger than primordial villages of face-to-face contact (and perhaps even these) are imagined' (1983). What this means, then, is that all nations, before becoming a geopolitical reality, are necessarily brought into being in and as an imagination through the discourses of and about that nation (Anderson 1983). In such a case, a critical engagement with Indian SF narratives inside the frameworks of their 'Indianness' and 'science fiction-ness' allows the creation of an imagination of the nation that spans across spatio-temporal dimensions since, in being SF and holding all the modal artefacts of SF, the genre allows an imagination of the Indian nation to overarch temporal distinctions of the past, the present and the future. The Indian nation, through such a critical intervention, 'comes into being' (Anderson 1983) as a pan-temporal entity, reaching both into its histories and futures from the current existential coordinates.

Further, if political realities of nations, as Anderson puts it, depend on imaginative constructions, the 'imagined community' of the Indian nation through SF can and often does hold severe political ramifications. The current volume seeks to find a place within such a theoretical framework and, alongside the aforementioned theorists, interrogate this entanglement between the Indian nation and SF. The idea for this book was conceived during an international workshop on Indian SF organised and hosted by SGTB Khalsa College, University of Delhi, in January 2021, where SF scholars from the world over came together and tried to figure out the possibilities of Indian SF. The book has been framed keeping in mind the spirit and mood of the discussions during the workshop. Its sixteen individually authored chapters and a conceptual prologue look at the different ways through which the nation, its histories, its presents and its futures have been imagined in and through the SF genre. The intent here is to continue, through the inclusion of various SF forms, from novels to graphic novels and films, the work that began previously through various critical interventions in the Indian SF genre. Along the way, the authors of these chapters question and interrogate the most probable aspects of the forms with an intent to build a conceptual foundation of a truly Indian SF. Towards the same, two distinct aspects of *form* and *content* arise across the chapters. Thus, the book is subdivided into two sections: Book I: Paradigms and Book II: Worlds. While the chapters in the first section seek to understand the theoretical paradigms and frameworks for a possible definition of Indian SF, those in the latter section apply these theoretical formulations to present the different ways in which the genre imagines and reimagines the nation across its temporal dimensions. Further, since there is an implicit desire in the conception of the present book to find a cohesive formulation towards understanding both Indian SF as an entity (or, perhaps, an act) in itself and the modalities that constitute multiple manifestations of this genre, each chapter is located within the context of a running narrative of Indian SF. This has been done by prefacing each chapter with an editors' introduction which seeks to first locate the chapter within the conceptual environment of its preceding, and at times succeeding, chapters and then complicate the theoretical, conceptual, philosophical and political prospects presented within that chapter. There is a hope that the reader of this book will not only find the presentations of the ideological positions by individual authors interesting but will also be able to develop newer possibilities of future research and critical engagements. The book, thus, is intended to come together as a singular cohesive whole, much like the Indian nation that navigates through both spatial and temporal diversities to form a singularity.

NOTES

1 Particularly, in its translated form by the SF scholar Bodhisattva Chattopadhyay for the *Strange Horizons* September 2013 issue. The story was first published in 1896 as '*Niruddesher Kahini*' (The Story of the Missing One) and later changed, in 1921, to 'Palatak Toofan' (Runaway Cyclone).

2 The hyphenated word is to bring to notice a different kind of a nationalisation where the discourse of the nation is, in quite definite terms, inserted, as it were, into the discourse of science fiction.

3 As Darko Suvin and Charles Elkins note, science fiction is not just about the scientificity of fiction or the fictionality of science, but in being produced and consumed within a particular set of (dominant) cultural mores it 'either reinforces, questions, or rejects the dominant culture by (tacitly or openly) endorsing the values and norms upon which the dominant culture rests or by endorsing alternative norms and values of past, residual cultures or future, emerging cultures' (2020). This allows science fiction as a genre to find immediate critical engagement with the cultural aspect of the spatio-temporal localities involved in its propagation. This is an idea that multiple chapters in the present book talk about.

WORKS CITED

Anderson, Benedict. 1983. *Imagined Communities*. London and New York: Verso.

Banerjee, Suparno. 2020. *Indian Science Fiction: Patterns, History and Hybridity*. UK: University of Wales Press.

Bose, Jagadish Chandra. 2013. 'Runaway Cyclone.' Translated by Bodisattva Chattopadhyay. *Strange Horizons*. http://strangehorizons.com/fiction/runaway-cyclone/ (accessed on 19 August 2021).

Dogra, Sakshi, and Shweta Khilnani, eds. 2020. *Imagining Worlds, Mapping Possibilities: Select Science Fiction Stories*. New Delhi: Worldview Publications.

Khan, Sami Ahmad. 2021. *Star Warriors of the Modern Raj: Materiality, Mythology and Technology of Indian Science Fiction*. UK: University of Wales Press.

Saint, Tarun K., ed. 2019. *The Gollancz Book of South Asian Science Fiction*. India: Hachette.

Suvin, Darko, and Charles Elkins. 2020. 'On Teaching SF Critically.' In *What Makes it Pop? An Introduction to Studies in Popular Fiction*, edited by Srinjoyee Dutta and Ritwick Bhattacharjee. New Delhi: Worldview Publications.

THREE PROLEGOMENA

Shweta Khilnani, Ritwick Bhattacharjee and Saikat Ghosh

A SCIENCE AND A FICTION OF OUR OWN

In his Nobel Prize acceptance speech titled 'The Solitude of Latin America', Gabriel García Márquez declares that '[t]he interpretation of our reality through patterns not our own, serves only to make us even more unknown, ever less free, even more solitary' (1982). Widely regarded as one of the greatest exponents of the magic realist genre, Márquez gestures towards the dynamic between the peculiar nature of a people's lived experiences and the narrative constructs used to represent their reality. Are there certain forms of expression better suited to negotiate particular cultural, social and political sensibilities? If so, how do these forms develop and evolve within the materiality of temporal and spatial paradigms?

As opposed to magic realism, which is indigenous to Latin America, science fiction (SF) is primarily a Western literary genre. Right from Mary Shelley's *Frankenstein* (1819; often regarded as the first SF novel) to the iconic SF pulp magazines such as Hugo Gernsback's *Amazing Stories*, SF developed and matured primarily in Europe and America. This does not imply that the topoi of SF are not present in literature from other parts of the world, including Latin America, parts of Southeast Asia and the Indian subcontinent. However, one can argue with a certain degree of conviction that SF first emerged as a self-conscious literary (and/or popular/pulp) genre of writing in the West. Moreover, SF has often been understood as a genre that aligned itself with the imperialist ideology. John Rieder, in his now-iconic book titled *Colonialism and the Emergence of Science Fiction* (2008), argues that SF rose to prominence during the precise period that witnessed the most 'fervid imperialist expansion' in the late nineteenth century. Rieder contends that as a product of imperialist culture, SF represents the West's technological will to power. Clearly, a preliminary reading of SF does not present it as an appropriate genre for capturing a distinctly postcolonial Indian sensibility.

However, the rich and diverse corpus of SF and speculative fiction emerging out of India enriches the existing body of SF writing, not simply in terms of volume but more so by way of forcing a reconsideration of some of the very definitive theories of this form of literature. It prompts an inquiry into the very ontology of science and how the discipline can be historicised in different cultural contexts. Almost simultaneously, it compels us to advance our apperception of the already exciting, rich but ambiguous, body of writing usually recognised as Indian literature. If we now return to the question posed in the very first paragraph of this prologue—regarding forms of narrative representation more or less suited to capture certain cultural or social realities—we can add further layers of nuances to that dilemma. Is SF an apposite genre of writing to represent Indian sensibilities and experiences? Within this question lie multiple other challenges: How is science conceptualised as a field or a form of knowledge within Indian culture and thought? What exactly does the term 'Indian' connote here? Undoubtedly, there is a rich body of theoretical postcolonial writing that caters to the latter question.[1] We are more interested in how SF narratives complement, supplement, contradict or question this already existing understanding of 'Indianness'.

The question of defining 'science' in science fiction has been the mainstay of several leading theories of the genre. Whether it is Darko Suvin's iconic phrase 'cognitive estrangement' or Carl Freedman's modification of Suvin's concept of 'cognition' to 'cognition effect'[2], their definitions of science fiction comment on the different connotations of science and the role played by the scientific imagination in such narratives. Recently, critics such as China Miéville and Suparno Banerjee have raised questions about the very ideology of science and rationality. The claim that SF is based on science and rationality, Miéville argues, is premised on 'capitalist modernity's ideologically projected self-justification' and 'not some abstract idea of science' (2009). In other words, he suggests that science itself is not a homogenous, universal category and, therefore, there is a need for a more inclusive and diverse understanding of science and rationality. Within a specific Indian context, Banerjee opines that multiple knowledge systems stake a claim to the epistemic role generally reserved for science in Western SF (2020). These include 'modern techno-science, dominant Indian mainstream Hindu/Vedic science and the nebulous realm of regional folk/subaltern knowledge' (Banerjee 2020). Through the course of Indian history, these systems have interacted with one another in complementary or antagonistic ways, producing a distinctly hybridised body of knowledge through which individuals make sense of the world around them.

The formal dynamics of SF allow this hybridity to prosper, resulting in a rich and diverse body of Indian SF writing, which at once reconstructs past(s) and imagines future possibilities. One needs to study Darko Suvin's famous understanding of science fiction as a literature of 'cognitive estrangement' to fully appreciate this dualism. According to Suvin, SF is characterised by the co-presence of estrangement and cognition; therefore, even as SF is replete with alternative worlds, these worlds are rationally constructed according to certain cognitive principles. In the case of Indian SF, this translates to a near-ideal union of rational modernity that places its faith in techno-utopianism and a traditional indigenous philosophy that has employed myth and folklore to negotiate external reality since time immemorial. As a result, it 'liberate[s] the texts from the constraints of realism and yet provide[s] a logical orientation' (Banerjee 2010). Owing to this unique feature of science-fictional narratives, they have witnessed new trajectories of evolution within the Indian landscape. The synthesis of myth, religion, superstition and folklore with the more characteristic motifs of SF such as space travel, time travel and utopia/dystopia has produced a hybrid form of SF, infusing it with a range of postcolonial possibilities.

Despite these theoretical configurations, SF does not have a considerable presence in the literary arena of the country, save for the last few decades. In the West, there is a clear literary and mass cultural lineage of SF narratives. While authors such as Mary Shelley, Jules Verne and H.G. Wells are regarded as the earliest stalwarts of the literary genre, pulp magazines such as *Amazing Stories* and *Astounding Stories of Super-Science* (later retitled, *Analog Science Fiction and Fact*) ensured that SF enjoyed a huge readership and fan base, thereby etching a place for itself within mass popular culture. Save for the recent surge of readership and academic interest in Anglophonic SF, it has been largely limited to a small niche, which was further constrained by language-specific readerships. (Some of the most prolific SF stories were written in regional languages such as Bengali and Marathi). Quite obviously, the causes were both sociological and logistical: the conditions of the market, the declining rates of fiction readership in general, the lack of a robust infrastructure for translation, et cetera. However, one often wonders if the issue at hand is more fundamental or ontological in nature.

India is often represented as a land of mystery and exoticism, and several contemporary authors of science/speculative fiction from the country have often observed that inscrutability is built into the very fabric of Indian reality. Anil Menon, in an interview with Charles Tan, remarks that India 'is one of those places that couldn't be, but it is. It is, but it could be so much more. It is Zeno's paradox given coordinates, a place that moves by standing still and rests through ceaseless motion' (Tan 2009). Similarly, Vandana Singh has often mentioned that her first exposure to science fiction was through Hindi pulp magazines consisting of stories about fairy tales and cosmic voyages among other things. However, this rich reservoir of source material, ideal for imaginative storytelling, somehow hasn't translated into a self-conscious and established tradition of Indian SF writing. One of the reasons behind this gap is obvious: our notions of science subvert traditional expectations of rationality and objectivity. In a worldview where an understanding of the outside world is mediated through a curious blend of technoscientific modernity and what can only be provisionally described as a tradition of myth, folklore, subaltern knowledge and religious belief, it is perhaps misplaced to trace a genealogy of 'science' fiction per se where the definition of science is distinctly Western and modern in nature. The specificity of cultural and social experiences results in a kind of writing that might bypass some of the typical 'hard' SF motifs characterised by the presence of advanced technology. At the same time, it produces imaginative, alternative worlds that are more reflective of the specific, local coordinates of places and lifestyles. Therefore, the chapters in this volume demonstrate, first, that a futuristic utopia or dystopia set in India invariably borrows from its precolonial past, second, that contemporary forms of surveillance are also informed by practices of exercising control used by the British forces and, third, that anecdotes from Indian classical texts are constantly reworked in many science- and speculative-fiction narratives.

While discussing the primacy of ancient myths and folklore within an Indian context, there is always the lurking danger of a certain sort of cultural appropriation, both from within and without. On the one hand, the rhetoric of a fetishised 'Oriental'/'Third World' experience often leads to essentialisation of nations, cultures and communities globally; on the other, tales from ancient texts are often appropriated by local political forces either to uphold certain conservative values or to assert the supremacy of the glorious Indian past. At the same time, such writing is often haunted by the spectre of the Jamesonian national allegory.[3] Is it possible to imagine a body of SF writing that can circumvent the expectation of the allegorical mode of representation? Sami Ahmad Khan believes that the re-emergence of SF in Indian Writing in English is a sign that it has 'grown out of the shadow of the (anti)hegemonic postcolonial agenda, which had usurped its original pulp self earlier [sic.], and now finally has the confidence to own up to its "lowly" roots' (2021).

This emergent genre-bending, hybrid nature of narratives has often sparked debate regarding the terminology to be used for this form of writing. While we have chosen to stick to science fiction as our preferred terminology—primarily for the sake of convenience but also because we believe it allows us to access a broader range of narratives and writing styles—alternatives like 'desi SF', 'Bharati SF', '*kalpavigyan*', et cetera, have been proposed by several critics and scholars of SF. Such labels attempt to unlock a range of postcolonial possibilities in order to develop a more productive and enabling understanding of this body of narratives. For instance, Bodhisattva Chattopadhyay argues that *kalpavigyan*, a term used by some Bengali writers, reveals marvellous possibilities as it uses the mythic as the 'source of alternative or unknown or advanced science' (2016). He contends that Indian SF or *kalpavigyan* articulates 'truths' or 'gyan' in sources that have been discarded by modern knowledge and reframes them in terms of science or *vigyan*, bringing into focus alternative, hidden knowledge systems. Vandana Singh rallies against the constraints imposed by the term science fiction, choosing instead to embrace speculative fiction, which allows the imagination to be unfettered by any expectations of fidelity to predefined notions of science. The politics of nomenclature notwithstanding, it is our belief that we need novel scholarly paradigms to study this ever-growing field of writing, and this collection of chapters is but a small step in that direction. Our aim is twofold: pay homage to the rich body of scholarly work on SF and simultaneously deconstruct some of it to cater to more culturally specific needs and frameworks. We begin this endeavour with a deep exploration of the very nature of science and its relationship with the external world. This will be followed by a more specific focus on how such dynamics are materialised in Indian SF of all forms and shapes.

LOOKING FOR ABSENCES AND CREATING THE REAL

From Aristotelian to Newtonian to Quantum, Science[4], as a set of epistemological actions, has tried to relate the mechanics of reality to human beings in as concrete and, for the lack of a better phrase, as *mathematically precise* a way as possible. It does this by entangling itself with absences: first by revealing them and then trying to fill them. In a sense, in *doing* Science, humans not only make present the absences they notionally encounter in their travels through the cosmos—physical, spatial or temporal—but also seek to fill the said absences. There is, then, in the very functioning of Science, an innate engine of desire that drives the scientific will forward: the desire to know, to fill a revealed *emptiness* and to understand the reality in which humans exist. Further, this quest is not merely limited to the applicability of Science through the building of machines but is also subject to the same intellectual impulses that have engrossed and fascinated the metaphysical philosopher and/or artist. Consider, for example, the Penrose-Hameroff theory. In the early 1990s, Sir Roger Penrose, a

Nobel laureate in Physics, and Stuart Hameroff, an anaesthesiologist and psychologist, proposed that human consciousness is not really the result of neural actions of the brain but rather, in a more complex turn, of the quantum processes that take place at a deeper level within-and-as the said neural connections and movements. One of the immediate implications of this proposal was the resurgence of the possibility of free will. The reason behind this implication, although inductive, was rather simple. Since, at the quantum level, particles function as waves[5] and, unless measured, can be found at all the probable places they can be at the same time,[6] they escape the determinism of classical mechanics implicit in the larger experiential world. If, in such a scenario, human consciousness *becomes* a result of the quantum processes inside/of the human brain, it too gets freed of the determinism of the universe and finds, after a long time,[7] the possibility of free will.

Despite its persuasive appeal, the Penrose-Hameroff theory provoked intense criticism from all ends of the philosophical spectrum, especially since there is, so far, no scientific proof to show that the non-determinism at the quantum level can be extrapolated to the experiential level, a level at which human consciousness functions. Even if the theory were true, there would still be a huge gap between the jump from the creation of consciousness to its function and figurations of the possible answers to the questions regarding the consciousness of consciousness and, further on, the consciousness of the universe.

Having said that, notwithstanding such criticisms and the possibly faulty conception of the theory ('possibly' because neither the physics behind the Penrose-Hameroff theory nor the question concerning its validity is within the scope of this book), it is interesting to note the presence, in the theory, of the desire (itself) to locate the materiality of human consciousness. Since the Presocratics, human consciousness, in one form or another, has been a mysterious entity despite its fundamental role in the creation of a human's Being and reality. It has been a frontier at which human knowledge systems have always faltered and functioned (even if barely), either at the most abstract or the utter mystical. This absence, in terms of the relation of human consciousness, has always been absolute and philosophers, theorists and artists have always limited towards its comprehension without really arriving at it. Yet, it has been both *a* real and *the* real, not only in the existential being as the human consciousness itself, but also in and as its activity of conversion from the noumenal to the phenomenal. That Penrose and Hameroff wish to whittle down this entity to a cognisable theoretical framework, and perhaps to a mathematical order as well, indicates both the scientific will to grapple with the most abstract of entities as well as the scientific method's purported role in filling in the gaps and configuring the Real. Machines might come later but what drives the Penrose-Hameroff theory is the desire to figure, in as concrete terms as possible, what has for long been lost in the mists of incomprehension. That these mists have been revealed in the first place through the scientific method, not only of Penrose and Hameroff's but also of all those who have come and questioned what consciousness is, vivifies the operations of desires in relation to the absences behind Science[8]. The question of the veracity of the theory is besides this intention. It does not, for the purposes of the current argument, matter if what Penrose and Hameroff propose is correct or not. What matters is the proposal itself: the intention that wishes to fill an absence[9]. There are, then, three impulses operating behind the actions of Science. The first is the human's encounter with the real and its consequent interrogation. At this point, the real is presented only as the experiential and has all its logic and methodologies of creating its experiential component hidden behind a veil. This leads to the second impulse: recognition of the veil as an absence and a subsequent desire to peer through it to look at the way the real functions. The third impulse, finally, is the intellectual push towards the satisfaction of previously evoked desire, first through theorisation and then through applications of mathematical methodologies for certitude. It is with this final certitude that Science first reorders the real for the human cogito and then recreates it. In a way then, in answering *what* reality is, Science also facilitates its creation; not, obviously, in an objective sense but *for* the human. Before the application of Science, the real (outside the experiential) is, for all intents and purposes, hidden and unachievable. In allowing concrete access, Science allows the real to *be*. If, for example, the Penrose-Hameroff theory is true, then the reality, concretely, is that human consciousness is a product of the quantum process in the neural functions of the brain. This is a reality that *becomes* and takes on a reality in itself (the reality of reality) for the human, one that has so far been missing.

While none of these ideas is really new or groundbreaking (in fact, most of them are common knowledge), insofar as this book is concerned, there is an imperative need to state them clearly for they have important implications for the definitional continuities (and discontinuities) of science fiction; definitional, not as much in terms of the delineation of generic intricacies of the varied forms of SF but to fashion a possible framework for the phenomenon itself. For it is only from within this framework that there lies a possibility of a different Cartesian location of the Indian science-fiction narrative. Concerning these three terms (Indian, Science and Fiction), what the aforementioned argument thus presents is, first, Science's entanglement with absences and, second, its revelation and subsequent creation of the Real through factical filling up of the said absences. Both these aspects are important for the interrogation of the idea of Indian science fiction: the first, to work on the 'fiction' part and, the second, the 'Indian'.[10]

Concerning the fiction part, the question that needs at least an interrogation, if not an answer, is what happens to this act or entity of Science when it finds an ostensible cosy companionship with fiction? For this companionship is not a simple assemblage. The fiction that attaches itself to science is not an unaffected entity but one that, in its attachment to Science, finds individuated modalities of action. In other words, SF is not just a simple combination of Science and Fiction but a product of a complex overlapping of the Being of either; it is a structure where the scientificity of Science bears upon the fictionality of fiction and vice versa. The implication of this complexity is quite telling. It allows the fiction part to be an absorbed extension of the Science part rather than a simple inclusion, even as the fictionality of the fiction works on the science. This entails that insofar as Science functions upon the Being of absences, the extension accorded by fictionality allows the presence of a double absence. SF, in a sense, makes present the absence within the actions of Science as the latter reveals and wishes to work on the absences of the world. It is not as if SF acts when Science fails. In fact, it is possible to think of SF, in the extensionality of the fictional, as Science working on itself. Thus, narratives of alien (not only as extra-terrestrial) beings, spaces, and time abound in this corpus of literature. All these elements become absences within the actions of Science on the world, presenting, in the process, a matrix of systemic lack. Take, for example, Vandana Singh's short story 'Yakshantriksh'. The story is about a person's encounter with a giant snake-like being *Yakshantriksh*, which supports all existence in and of the Milky Way galaxy, perhaps even the entire cosmos. For the major part, the story lacks action but deals with the affectation of the knowledge of the being itself. What is interesting is that Singh, a physicist, forms this being out of dark matter and tachyons. It is interesting since either of these things that makes the *Yakshantriksh* are entities that science cannot comprehend. Both dark matter and the tachyon particle are hypothetical concepts that answer a few questions with respect to the universe but are themselves unknown. While physicists are sure that there is both dark matter and the tachyon, they are yet to know what these things actually are. Thus, though they explain certain absences, they themselves become absent. Singh's *Yakshantriksh* plays on this second layer of absence and gives it form. In other words, the fictionality of this great serpent-like being first becomes an acknowledgement of this double absence and then its own revealing. In an interesting parallel to Science itself, which shows what is beyond the limits of human knowledge, the *Yakshantriksh* does not show where science fails but what lies beyond it. As with the Penrose-Hameroff theory, thus, there is an equal possibility of this gargantuan being to be real.

The idea of SF's revelation of a double absence, however, is not simply about the possibilities of that particular SF element being real. In fact, the deeper implication is about both reality and a human's location within it. If Science, through its operation in and through the absence it locates, allows the creation (in order of a recreation *for* the human) of reality, what happens when the result of the desire to fill the absence is absence itself? Not within the same layer but beyond it, like the failure of either dark matter or tachyons to *be* actual explainable objects even as they definitively relay the mechanics of other intricacies of existence. Whatever the answer to this is, there is, within the limits of this question, an implicit knowledge of the complexity of the real itself, especially in terms of the reluctance to fall within comprehensible categorisations. SF, in a sense, reveals a reality that fundamentally resists classificatory relations. For the human, located within this incomprehensibility of reality, SF, in turn, allows an absolutely fantastic mode of reality, where the Scientific method is not defining (in terms of constricting) aspects of the real anymore but simply letting go for absolute creations. In the process of Science turning its action on itself (in and as SF), humans are able to figure their own realities with the absolute freedom of fictionality along with a mechanised procedure of Science. It allows, thus, not just a recreation but creation itself, and through it, a renegotiation of all that Science has already created. The *Yakshantriksh*, in that sense, allows not only the creation of a universe where the human is an infinitesimally small part of a greater being but also a renegotiation of the reality where the earth finds itself, at least so far, singular. The effect of this creation ranges from philosophical presentations of the meaning of life (for life, in the shape of the *Yakshantriksh*, is grander than imagined) to possibilities of connecting with the entire universe (as everything becomes a part of the *Yakshantriksh*).

The spatial aspect of SF, here in the form of its Indianness, also stems from an allied argument, as has been stated earlier. First, since Science begins its operation in entering the real to detect classificatory absences, the real, as a catalytic playground for Science, becomes an important modulator for it. This means that aspects, objective and subjective, which constitute the real, necessarily and simultaneously moderate the absences that Science reveals. Such moderations, in turn, bear upon the operations of Science towards the possible alleviation of these absences and the subsequent recreation of reality.[11] The Indian reality, thus constituted by its geographical position, historical evolution, governmentality and postcolonial formulation, necessarily affects not only the kind of Science that is done in it but also the recreations of that reality post the procedures of the Scientific. Amitav Ghosh's novel *The Calcutta Chromosome* is perhaps an interesting example of this idea. It talks about a system of scientific procedures that is both indigenous and peculiar to India and allows, albeit hidden under the Western methods of scientific enquiry, different characters near-immortality. This Science, Ghosh shows, is something that the West does not have recourse to as it finds being within *very* Indian elements of existence. While the novel is decidedly science-fictional, the impulse behind the presentation of a fundamentally different scientificity cannot be ignored. Second, and perhaps more importantly, these Cartesian coordinates of the nation, in affecting the manoeuvres of Science, also act upon the structures of SF as Science turns itself on itself. What is created through Indian SF, then, is not just a copy of a larger conceptual entity but something singular. The renegotiation, implicit within the systems of SF, similarly becomes allied to the existential conditions of the nation. Ghosh's novel is, once again, an example of this alignment. His SF effectively reconditions the Indian reality within scientific possibilities of attaining immortality. *Yakshantriksh* too becomes a rather good presentation of this singularity of Indian SF. The narrator reveals that the cosmic being has entered into the consciousness of many humans across national boundaries. But, since the narrator (as Singh herself) is Indian, the being becomes a chimerical facsimile of two Indian mythological beings—*yaksha* and *Ananta Nag*—even as it negotiates the double absence. The reality of the *Yakshantriksh* then is decidedly Indian. It is this singularity, therefore, that decries the necessity of an Indianness within the SF produced from within the nation.

Obviously, this argument can be used to truncate the entire corpus of SF literature. Each marker of reality, national or otherwise, can similarly be used to moderate generic SF. Perhaps it should be. But that is an argument that needs its own space. For the purposes of this book, as the reader proceeds to read through the following chapters, two things become extremely crucial. First, the consideration of the Indian SF as *Indian* SF and, second, perhaps more importantly, the comprehension of SF as not just a category of narrative but, in its complex synthesis of Science and Fiction, a thought or a mode of being, especially since it is within this wellspring of Being that SF finds intricate relations to the aforementioned cultural aspects. Having said that, a wide-ranging interrogation of the different dimensions of Indian SF demands, as a provisional starting point, a contextual frame within which Indian SF may be seen to have evolved. Allowing for some necessary recapitulation of details shared previously, the following section is intended to offer a broad blueprint of the shifting concerns, methods and creative horizons that have characterised the historical trajectory of Indian SF.

REVISIONISM IN POST-LIBERALISATION INDIAN SF

Except for Henry Meredith Parker, no nineteenth-century SF writer in India had dared to visualise the twenty-first century. This is remarkable because almost all the colonial SF, whether written by sahibs or desi enthusiasts, was futuristic and utopian in its content. Some did envisage a nominally 'free' country that naively remains indebted to trajectories of modernity and progress introduced by its erstwhile European masters. Parker's 'The Junction of the Ocean: A Tale of the Year 2098' (1850) is not set in India. It is, however, an interesting exception to the other stories on two significant counts. One, the story is dystopian and narrates a hair-raising but *real* possibility of the oceans flooding and eventually swallowing large masses of inhabited land. Two, the story questions large-scale interventions of industrial technology and modern governmental priorities by portraying the Panama Canal project as a doomed attempt by Europe to selfishly link the oceans to serve its own commercial interests. The story offers a parable of scientific overreach, technological mismanagement and calamity of a scale and intensity that can match the bleakest doomsday scenarios.[12]

Parker published his story at a time when SF had no distinguishable presence for its readers and his gifts as a writer did not merit any serious consideration beyond commonplace curiosity and the pursuit of fanciful diversion. The world had not yet suffered a tsunami that would symbolise, a century and a half later, the precarity of modern existence for large sections of its population. Hence, it is only in retrospect that one can acknowledge the prescient critique of colonial modernity in this work of fiction or see it as a testament of its own time.

In sharp contrast to Parker, Indians who dabbled in SF appear in awe of the majestic accomplishments of nineteenth-century science and technology while simultaneously fantasising about themselves in the roles of minor yet important subjects of the scientific enterprise and modern age of enlightenment. Concepts and epistemological hair-splitting from the shastras and sutras too were sometimes marshalled to argue about the autonomy of scientific processes and their pursuit of objective truth. As a result, scepticism towards colonial modernity could go hand in hand with the conviction, howsoever misplaced, that science and its institutional practices were free from bias and discrimination (Chattopadhyay 2016).

The Nehruvian endorsement of a techno-industrial path to modern progress can be seen in continuity, and almost all the SF written in the decades immediately following India's independence is hence surprisingly apolitical. Leaving aside some of Narayan Dharap's and Premendra Mitra's edgy fantasies and Satyajit Ray's tributes to the works of Wells and Verne in the Professor Shonku series, the SF published in the pre-liberalisation era was largely didactic and preached a reverential approach to visions of technologically driven progress and deterministic models of society and history. It may seem quite remarkable that Indian writers remained inert to the critical influence of counterculture in the West that produced, for instance, Philip K. Dick's gloomy and surrealist interrogation of paranoid state surveillance and precog in 'The Minority Report' or Arthur C. Clarke's agnostic parable of space reconnaissance in *Rendezvous with Rama*. In fact, they resolutely championed statist initiatives to control scientific endeavour and technological innovation. To a large extent, the insularity of Indian SF in the early decades of Independence mirrors the social insularity of Indian science itself. Upamanyu Pablo Mukherjee notes this in his recent survey of Indian SF in the decolonising era when he describes the development of a Nehruvian paradigm of scientific thought and its eventual crisis in terms of its three components: 'ideologies of modern development, the militarization of science and the location of scientific practices in a polycentric, uneven, field of knowledge' (Mukherjee 2020). However, instead of explaining the narrow templates of Indian science fiction by solely referring them to the post-Independence state's symbolic attempts to cultivate a scientific temper, a genuinely historicist approach will dwell on factors such as the disconnect between science and large sections of the Indian masses, the lack of easy access to science education and research, and the exclusion of women and subaltern groups from scientific endeavour; these are factors that impeded the growth of an autonomous cultural discourse on postcolonial science and its relationship with other dimensions of Indian reality.

Post-liberalisation of the Indian economy, the sociological dynamics of scientific culture changed rapidly and drastically. Science-driven reality impacted the lives of the masses in a far more comprehensive way, albeit obliquely, through technological innovations in communication and media. These innovations brought the world to our doorsteps and allowed freer contact between diverse cultures. More importantly, the Digital Revolution created unexpected virtual avenues for self-expression and exploration. The generations that grew up within the experiential grid of personal computers, satellite television, mobile phones and smart devices seemed culturally hardwired to renegotiate the terms of their reality with a burgeoning paradigm of mass-produced technological consumables. As one of the first-generation women writers of Indian SF, Manjula Padmanabhan so eloquently observes in her Foreword to *The Gollancz Book of South Asian Science Fiction*:

> [W]e live in an era where only a whisper thin membrane separates science fiction from science fact. Some of us are living in the digital Other Worlds of our parents' nightmares. Some of us are fighting wars at the pixelated boundaries of countries we can no longer name. Some of us are being treated by virtual doctors who visit us on our smartphones. Others are finding love in the glow of laptop screens. (xii)

The inclusiveness of the digital space allowed a plurality of voices to emerge and hitherto invisible forms of subjecthood or agency to be represented in SF writing, even as the terms of science fiction underwent a range of critical revisions in the hands of new SF writers.

Curiously, the new generation of SF writers has not been averse to drawing inspiration from the Puranas and epics while also tapping into the equally rich mosaic of folklore and local legends to produce stories and idioms that connected with the masses culturally. Contemporary SF author Vandana Singh has repeatedly invoked the importance of the oral epics by reworking them in her stories to establish a series of critical epistemological dialogues with Western science and rationality.[13] However, while myth-steeped multiverses are reasonably staple in contemporary Indian SF and speculative fiction, critical attitudes do not automatically find their way into them. At its worst, the contemporary use of myths can be ideologically revivalist or present an ahistorical version of a technologically governed society that transforms contemporary history into a consumable spectacle. Such dangers, in fact, may be assumed to be all too real in a society where consumerism fuels the fascination with technology. Yet, at its best, SF writers' openness to mythology allows them to stage dramatic encounters between different temporalities and weave remarkably intricate allegories of the past and present. The drama of time-consciousness is indeed an integral experience of a myth-nourished culture. Hard science belongs to only a few temporal registers in narratives that straddle or incorporate multiple temporalities. A time-consciousness that emerges from a modern, technologically determined set of social and cultural practices can be made to confront a different time-consciousness that exposes its limits and questions its certitudes. Critically distinguished SF and speculative fiction from India have explored precisely such a possibility.

The new wave of Indian SF has also broken with the past in incorporating other genres and registers of popular writing. Detective fiction; children's adventure stories; horror fiction dealing with local legends of vampires, monsters, werewolves, shapeshifters and magicians; alternative histories and teen or young adult romances have all found their way into the many dimensions of contemporary Indian SF from time to time. The imaginative traffic across generic boundaries is a crucial feature of post-liberalisation SF, projecting its appeal beyond the clichéd expectations of a conventional community of SF readers and exploring new catchment areas for diverse sensibilities that were hitherto excluded from any cultural relationship with SF. The blending of SF with other fantasy genres also happened in the West, especially in the prominent genre-bending works of Ursula K. Le Guin, Stephen King, Suzanne Collins, Margaret Atwood and George R.R. Martin. While writers often try to explain the crossover moments in their writing careers as outcomes of their decision to break through stereotypes or the need to address a larger readership, one suspects that the strategic thinking of global publishing imprints and entertainment media platforms has also had an important role to play in promoting genre-bending fiction. In the Indian context, however, the incorporation of multiple genres with the new SF appears to be comparatively more organic, wherein each register of fictional possibilities, albeit different, mirrors the other and imparts a 'horizontality' to the multiplicity of generic topoi on display.

The horizontality can also be seen as a function of a new kind of moral ambivalence in contemporary Indian SF writing. Moral ambivalence, or what could more accurately be described as a novel moral construction of subjecthood, one that makes the older moral equations seem simplistic and passé, is quite possibly the source of the most crucial form of revisionism seen within this sphere of writing in the decades following liberalisation. All popular genres of storytelling and writing have conventionally tended to rely on the schema of a conflict between the forces of good and evil. Indian narrative traditions have borne the burden of the good versus evil schema with far greater conformism than is seen in the West. Detective and adventure fiction, the two modern genres most frequently utilised to stage obvious confrontations between good and evil, have consistently shared an affinity with science fiction. In fact, all the moral dilemmas related to the practice, scope and visions of science have been conventionally accommodated within this schema, based on which a syntagmatic chain of binary themes can be easily imagined: use versus abuse of science, humanitarian scientists working for people's welfare versus the conceited and egoistical charlatans, science versus magic/superstition, humans versus aliens, human intelligence versus machines and so on. When they are uncritically allowed to structure the narrative thematics, these binaries reinforce conservative notions of alterity and nurture attitudes of hostility or blindness towards different categories of otherness. Consequently, cultural or epistemological subversion becomes a remote, indeed impossible, choice in works that conform to this schema. Moral ambivalence liberates narratives from an underlying structure of conservatism and opens the doors to subversion, mimicry and re-examination of moral ideas and, most importantly, the historicisation of truth. According to contemporary SF author Samit Basu, moral ambivalence is a growing trend in Indian SF and speculative fiction. To illustrate this phenomenon, he lists in his top-shelf contemporary reads within the SF genre at least four recent Indian novels displaying moral ambivalence: *The Beast with Nine Billion Feet* (2009) by Anil Menon, *The Devourers* (2015) by Indrapramit Das, *Cult of Chaos* (2015) by Shweta Tancja and *Dark Things* (2016) by Sukanya Venkataraghavan.[14] Each of these novels redefines our relationship with 'other' or altered states of being while also challenging a unidimensional temporal state of consciousness without resorting to hackneyed ex machina such as time travel or parallel universes that were formulaic inclusions in earlier SF.

Yet, all these observations about post-liberalisation Indian SF pertain, in the main, to works written in Indian English. Regional language traditions of SF and speculative fiction are bound to add another layer of complexity to our analyses. Though SF written in regional languages has not been prolific enough to discern distinct patterns of evolution or paradigms of change, a rich and influential legacy of fantasy and adventure literature written in some of the culturally prominent bhashas of the pre- and immediate postcolonial period, especially Bengali and Marathi, confronts us. In Bengali, besides Ray and Mitra, other established modern authors, including Rabindranath Tagore, have frequently dabbled in genres like detective fiction, horror fiction and children's fiction. The literature in these genres is recognisably and unapologetically influenced by much popular fiction published in nineteenth-century England but tries to periodically secure an Indian flavour in its content and subject matter. SF also looks back to a minor tradition in the pioneering works of Adrish Bardhan, Dilip Raychaudhuri, Anish Deb and Muhammad Zafar Iqbal, who together edited little magazines and anthologies dedicated to science fiction, translated the iconic works of the Golden Age and wrote stories that absorbed and reflected, from time to time, global innovations in the genre.

In ironical contrast to this rather rich and diverse history, though, is, once again, the sheer absence of a body of theoretical discourse on Indian science fiction. Barring some outstanding efforts made in the recent past to conceptualise explicitly postcolonial categories such as *kalpavigyan*, that too by academicians based in the West, there has been none to very little local engagement with the complexities of SF writing.[15] While this relative lack of critical interest in Indian SF (indicating its severely marginalised status in the modern literary culture of the Indian academia) suggests, perhaps, freedom for new authors to experiment without having to confront a rigidly established set of conventions, it simultaneously disallows the formation of a tradition within which newer, even if more experimental, authors can write and be read. The present book wishes to plug this leak with the hope that it will allow the Indian literary cultures to think about Indian SF more as a legitimate field of critical enquiry.

NOTES

1 While an extensive study of postcolonial theory is truly beyond the scope of this collection of chapters, it is a rich and evolving body, including works by Bennedict Anderson, Bill Ashcroft, Edward Said, Homi Bhabha, Gayatri Spivak, et cetera. For a more specific discussion of Indian SF vis-à-vis postcolonial theories, see Suparno Banerjee's *Indian Science Fiction: Patterns, History and Hybridity*.

2 Carl Freedman argued that Suvin's understanding of cognition in his iconic phrase 'cognitive estrangement' was too rigid and might exclude certain works from being classified as science fiction proper. Therefore, he proposed the term 'cognition effect' to possibly include texts that do not adhere strictly to the principles of cognition. See Carl Freedman's *Critical Theory and Science Fiction*.

3 Fredric Jameson argued that in the case of 'third-world' national allegory, the 'story of the private individual destiny is always an allegory of the embattled situation of the public third-world culture and society'. This definition came under criticism, primarily from Aijaz Ahmad for providing a reductionist view of this kind of literature.

4 Note the capital S. The Science spoken about here is not just the Western idea of science but ProtoScience, as spoken about in the sixth chapter of this book.

5 This is a rather colloquial explanation of the quantum wave function.

6 The infamous Schrodinger's cat experiment is an explication of this probabilistic and non-deterministic nature of quantum entities.

7 The length of the absence of free will is, by and large, due to the determinism of classical mechanics. The idea is that if a person knows all the initial conditions and the laws of a system, they can calculate the path an entity in that system can take. The processes of human consciousness—insofar as they make humans human, subject to the same physical determinism of nature—thus gets rendered calculable.

8 This is very similar to Hegel's dialectical science.

9 Risking repetition, obviously, this absence is not an absence of nature but a void in the human comprehension of it that science reveals.
10 Clearly, a triage reveals the prima facie importance of the concept of Science discussed before as the governing term of the three, for Indian science fiction is markedly different from Indian fiction. Even if the former finds a place inside the latter, it is still something that, just with the inclusion of science, stands out on its own.
11 Not only does the previous section speaks about this in some detail but the different chapters of the present book showcase it through different aspects.
12 Mary Ellis Gibson, ed. 2019. *Science Fiction in Colonial India, 1835–1905: Five Tales of Speculation, Resistance and Rebellion*. London: Anthem Press. See the discussion of the story in Gibson's wide-ranging introduction to the anthology (pp. 1–28).
13 Vandana Singh belongs to the generation of SF writers who oversaw the transition of Indian SF from its traditional investments in form and subject matter to a new wave that broadened its speculative horizons. Singh has often been a spokesperson of this new wave in her non-fiction essays, blogs and interviews, wherein she has offered deep but accessible insights into the redeployment of myths as models of epistemological critique. See, for example, her chapter 'A Speculative Manifesto', published as an afterword in her 2008 collection, *The Woman Who Thought She Was a Planet and Other Stories*. New Delhi: Zubaan Books and Penguin India. Also see Malisa Kurtz. 2016. '"Alternate Cuts": An Interview with Vandana Singh'. *Science Fiction Studies*, 43(3): 534–545.
14 From an interview with Gautham Shenoy for FactorDaily's New Worlds Weekly series, published on 11 November 2017 under the title 'No poster and no flag'. https://archive.factordaily.com/samit-basu-interview/
15 Two works, in particular, must be cited as examples of the rare but useful critical attention that has come the way of Bengali SF. See Bodhisattva Chattopadhyay. 2016. 'On the Mythologerm: Kalpavigyan and the Question of Imperial Science'. *Science Fiction Studies*, 43(3): 435–458. Also see Atanu Bhattacharya and Preet Hiradhar. 2014. 'Own Maps/Imagined Terrain: The Emergence of Science Fiction in India'. *Extrapolation*, 55(3): 277–297. But that they are primarily on Bengali SF need not be reiterated.

WORKS CITED

Banerjee, Suparno. 2010. 'Other Tomorrows: Postcoloniality, Science Fiction and India.' PhD Diss., Louisiana State University.

—. 2020. *Indian Science Fiction: Patterns, History and Hybridity*. Cardiff: University of Wales Press.

Chattopadhyay, Bodhisattva. 2016. 'On the Mythologerm: Kalpavigyan and the Question of Imperial Science.' *Science Fiction Studies*, 43(3): 435–458.

Ghosh, Amitav. 1996. *The Calcutta Chromosome*. New Delhi: Ravi Dayal.

Khan, Sami Ahmad. 2021. *Star Warriors of the Modern Raj: Materiality, Mythology and Technology in Indian Science Fiction*. Cardiff: University of Wales Press.

Márquez, Gabriel Garcia. 1982. 'The Solitude of Latin America.' Nobel Prize. https://www.nobelprize.org/prizes/literature/1982/marquez/lecture/ (accessed on 15 July 2020)

Miéville, China. 2009. 'Afterword: Cognition as Ideology: A Dialectic of SF Theory.' In *Red Planets: Marxism and Science Fiction*, edited by Mark Bould and China Miéville. Middletown: Wesleyan University Press.

Mukherjee, Upamanyu Pablo. 2020. *Final Frontiers: Science Fiction and Techno-Science in Non-Aligned India*. Liverpool: University of Liverpool Press.

Padmanabhan, Manjula. 2019. 'Foreword: Spice-Ship to Infinity.' In *The Gollancz Book of South Asian Science Fiction*, edited by Tarun K. Saint. Gurugram: Hachette India.

Parker, Henry Meredith. 1835. 'The Junction of the Ocean. A Tale of the Year 2098.' In *Bengal Annual: A Literary Keepsake*. Calcutta: Samuel Smith & Co.

Rieder, John. 2008. *Colonialism and the Emergence of Science Fiction*. Connecticut: Wesleyan University Press.

Singh, Vandana. 2017. 'Yakshantriksh.' *Lightspeed*, 85. https://www.lightspeedmagazine.com/fiction/yakshantariksh/ (accessed on 24 August 2021).

Tan, Charles. 2009. 'Exclusive Interview: Anil Menon.' *SF Signal*. https://www.sfsignal.com/archives/2009/11/exclusive_interview_anil_menon/ (accessed on 20 October 2020)

Book I

PARADIGMS

Chapter 1

STEAMPUNK PROBES: PARODY AND THE ALLEGORICAL RETRIEVAL OF HISTORY IN SUMIT BARDHAN'S *ARTHATRISHNA*

Saikat Ghosh

INTRODUCTION

By Editors

Even as SF finds its roots within the more scientifically and industrially developed Western nations, the Indian reformulations of the genre have, over the ages, evolved to include not just specificities of Indian realities but also processes of replying to all of West's colonial incursions—historical or discursive. In fact, by using the very instruments that the colonial West (read the British) has birthed, Indian SF narratives have shown possibilities of existential alterities to ensure inscriptions of renegotiations with the very temporality that has sought to cage it within colonial identities. In a sense then, Indian SF, primarily the postcolonial variant, reworks the formal systems of SF itself to ensure both synchronic and diachronic (re)emergence of the Indian nation outside the frameworks of its erstwhile colonised identity.

The alterity implicit within these narratives is then of an ontological variety that allows for concretely singular and specific national presentations and re-presentations. This is done with an essential re-historicisation: a procedure through which history itself is rethought as something else than what it is. While there are multiple ways by which this happens, and different narratives have used different tropes towards the same, the entanglements with absences within the framework of SF have always ensured even the possibility of such. It is this possibility that Indian SF exploits for the presentation of its existential alterity. Obviously, this alterity is a difference to not only what historically *is* but also what could *have been*, for this realises, in ways that real-isations happen, differences of imaginations of the nation and, extending from it, the political reality of the nation itself (Anderson 1983).

Saikat Ghosh's chapter, through the reading of Sumit Bardhan's *Arthatrishna*, speaks about the presentations of one such form of alterity. Not only does Ghosh speak about the possibilities of difference implicit inside the steampunk genre of *Arthatrishna* but also the changes that Bardhan brings to the conceptualisation of steampunk itself through his novel. What results, then, is the essential re-historicisation of colonial Bengal allowing it to be imagined outside the discursive limits of British and Western conceptualisations.

****

> To articulate the past historically does not mean to recognize it 'the way it really was'. It means to seize hold of a memory as it flashes up at a moment of danger.
>
> —Walter Benjamin

Stylistic and discursive constructions of the past are always motivated by the present experienced as a crisis. Those who are culturally involved in framing the crisis as a set of questions and attempting solutions are invariably thinking about a future. If the questions lead to aporia or dead ends of the imagination, the tendency to *re-territorialise* the future with glamorous debris from the past, or to nostalgically wear the present inside out as past, is a compulsive one. In such a case, the crisis continues to underlie anxieties and gets registered in current social conflict as well as political manoeuvring; however, cultural production temporarily detaches itself from the crisis and participates in a commodification of time that results in 'ersatz nostalgia' (Appadurai 1996).[1] The peculiarity of this problem has been noticed while analysing fantasies that are at least partly shaped by the fashion-driven mass cultures of late capitalism. Since the 1980s, the appeal of retro-futurism in cinema, literature, art, visual design and advertising has steadily intensified and has even gained currency within youth subcultures from time to time. Retro-futurism encodes Culture as a series of ideological operations through which the present as a crisis is acknowledged and simultaneously evaded within imagined temporalities that continuously enact a journey back to the future by seeking traces of a viable or desirable future in discarded/alternative trajectories of the past.[2]

At the turn of the century, a steampunk style of explicitly retro-futuristic art and fashion emerged in the West. Citing some of the most advanced mechanistic inventions and risqué emblems of nineteenth-century industrial Europe, Steampunk tried to accomplish an imaginative fusion of the past with futurism borrowed from SF. In fact, the sense of the past itself was derived from literary sources, such as the works of H.G. Wells and Jules Verne whose SF novels are seen as precursors to steampunk classics such as Gibson and Sterling's *The Difference Engine* (1990). Recent scholarship on the steampunk-inspired literature has indeed noted the ways in which it harks back to a 'past that never was' (Taddeo and Miller 2013; Bowser and Croxall 2016). Even so, academic investigations have been blindsided by a lazily Eurocentric assumption that the steampunk assemblage of signs and props that refer to the nascent advance of industrialism in nineteenth-century Europe is utilised by the works in the genre to stage a fantastic recovery of precursory moments in the history of industrialisation that could have yielded an alternative to the present reality. This is perhaps based on the fallacious assumption that industrialisation proceeded along a singular trajectory, governing a unifying set of practices that historically shaped all the impactful consequences in the present reality. In fact, to historically recall that the most zealous advocates of industrialism in the nineteenth century were themselves privy to the colonial policy of dismantling non-European native forces of industry and scientific innovation in the colonies is to *also* see the clunky, eccentric pageantry of steampunk machines as a parody of a grand narrative that had hoped to direct the technological and productive forces of the nineteenth century towards a world-imperial order. The lens of retro-futurism precludes this double vision because it does not engage seriously with the production of steampunk literature in non-European cultures and languages. Instead, it superficially and fallaciously conflates observable global participation in steampunk creativity with a mass-cultural endorsement of the European theme of retro-futurism and its commodified fantasia of time.

Part of the problem lies with globalisation itself. With globalisation, the West's logocentric re-arrival in the late twentieth century marks the rhetorical 'end of history' (Fukuyama 1992).[3] Retro-futurism is its handmaiden in the sense that its key ideological operation consists in the transformation of historical time into aesthetic time. Together, they conjure up a nineteenth-century past for the world in which the temporal topography is undifferentiated, sans dialectical tensions and mechanically governed by Greenwich Mean Time—a 'homogenous empty time' of a world immersed in nascent industrialism and forces of modernity unleashed by the West—instead of the historically contested and fraught experience of industrialism in a world wherein the West was not the sole actor or subject.

Diagnosis of the problem does not automatically aid us in freeing steampunk literature from the ideological prison-house of retro-futurism. And yet, the need for a critical reappraisal of this style, beyond its hyperreal signatures in the fashion and advertising sectors, is made rather obvious when we consider the current reinvigoration of steampunk through literature that is being produced away from the West, across postcolonial literary cultures. Steampunk novels have recently appeared in languages that have hitherto served at the vernacular margins of imperial or national imaginaries.[4] One such example is Sumit Bardhan's Bengali SF thriller *Arthatrishna* (2019), a work that is currently being promoted as the first steampunk novel in a language that offers, as legacy, a remarkable range of cultural resonances when we fully consider its relationship of intimate otherness to nineteenth-century European fictions of adventure, crime, scientific speculation and rational conjecture.

It will be my effort to convey, through the course of this chapter, the ways in which *Arthatrishna* reinscribes the semantic landscape of the steampunk novel with meanings and potentialities that have traditionally constituted the epistemological field for the most rigorous historical fiction, thus freeing steampunk from an indentured association with the reified notion that pasts may be recoverable and reusable through the aura cast by objects that would otherwise be considered obsolete.

FORMULA AND MULTIVALENCE IN THE PLAY OF GENRES

That *Arthatrishna* is both a novel experiment as well as a child of Bengal's colonial past is evidenced in the numerous generic debts it accumulates as its story courses forward. It is set in the period just prior to India's independence, marked by the insecurities of the Second World War, the worst ravages of famine and unemployment in Bengal, the hollowing out of the colonial metropolis Calcutta where economic opportunities have been reduced to a trickle, a peak in the coercive aggression of the colonial state and an exponential rise in petty urban crime that made the native upper classes deeply suspicious of the underlings. The setting is identical to that of Sharadindu Bandyopadhyay's Byomkesh Bakshi series of detective stories and novellas. Indeed, Sumit Bardhan pays tribute to Byomkesh by naming his detective protagonist Dhurjati, another name for the maverick Lord Shiva, whose third eye is believed to have the power to penetrate through all webs of deceit. Both Byomkesh and Dhurjati are *satyanweshis*, or truth-seekers, with the airs of a renunciate. Both are paired with less gifted but perceptive companions who also function as narrators of their respective peers' exploits. The similarities extend up to their immediate predicament of being bachelor tenants in rented pensions within central Calcutta's petty-bourgeois neighbourhoods. Both are eccentrically obsessed with the laws of deduction and seem to operate within a well-worn template offered in Arthur Conan Doyle's iconic Sherlock Holmes adventures. Yet, unlike Byomkesh's Calcutta wherein the ubiquitous presence of the colonial state was registered as a mere fact of social, and to a much lesser extent, political life, Dhurjati's Calcutta is the emblem of the colonial uncanny.[5] Its industrial past lies in ruin and its once prosperous commerce has been laid waste by wartime inflation and hoarding. The warehouses on the banks of the Hooghly lie empty and unused, except as squalid sites of refuge for fugitives or as secret meeting places. The city slumbers or sluggishly goes about its routines in the daytime but comes alive in a restless air of devilry and daring after sundown, even as it fattens and thrives on the illicit trades and nocturnal labours of the hapless. It is a city of night, reminiscent of China Mieville's surrealist rendering of London as Bas-Lag in *Perdido Street Station* (2000).

The abrupt foreclosure of industrial progress in the 1940s Calcutta precipitated a historically significant period of crisis and upheaval. However, it is rare to come across literary accounts of that period, realistic or otherwise, that leverage the impulses of this crisis to explain the social and cultural transformations that took place during the fag end of colonial rule. In *Arthatrishna*, this crisis acts as a fitting backdrop for the introduction of steampunk elements. The forlorn and alienated existence of the Indo-British Clockworks, a commercial establishment housing archaic mechanistic inventions and other curious objects dating back to the times of Charles Babbage, symbolises a past ruined by colonial greed. On deeper discernment, however, it turns out to be a past that has already been visited by the spectral future of computers and robotics. Humanoid brass machines, programmed through Hollerith Cards, are objects of a clandestine ongoing trade that holds the key to an extraordinary theft committed in the premises of the establishment. To simple-minded onlookers, the Indo-British Clockworks is a mere museum of steampunk paraphernalia; but to Dhurjati, the intriguing traces of the past signal the moral and civilisational obsolescence of industrial modernity. The proper understanding of this obsolescence becomes a precondition for the detection of the motive, instrument and modus operandi of the theft.

Fairly early in Dhurjati's investigation, it becomes clear that the thief managed to access the closely guarded premises of the Clockworks by landing an aircraft on its rooftop. Aeroplanes were a common sight in Calcutta's airspace during the Second World War. Commissioned military planes shipping combatants, cargo and officials were being used by the colonial government regularly. But a common citizen had no access to commissioned aeroplanes. Hence, Dhurjati concludes that the thief would have used a Giffard Airship, a helium-propelled smaller cousin of the monstrous Zeppelin and a familiar junk item of wonder in the steampunk imaginary, to accomplish the task. The stolen item, a brass robot, also provokes the reader's curiosity because, like the airship, it is an unused item leftover from the hyped futuristic experiments of nineteenth-century pioneers. While the British merchants and agents of the state have no use for airships and brass robots, except to collect them as memorabilia, Dhurjati correctly deduces that someone from the native milieu may be involved in repurposing junk technology for sinister ends.

The quest to uncover the thief's identity leads Dhurjati and his companion to the discovery of a spate of murders and uncertain threats that cannot be clearly connected but indicate the presence of a formidable and shadowy adversary who acts upon complex motives and is willing to improvise at every step. At the behest of Soumendranarayan, a chance acquaintance who feels threatened and solicits professional assistance, the duo visits the provincial estate of Dulmigarh where it is fortuitously discovered that Soumendranarayan's toddler son Upen owns a brass robot that has started malfunctioning. Dhurjati closely observes Upen playing with his mechanical toy and begins to comprehend the mysterious motive of the theft.

Two observations on the relationship between technology and agency become pertinent at this point. First, the *use-value* of discarded mechanistic props from the steampunk imaginary is resurrected by those who have no access to more updated technology. Disenfranchised native subjects of the Empire improvise with abandoned machines and invent novel uses that may be imperceptible within a more evolved discursive paradigm of technology, thereby disrupting, and momentarily subverting, the discursive framework itself. Second, to comprehend improvisation, one must observe elements of a system *at play*, detached from the system's own episteme or 'condition of possibility' (Foucault 1972). Upen frees the brass robot from the uses to which it had been originally intended and, in turn, guides Dhurjati into a world of parodic adaptations wherein the concealed motive for stealing junk robots can be found.

In his influential work *The Savage Mind* (1966), Claude Lévi-Strauss described the observable forms of creativity in non-European societies as bricolage, a process involving heuristic repurposing of available signs to accomplish 'concrete' tasks, and culturally distinguishable from Western modernity's reliance on totalising conceptual systems that govern all aspects of its civilisational knowledge and self-representation. Even though Lévi-Strauss questioned the stability of this distinction, he wished to retain it as an analytic model because it helped him explain the mode of construction in myths. For our purposes, it allows us to see a specific valence of the dialectic that conditions cultural differences in the colonial encounter between Europeans and the colonised peoples. In the novel, both the adversary and Upen, as bricoleurs, have counterposed the pursuit of technology-as-signs (semiotic and syntagmatic) to the colonial state's pursuit of technology-as-system (symbolic and paradigmatic). Owing to the asymmetry of power relations between the colonisers and the colonised, the dialectic cannot acquire a real resolution. In the real context of colonialism, the semiotic will necessarily have to submit itself to the symbolic. Its psychic and cultural survival is predicated on *play* or, in the broadest sense, playfully *mimetic* gestures. It is in this sense, too, that steampunk is adapted into the novel as a bricolage with intermittently parodic references to colonialism's 'mimic' modernity (Bhabha 1994), which, in its own turn, relates to the nineteenth-century industrial past of Europe as a 'sign of the inappropriate' that 'poses an imminent threat to both "normalized" knowledges and disciplinary powers' (ibid.).[6]

The child figure in the novel is another trope derived from the extant tradition of detective fiction in Bengali. Satyajit Ray's precocious child figures such as Mukul (*Sonar Kella* 1971), Ruku (*Joy Baba Felunath* 1975) and Bablu (*Phatikchand* 1983) function within a given template wherein their make-believe universe runs parallel to the precarious reality that the adults surrounding them are forced to contend with. Scholars who have studied the specifically Bengali cultural phenomenon of publishing detective fiction in literary magazines catering to children and teenagers, and hence the concomitant necessity of fusing children's fiction with detective fiction, have emphasised the disciplinary aspects of such an exercise to suggest the construction of an 'ideal child-subject' that, under the tutelage of the adult detective, is expected to attain a normative 'adolescence without entirely endangering the qualities of a vulnerable childhood' (Chowdhury 2015). *Arthatrishna*'s Upen is seemingly at ease within this company of child figures; however, unlike them, he functions almost without adult guidance. His protector cum companion is the robot, which is also 'controlled' by him because he understands the robot's mechanism and the Hollerith cards that are used to dictate its behaviour. Upen's relationship with the robot is that of a playmate, and the robot is programmed to reciprocate his gestures in various ball games. When the robot starts receiving remote heliographic signals and behaving erratically, he realises that an adult is at the source of the mischief. Upen's intuitive grasp of the problem eventually helps Dhurjati in connecting the heliograph with a respected geologist who had encamped in the vicinity and, on further investigation, turns out to be the arch adversary. Upen's moment of truth dawns upon him within the improvisational context of play; he realises that someone else is also trying to 'play' his pet robot. To help with the investigation, he is not required to cross the boundaries of his make-believe universe or engage with problems that concern the adults. There is no suggestion of a normative passage to adolescence or any impending moment of disillusionment that may undermine his credulity.

ALLEGORY AND ALTERITY

Distinguishing 'allegory' from 'symbol', Paul de Man famously argued that allegory accommodates temporality, anteriority and difference, whereas symbol works through a mystification of time and history and promotes the romantic (and false) identification of a subject with an object (de Man 1983). This distinction becomes important while reading novels that use fantasy as a mode of defamiliarising and denormalising the experience of reality. In relation to the real, the fantastic either adopts a language of symbolism or chooses to assemble an allegory. The distinction between the two choices has a bearing on the question 'who claims alterity?' (Spivak 2012).[7] In an allegory, it is possible to seek an answer to the question by examining and re-theorising the ideological abstractions that determine the concrete experience of history.

In terms of its standard plotting, *Arthatrishna* gives in to a juridical order that is predicated on the sanctity of private property. It invokes and endorses age-old attitudes of distrust and condemnation against the figure of the mad, itinerant professor whose boundless greed and pathological urge for revenge drive him to commit a spectacular series of crimes that cannot go unpunished. However, when Dhurjati discovers the identity of his adversary, Professor Sukumar Ghoshal, he is intrigued by the details of the scientist's life. These details are expectedly fantastic but also overlap with history, and in being so, invite the reader to re-encounter history more reflexively. Sukumar had been a brilliant protégé of the legendary Belgian Jesuit missionary and scientist Father Eugene Lafont.[8] Trained at St Xavier's College, one of the prestigious institutions of colonial Calcutta, Sukumar intends to conduct breakthrough research in Physics and earn permanent fame. Yet, his aspirations are cruelly thwarted when the University of Calcutta denies him a fellowship he deserves, awarding it instead to his wealthy friend Nripendra, who is less gifted than him. Nripendra is the scion of an influential landed family that has close relations with the colonial government and the British commercial establishments. Sukumar tries to sustain his research through independent means but is repeatedly shunned by the official scientific establishment. The futility of his endeavours forces him to abandon physics in favour of geology, a discipline that provides him modest means of income through teaching positions in provincial colleges and occasional surveys commissioned by the colonial government. During one such survey at Dulmigarh, a chance discovery of rich deposits of the mythical adamantine pushes Sukumar to transgress the limits of law. He begins to secretly nurture the ambition of mining the adamantine and smuggling it out to enemy nations that can use it as a superior alternative to steel in the manufacturing of weapons and military infrastructure. The thriving illicit war trade allows him this opportunity. Precipitously, it turns out that the Dulmigarh land is owned by Nripendra's family; hence, a pragmatic decision is taken to hatch a conspiracy against the landowners and dispossess them of their title, even fantasising spectacular retribution against Nripendra. His desperation leads him to embrace alchemy, thaumaturgy and the discredited chemistry of phlogiston.[9] To mount a murderous attack on the estate, Sukumar busies himself with the task of raising an army of *pisacha* (indigenous flesh-eating zombies) and *krashpashu* (mutant monsters). In exchange for samples of adamantine, he receives a squad of terrifying *tsuchinokos* (mythical reptiles) from the fascist Japanese government. He marshals his 'non-human' forces against the estate owners and succeeds in killing Nripendra. His triumph is incomplete, however, as Nripendra's son, Soumendranarayan, is stationed far away from home at the time of the attack and thus manages to survive. Sukumar rallies for a comeback with the plan to mechanically manipulate Upen's robot into murdering Soumendranarayan and the remaining members of his family.

In a symbolic narrative, Sukumar could be constructed as an inverted ideal in the image of the romantic anti-hero, estranged from the reality principle by forces that seek to destroy his creative potential, asserting that potential in a negative form that seeks the annihilation of self and the world. But in *Arthatrishna*, he is a wily and unheroic survivor who seizes opportunities that lie outside the legitimate sphere of scientific practice because his relationship with colonial science has never been an organic one. As a colonised subject from the working class, he has always been an outsider, both culturally and economically. Despite his talents, he has ceaselessly struggled to acquire a foothold in the very institutions that discriminate against him. Hence, he does not ingenuously bear the burden of an ethos that he is condemned to betray. Instead, his actions mirror the remorseless aggressions of colonial science and explode the myth of an ethos. To raise resources, Sukumar unhesitatingly gets involved in the trafficking of mutants and patronises petty crimes against people less fortunate than him. Far from posing himself as a rebellious antithesis to the hypocritical moral order of colonial society, Sukumar willingly embodies its mimic excess and cloaks his intentions through a 'sly civility' (Bhabha 1994).[10]

If Sukumar's transgressions are conditioned by the cynical reason that shapes colonial power relations, the provincial abundance of monstrously deformed mutants and *pisacha* allegorically refers to the primitive accumulation of capital in colonialism. The anthropogenic famine of 1943, which is estimated to have caused three million deaths in the Bengal province, left a huge penurious population of starving, malnourished and pestilence-ridden rural poor in its wake. The scale of damage to life and livelihood was so colossal that it proved a turning point in the fortunes of India's struggle for freedom from colonial subjection. Yet, Calcutta's affluent classes remained largely indifferent to the common people's predicament, merely viewing from a distance the misery of disorderly hordes spilling on to the city's streets with cries of hunger, and feeling vaguely threatened by the fear of disease and violence. The phobic gaze of the urban gentry is allegorically transferred on to the attack of the *pisacha* and *krashpashu* on the residents of the Dulmigarh estate, its visceral scenes of violence evoking the horror of broken bodies and bonded souls.

The official narrative of India's anticolonial struggle notwithstanding, an allegorical reading of the novel helps excavate the fossilised class and caste relations and the resilient cultural distrust of difference that is only obliquely indicated by the rapid emergence of a comprador spirit within the bourgeois elite and the political fracturing of the idea of a sovereign people. In Dhurjati's final battle with Sukumar, loyal *garudas* (the native equivalent of the steampunk gryphon), who have already served as subalterns in the British colonial army, willingly sacrifice themselves to secure the lives of the privileged humans.

CONCLUSION

The allegorical design of *Arthatrishna* is not limited to the recovery of the margins that frame the authoritative and normative articulation of colonial modernity. Its scope goes beyond postcolonial critique. It demonstrates the allegorical role of steampunk literature in retrieving the temporal signs of modernity and unpacking the subjectivities that inhabit and express the repetition of these signs as differences. Modernity is birthed by the antinomian desire to cut away from externally enforced codes and predetermined felicities. The inexhaustible drive to innovate, experiment and mark off as separate comes with that most modern of gestures—disavowal. But in disavowing its connection with the anterior sign, the modern subject ends up paradoxically eliminating its own signification of difference. Every new thing presents itself as modern, dispossessed of its historical signature. The obsessive presentism of the modern has created incalculable difficulties in the historiographical conception of modernity. The only way out, as Walter Benjamin contra Baudelaire remarks, is to value the 'interruptive stasis of the image [from the past] over the continuity of temporal succession' (Osborne and Charles 2021). In other words, history interposes itself with the present as uncanny, as the image of a distinct other that embodies the latent anxiety of the present moment. Functioning within a steampunk imaginary, *Arthatrishna* offers an assemblage of uncanny images derived from the recesses of phobic memory that continuously reacts to the disruptive circularity of the present time in which technology dissolves our subjectivities, only to parodically reconstitute its impulses.

NOTES

1 According to Arjun Appadurai, mass advertising and other modern forms of consumer appeal are engaged in a commodification of time that manifests itself in a simulacra of periodicities whereby temporal flows are experienced as nostalgia for a loss that never actually took place or 'for things that never were'. This fabricated nostalgia, through which the consumer gets sentimentally drawn to commodities with a retrospective aura, is designated as 'ersatz nostalgia'. See Arjun Appadurai. 1996. *Modernity at Large: Cultural Dimensions of Globalization*. Minneapolis: University of Minnesota Press.

2 The cultural exhaustion of late capitalism and the melancholic reconciliations of most strands of utopian thought with their pragmatic counterparts is also reflected in science fiction's forfeiture of wonder and optimism. Answering his own question 'can we imagine a future?', Fredric Jameson concludes thus: 'What is indeed authentic about it [science fiction], as a mode of narrative and a form of knowledge, is not at all its capacity to keep the future alive, even in the imagination. On the contrary, its deepest vocation is over and over again to demonstrate and to dramatize our incapacity to imagine the future.' See Fredric Jameson. 1982. 'Progress Versus Utopia; Or, Can We Imagine the Future?' *Science Fiction Studies*, 9(2): 147–158.

3 The fall of the Berlin Wall in 1989 prompted a triumphalist commentary in Western media that saw the event as presaging the political dissolution of the Soviet Bloc and the end of communism as an ideological challenge to a globally integrated market economy controlled by the liberal nations of the West. An attempt to philosophically dignify this triumphalism was made by the US-based political scientist Francis Fukuyama. Fukuyama corrupted and caricatured Hegel's view of history as a dialectical forward march in world society's universal realisation of objective reason to suggest

that history's forward march had come to an end with the decisive defeat of communism and the universal hegemony of Western liberal democracy. The specious invocation of the West as the subject of world history and liberal democracy as its object provoked sharp reactions from Fukuyama's critics and interlocutors. See Francis Fukuyama. 1992. *The End of History and the Last Man*. New York: The Free Press.

4 Mainstream publishers of SF have ignored the need to publish steampunk fiction from non-Anglophone cultures and languages. However, independent publishers based in smaller US cities have lately shown some interest in commissioning translations and publishing anthologies of some representative works from emergent cultures of steampunk in South Asia, China and sub-Saharan Africa. For instance, see Sarah Hans, ed. 2014. *Steampunk World*. Dayton, OH: Alliteration Ink.

5 To the cultural historian, the spatial and architectural design of colonial Calcutta offers symptoms of pathologies that have characterised, from time to time, the relations between the state and the various orders, communities and classes of its subjects. Lately, several studies have drawn attention to the ways in which the colonial state's attempts at imposing a sanitary and civic order to routine life in the city was met with resistance and the subversive reordering of space, activities and agency. Some, like Swati Chattopadhyay (2005) have argued that resistance can only be inferred through symptomatic readings of testimonies and eyewitness accounts by administrators and people making official visits to the city. Their confounded sense of the city is articulated through depictions, among other things, of the extraordinary transformations of space between day and night when the familiar metamorphoses into the unfamiliar. See Swati Chattopadhyay. 2005. *Representing Calcutta: Modernity, Nationalism, and the Colonial Uncanny*. New York: Routledge.

6 British colonialism produces a discourse of authority that is marked by ambivalence. It authorises disciplinary and regulative practices that appear to reform and civilise but end up producing farcical 'effects' of the post-Enlightenment ideals of liberty and secular conscience in the colonies. The discursive limits of this authority are not shaped by the British Constitution, but by the imperatives of maintaining colonial dependency. Homi Bhabha refers to the performative acts of colonial regulation as 'mimicry'. He argues that this mimicry profoundly destabilises the moral authority of the colonial discourse by eliciting 'another knowledge of its norms'. See Homi Bhabha. 1994. *The Location of Culture*. New York: Routledge, 121–131. For a comparable analysis, see Uday Singh Mehta. 'Liberal Conventions and Imperial Exclusions.' In *Liberalism and Empire: A Study in Nineteenth-Century British Liberal Thought*. Chicago: The University of Chicago Press, 46–76.

7 While recognising that fantasies can effectively interrogate the truth claims of conventional history, we must exercise necessary caution to ensure that such interrogations do not obfuscate the historical sign of alterity or appropriate the sign into a privileged, vantage-point utterance. Gayatri Spivak's plea to evaluate postcolonial texts as 'alternative histories'

by closely attending to the ways in which their signs are framed, gendered or ordered in relation to the 'centrifugal potential of the plurality and heterogeneity native to the subcontinent' can be applied to the reading of fantasy and speculative fiction. See Gayatri Chakravorty Spivak. 2012. *An Aesthetic Education in the Era of Globalization*. Cambridge, MA: Harvard University Press.

8 The historical figure of Fr Eugene Lafont is relevant to a critical discourse on science in colonial India. Besides being a legendary teacher, Fr Lafont was a zealous advocate of science education and inspired three native pupils J.C. Bose (physicist), Prafulla Chandra Roy (chemist) and Pramatha Nath Bose (geologist) to earn international fame through pioneering research in their respective fields. The physicist Bose is also credited as the first native writer of science fiction. Fr Lafont collaborated with social reformer and physician Dr Mahendralal Sircar to establish the Indian Association for the Cultivation of Science (IACS) in 1876. Both wished to create an ethos and ecosystem for scientific practice in Indian institutions.

9 Phlogiston, an element believed to aid combustion, dominated the work of seventeenth-century German scientists Joachim Becher and George Ernst Stahl. Stahl insisted that phlogiston could be combined with calx to produce metals. Eventually, Antoine Lavoisier's attempt to prove the theory of Phlogiston wrong led him to discover oxygen and oxidation.

10 Native resistance to colonial authority through the 'refusal to satisfy the colonizer's narrative demand' (Bhabha 1994) is how Homi Bhabha describes the idea of 'sly civility'. The native's public actions subversively embody the splitting and doubling of the discourse of colonial authority and expose the limits of the 'civilising mission' invoked by the authority.

WORKS CITED

Anderson, Benedict. 1983. *Imagined Communities*. London and New York: Verso.

Appadurai, Arjun. 1996. *Modernity at Large: Cultural Dimensions of Globalization*. Minneapolis: University of Minnesota Press.

Bardhan, Sumit. 2019. *Arthatrishna*. Kolkata: Kalpabishho.

Benjamin, Walter. 1966. 'Theses on the Philosophy of History.' In *Illuminations*. Translated by Harry John. New York: Schocken Books.

Bhabha, Homi K. 1994. *The Location of Culture*. New York and London: Routledge.

Bowser, Rachel A., and Brian Croxall, eds. 2016. *Like Clockwork: Steampunk Pasts, Presents, and Futures*. Minneapolis: University of Minnesota Press.

Chowdhury, Sayandeb. 2015. 'Ageless Hero, Sexless Man: A Possible Pre-history and Three Hypotheses on Satyajit Ray's Feluda'. *South Asian Review*, 36(1): 109–130.

de Man, Paul. 1983. 'The Rhetoric of Temporality.' In *Blindness and Insight: Essays in the Rhetoric of Contemporary Criticism*. Revised 2nd ed. London: Methuen.

Foucault, Michel. 1972. *The Archaeology of Knowledge*. Translated by A.M. Sheridan Smith. London: Tavistock Publications.

Fukuyama, Francis. 1992. *The End of History and the Last Man*. New York: Free Press.

Lévi-Strauss, Claude. 1966. *The Savage Mind*. Translated by Doreen and John Weightman. Chicago: The University of Chicago Press.

Osborne, Peter, and Matthew Charles. 2021. 'Walter Benjamin.' In *The Stanford Encyclopedia of Philosophy*. Edited by Edward N. Zalta. Stanford, CA: Metaphysics Research Lab, Stanford University. https://plato.stanford.edu/archives/fall2021/entries/benjamin/ (accessed on 26 August 2021).

Taddeo, Julie Anna, and Cynthia J. Miller, eds. 2013. *Steaming Into a Victorian Future: A Steampunk Anthology*. Plymouth, UK: The Scarecrow Press.

Spivak, Gayatri Chakravorty. 2012. *An Aesthetic Education in the Era of Globalization*. CA, Massachusetts: Harvard University Press.

Chapter 2

PARALLEL 'DISCOVERIES': (RE-)CONSTRUCTING THE 'SCIENTIFIC' ENTERPRISE IN *THE CALCUTTA CHROMOSOME*

Jaya Yadav

INTRODUCTION

By Editors

Alongside presentations of historical alterity, procedures of re-historicisation(s) become rather central towards the renegotiation of postcolonial Indian Being as well, especially since such existences always tend to end up in the lap of colonial history despite their paradoxical absence from it. In a sense then, while the 'postcolonial' Indian finds itself anchored inside its (own) colonised historiography, it is also on the fringes of that history. The major reason for this outsideness is coloniality itself. History, in other words, has been and is still being written by colonial powers. Even when there have been resistances to such historiographies, the very fact that they have been systems of answering back, as it were, betray their dependence on coloniality.

In such a scenario, how does one go about untangling this paradox of spatio-temporal being? One answer, rather obviously, is to drop this temporality altogether. But, even as postcolonial theorists have tried to nominate multiple modalities to postcolonial existences veritably outside the boundaries of colonial history (and, indeed, historiography), the post-ness of such existences never seems to let go. The present Indian identity, for example, is still always marked against a colonial Indian identity (in acceptance or rejection), and there seems to be little that theory can do to change it. The second option is a form of amnesia: an essential forgetting of a major chunk of being-in-historical time and looking even farther back for narrative continuity. But, such movements are, if nothing else, merely hopeful, because subjective amnesia does not negate objective causality. What is in the present is an inevitable causal effect of the events that have happened, including the violent imperial/colonial ones. In its disruption of historical continuity, colonisation has, in other words, left its own smorgasbord of complicacies that cannot be overlooked or essentially forgotten.

The third and final option is a form of re-historicisation that Jaya Yadav's present chapter talks about. It is neither an answering back in the form of a rewriting nor either of the other two processes. Instead, this time it seeks to relocate colonial history from the colonisers to the colonised. In such, there's neither a fundamental change nor a disruption to the coloniality, but a literal renegotiation of the same. In this chapter, Yadav not only shows the need for this re-historicisation but, through the reading of Amitav Ghosh's *The Calcutta Chromosome*, also shows how SF, in its form as well as function, allows such re-presentations.

****

> Not making sense is what it's about—conventional sense that it. Maybe this other team started with the idea that knowledge is self-contradictory; maybe they believed that to know something is to change it, therefore in knowing something, you've already changed what you think you know so you really don't know it all: all you know is history. Maybe they thought that knowledge couldn't begin without acknowledging the impossibility of knowledge.
>
> —Ghosh (1996)

Since historiography as a discipline has witnessed several ruptures, digressions and transformations over time, (re-)locating the process of history writing in a postcolonial world invites new readings of colonialism and a revisitation of a large number of Orientalist[1] texts written by the colonisers. In such a scenario, connecting the precolonial past to the contemporary era, Ghosh's *The Calcutta Chromosome* (1996) interrogates the binaries created in the world of the 'scientific' coloniser, working in British-ruled territories of the subcontinent and seeking to 'rationalise' those around him. In fact, Ghosh's inflexions into the genre of science fiction (SF) posit alternative readings of history through a departure from thematic concerns that maintain the hegemonic discourse of the exemplification of Western neocolonial concerns as can be seen in a multitude of literary and on-screen representation[2]. *The Calcutta Chromosome* acts as a counternarrative, redefining what constitutes SF, and questions those who have controlled the pervasive narrative between 'science', power and 'knowledge'. Traditional models of writing have occupied a central space in both literary and scientific canons that envision the white man at the centre of 'discovery' and research. *The Calcutta Chromosome* reinvents an interdisciplinary approach in order to decode a historiographical journey in 'the heart of darkness'[3] within the Indian subcontinent, addressing concerns of the nation-state as well as alluding to indigenous narratives of myths, folklore and time travel. This is reflected in Suparno Banerjee's understanding of Indian SF, where he writes,

> [The] genre is influenced simultaneously by the 'cognitive' mode of Euro-American SF as well as by the ancient precritical traditions of myths and legends of the country such as fantasy, ghost stories, folk tales, fairy tales and mythological narratives. SF in India, especially in the postcolonial era (after 1947, when most of the works in English were written), is a creation of a society at once driven by a fast-growing materialistic industrial economy as well as the metaphysical and pastoral traditions that have existed for millennia. These works subtly challenge the normativity of Occidental literary forms and ideas, yet never fully reject the main SFal generic tendency, which Darko Suvin describes as 'cognitive estrangement.' (Banerjee 2010)

Using these paradigm shifts in SF, this chapter (re)locates issues of agency, power and 'knowledge' through a focus on Ghosh's intricate mapping of the intersections of various 'quests' across time, geographical spaces and ideological frameworks. This helps reshape and deconstruct the label of 'science' through a lens that amplifies the voices of those who lie at the 'footnotes of history'[4]. A superficial reading of the text prompts the reader to trace the life of the Nobel laureate Ronald Ross while he lived in British India and travelled across northern parts of the country to conduct malaria research. A closer reading of the novel, however, sheds light on two central local characters Mangala and Laakhan who live across time from colonial to postcolonial India. Their ability to metamorphose their 'avatars' into different people across different periods foregrounds their agency and experience, which is central to the narrative, instead of following a linear and simplistic trajectory of Ross's life and work in India. Though the novel outlines Ross's 'observations' with references to his real notebooks he kept while he was in India, it fleshes out the nameless lab assistants and people he experimented upon as Mangala and Laakhan. In an ironic rewriting of events, it becomes evident that Ross is the being who is being experimented upon and not the colonised local Indian population. It is this retrieval of Mangala and Laakhan from the annals of Western 'empirical' history that provides the aforementioned parallel reading of history and science. The binaries between what is perceived as 'Western' and, therefore, 'modern' versus the indigenous or 'primitive' are undone throughout the text as it acts as an alternate history often told through Ross's perspective.

The process of this retrieval stems from Ghosh's oeuvre, which has often been described as anthropological and historical fiction. This chapter argues that the shifting boundaries of SF, namely in the context of the subcontinent, allow for an interdisciplinary approach to illuminate strains of historiography, postcolonial theory and critiques of hegemonic models of SF. Often, SF cites neoliberal concerns of conquest and territory warfare through technology in futuristic dystopian or utopian worlds. On the other hand, Ghosh's choice of delving into the past is one where the colonial subcontinent is neither fully dystopian nor utopian. *The Calcutta Chromosome* highlights critical moments in colonial history and turns the narrative dramatically around. There is no straightforward hierarchical relationship in place in coloniser/colonised and oppressor/victim binary but a portrayal of the dialectical nature of colonialism. Ashis Nandy in *The Intimate Enemy* writes, '[T]he West is now everywhere, within the West and outside; in structures and in minds' (1983). SF becomes a tool to relocate oneself in histories that have been coloured by the coloniser and through SF; it is also a tool to harness and explore power in this mode of historiography through a deconstruction of colonial discourses. Distinct boundaries between fact and fiction become blurred in the contestation of what is 'science' and who controls the tools to operate it? Furthermore, who has the agency to retell it?

The Calcutta Chromosome won the Arthur C. Clarke award in 1997, cementing its reception in the world and contesting between overlapping genres of SF, world literature and Commonwealth literature. The primary thematic concerns of the novel provide a theoretical springboard to examine the larger questions of 'discoveries', disease and travel. The novel follows multiple journeys of the characters of Antar, a technician working in a 'global public health consultancy' International Water Council, from where a senior colleague named Murugan goes missing while searching for the 'Calcutta Chromosome'. Their interwoven journey runs concurrently to Nobel laureate Ronald Ross's in a narrative mingled with themes of time and travel across the world. The novel is not simply a fictional retelling of Ross's time in India as a medical officer and tracing events leading to his 'discovery' of the malaria vector. Rather, it is a problematisation of science and the colonial project, positing an alternative history by using fiction as historiography. The novel does not function as a chronological retelling of these events in an anthropological manner. Instead, it sheds light on other 'real' events that may or may not have taken place alongside Ross's 'discovery'.

To undercut the dominant narrative of Ross's 'discovery', Ghosh circumscribes a timeline of global events that orbit around two central characters: Mangala and Laakhan. They are also equal, if not superior scientists in their own right, as they combine their cult practices with traditional knowledge, interjected with the tools of the coloniser's laboratory through Ross. To Ross, they are part of his larger scientific enterprise, even though they cannot communicate to him much as he speaks to them in his pidgin Hindustani. Whereas, to the reader, they orchestrate various relevant episodes of research without any underlying concern to highlight their names or existence. Their alternative knowledge system moves away from rigid binaries between what is perceived as 'Western' and therefore 'modern' versus the indigenous or 'primitive', terms that recur in Ross's own diaries written during this period. His writing and voice are not what dictates the tone of the text, and his own shortcomings as a narrow-minded colonialist, whose sight is coloured by parameters of being a white man, has often dominated his literary discourses.

Tracing the history of SF, one may begin from Thomas More's *Utopia* and later on to Julius Verne's *From the Earth to the Moon*, which contained a propagandist, imperialist agenda and belief that 'new found' lands were to be discovered. In stark contrast, *The Calcutta Chromosome* transports the reader from a near future like existence with more advanced technology to colonial India, in the heart of Calcutta, which becomes the epicentre of discovery and delirium, both in the past and the present. One must also note that instead of using magical realism to reveal a world where science or understanding of a difference as a form of 'reason' functions not as opposites, Ghosh intertwines them to create complementary tangents to a broader spectrum where science is not a unidimensional arena. The use of SF in this narrative, which revisits the colonial enterprise and its inflexions, does not glorify Western notions of science. Instead, Ghosh uses the 'translocal' and diasporic figures to deconstruct such narratives. The traveller here is not an alien intervention used for fictionalising history. In fact, it is 'Indianised', and it exemplifies a colonial world filled with Bhabha's 'Third Space(s)', as Indians are the ones who are using Ross to achieve their own long-term goals, a trope that also recurs in Ghosh's earlier novel *In an Antique Land* (1992). Ross does not merely represent the coloniser, but rather a figure, who has been (mis)placed in an intricate matrix of time, travel and history, in an overarching framework of 'Indian' 'science' and ancient systems of knowledge. Ghosh underlines and attempts to reverse this system of knowledge and power through *The Calcutta Chromosome*, which takes the reader on a journey of (re)discovery that continually redefines what constitutes 'modern' medicine, 'development' and 'knowledge'.

The novel's introduction to its title is through an initial engagement with its contemporary time period portraying the life of immigrants in the United States. This is with the assumption that the reader shares biases against alternative readings of history and a defence for the need for the 'absurd' through Murugan, who shuttles between being the primary and secondary narrators with Antar, the Egyptian origin New Yorker living alone in the city. The first line of the novel sets the tone for the rest of the fictionalised events: 'If the system hadn't stalled Antar would never have guessed that the scrap of paper on his screen was the remnant of an ID card'. The use of 'if' acts as a device to focalise future events in the various travels undertaken by the characters. The overarching themes present an interesting interplay of multiple histories, different modes of 'science' as well as cults and rituals, pluralising perceptions and pushing the definition of 'science' and scientific research.

Antar begins his typical day, set in the near future of the year 1995, which is the publication date of the novel. A futuristic artificial intelligence search engine named Ava scans an old ID card with the name Murugan, an old colleague of Antar's who has been missing for several years. The last place he had been seen was in Calcutta, a city that becomes the central site for rediscovering a rich past in the ever-shifting narrative. Antar has flashbacks of his conversation with Murugan who repeatedly argues for a space of his own reading of history wherein Ronald Ross's discovery of the malaria transmitter anopheles was not self-determined research.

Murugan believed that several other people used Ross as a catalyst in their own pioneering research efforts. Ghosh terms this as 'interpersonal transference', which echoes the Hindu philosophy of reincarnation. Mangala and Laakhan, too, are seen putting on different 'avatars' during different periods in history. It is important to note that the foils, or rather fellow scientists, are not Ross's competitors from other European countries but are everyday Indians who also simultaneously work as lab assistants to Ross. His character does not represent an extension of the 'white man's burden' prototypical hero but an intentional experiment by those participating in the cult-like counterscience movement that sought to be invisible. The other two major characters, Mangala and Laakhan, are at the heart of this research. Though socially marginalised in nineteenth-century India because of their castes, they are the powerful agents of discovery. They appear to be in control of Ross's day-to-day life in the laboratory and, as the reader discovers, even the novel, which becomes almost metatheatrical in the end. Mangala and Laakhan are not conditioned by Western empiricist notions with the emphasis on empirical 'proofs' due to their non-Western cultural paradigm of knowledge.

The overlapping parallels of the traveller, as the reader, Murugan, and Antar follow routes of travel in order to retrace a larger overarching narrative of subverting colonial hegemony and legacies of the empire. Since the medium of the language, in the novel, is in English, one can argue that it functions on a dual level. First, it may be read as a form of 'writing back to the Empire'[5], and second, it undoes the power the Empire holds by deconstructing the genre of travelogue writing popular especially during the nineteenth century. The subtitle of the novel, *a novel of fevers, delirium and discovery*, uses the nineteenth-century form of travel writing to take the reader from Victorian London to colonial Calcutta, where the fears and concerns of the empiricist, 'enlightened' white man are physically and ideologically transported to South Asia where port cities such as Calcutta become the repositories of scientific workplaces and laboratories often credited to colonial intervention.

It is important to note that the participation of the locals has to a large extent been overlooked in both fictive and non-fictive accounts in history where knowledge was not a linear process of passing down from the coloniser to the colonised. *The Calcutta Chromosome* does not depict the colonised people as silent or nameless, as they are portrayed in Ross's journal entries. Calcutta becomes an inverse laboratory where Mangala, who was found at the Sealdah railway station, and Laakhan, who masquerades as a 'dhooley bearer', become ingenious laboratory assistants to Ross. The duplication and reversal of their roles become more pertinent in colonial India. Murugan notices that their inclusion in his journals is not merely coincidental as it appears as though Mangala knew that induced malaria could cure syphilis. Again, this becomes counterfactual to Julius Wagner, another recipient of the Nobel Prize for curing syphilis by the same method. Theoretically, therefore, Calcutta is never far away or wholly an Othered place from Europe as Norma Evenson writes in 'The Hybrid Metropolis'[6]: 'Port cities such as Calcutta, Madras and Bombay were physical and social hybrids virtually from their inception. Founded as new towns by the British in the 17th century, subsequently attracting sizable Indian populations, these colonial centres were neither typical British nor typical Indian settlements' (1992). The hybridity formed here is akin to Bhabha's 'third space', where these newly formed cultures are a physical and metaphorical space for the coloniser and the colonised to form a dialectical relationship than a simple oppressor versus suppressed one.

As the plot moves back and forth spatially and textually across time, these themes become more evident. When Murugan arrives in Calcutta, he runs into Urmila and Sonali, two journalists who were reporting on a famous writer Phulboni who, one later learns, is also connected to the Mangala-Laakhan narrative. The reader learns that Mrs Aratorunian, an Armenian landlady, gives Murugan a place to stay at her house in Robinson Street, where Ross used to live in the previous century. In a series of chaotic events where Murugan finds Mrs Aratorunian's house and all his possessions were sold, one suddenly realises that in the contemporary age Mangala has been reincarnated as Mrs Aratorunian and Laakhan as Romen Haldar, reversing the roles of these previously marginalised characters into figures of power and class privilege in twentieth-century Calcutta. Barbara Romanik[7] writes, 'Clearly, the subversive way in which the members of Mangala's cult living and use #3 Robinson Street deflects the social, political and economic power these colonial mansions once represented' (2005). Gender roles and their reversal play an important part in *The Calcutta Chromosome*. Mangala may, in North Indian society, be placed lower due to her occupation as a sweeper, but she is the catalyst for major action that fuels scientific research. Laakhan, too, recurs in different times at different places as various reincarnations as he embodies, along with the figure of Mangala, the other domain of science, knowledge and power. The fact that this alternative history validates other sources of comprehension and understanding that exist simultaneously with Western forms of empiricist knowledge defies existing notions of what constitutes science. The other women, Urmila and Sonali, are working and independent. Tara, Antar's neighbour, also is a woman empowered in her own right, though dislocated geographically.

It is imperative to emphasise that during colonial rule, individuals and communities questioned the empire through various acts of subversion. One must note that colonial trade which made the imperialist conquest possible and the magnitude of the British Empire plausible was based on maritime technological advancements. This was closely associated with developments made during the industrial age. The colonies and their people too were shareholders and participants in these developments. Ghosh uses fiction as a site where the reader too becomes a literal and metaphorical traveller.

Ghosh's experimentations with the reconstruction of time in *The Calcutta Chromosome* as cyclical and not linear call for a comparative reading of history as histories in the field of SF, which allows for such experimentations in form and style, challenging linear, 'structured' narratives. The fragmentation of time in the novel grants the reader to fill these gaps with their own understanding based on alternative forms of history presented to them on paper. The crevices are unveiled behind the mechanisms of colonialism through a contradictory retelling of history. The questions of this 'new' world order connected to an old, which challenges Eurocentric understandings of the world, find space in *The Calcutta Chromosome*. Though Ghosh distances himself from calling his work postcolonial[8], one cannot isolate him from tools that this school of theory provides to deconstruct new reconstructions. The narrative technique of time that is not chronological keeps the plot shifting constantly and engages the reader.

Ghosh unmasks the façade of the greater good of humanity of medical research and shows the steeped materialistic reality of the 'noble' pursuit. The colonial empire evidently flourishes due to its exploitation of citizens of those 'antique' lands; they were never given credit for and are not found in the annals of history as anything other than a subjugated community only fit to be ruled and governed by the white man. The white man's burden and religion play a key role in perpetuating the hegemonic discourse of white Western superiority. *The Calcutta Chromosome* dismantles this view of power functioning vertically. As one sees, knowledge is a permeable process in which the coloniser and the colonised take an active part. No one is superior and all-knowing all the time or marked as 'true scientists' simply based on the colour of their skin. 'Irrationality' and 'rationality', in the novel, are not antonyms but are, rather, terms of different perspectives. Ghosh allows the reader to first doubt and later on believe in Murugan's convictions. His concerns are not ours in the beginning, but as the plot moves forward, one also begins to feel his doubts regarding Ronald Ross.

The elements of historiography in *The Calcutta Chromosome* pluralise the domain of what constitutes a SF novel while also allowing it to function as a historical one. *The Calcutta Chromosome* cannot be reduced to a single genre. Multi-layered and at times even challenging to understand, the novel becomes a medium to understand other histories, representations and misrepresentations of various famous episodes that have been unquestioningly accepted as the 'truth'. Whereas one learns through *The Calcutta Chromosome* that truth is an eternally subjective viewpoint that is alterable and changing, the novel raises far more complex questions regarding science or the techniques of history retelling. *The Calcutta Chromosome* challenges fundamental values of human existence that blur the binaries between reality and fiction. It proposes a past linked closely to the future that seeks to unravel and demystify the science that seeks to help humanity while at the same time frightens and controls it. The characters are globalised, even if they exist two centuries ago, which emphasises the interconnectivity of the world.

Ghosh navigates through time and genre to weave intricately detailed characters spread across continents, in the colonial past as well as technologically advanced future. He writes, '[T]he mid-19th century was when the scientific community began to wake up to Malaria' (Ghosh 1996), which was only the beginning in the eyes of the Western world. Murugan says to Antar, 'Here's Ronnie, right? He thinks he's doing experiments on the malaria parasite. And all this time it's he who is the experiment on the malaria parasite. But Ronnie never gets it; not to the end of his life' (ibid.). In a way, the reader meets a similar fate like Antar's: a thriller-like ending. (Antar does not know he has been part of a greater scheme of things throughout the whole period.) Both texts turn the gaze of the traveller inward towards the reader. The past seen through the traveller's eyes serves as a looking glass to see inflexions of the present onto the past. Overall, the theory of knowledge finds interesting paths in *The Calcutta Chromosome*, where the reader carries on the journey, past the traveller's existence on the pages, as does Ghosh as narrator and author, symbolising new forms and styles in travel writing by recreating the figure of the 'pioneering scientist' cum traveller as ever-shifting to meet the emergent concerns of a postcolonial, or arguably a neocolonial, world.

NOTES

1 Edward W. Said in his seminal text *Orientalism* explicated the discourse employed by the Occident to create definitions of the Orient through scholarship to justify imperialist agenda.

2 The West, namely the US, has produced several box office hits that are thematically SF, such as *Avatar* (2009), *The Guardians of the Galaxy* (2014), *Edge of Tomorrow* (2014), to name a few.

3 Taken from Joseph Conrad's novel *Heart of Darkness* (1899), where the continent of Africa is seen as the 'other', away from 'light', 'reason' and civilisation, similar to notions of the subcontinent nurtured by colonial rulers.

4 Scott McClintock in his essay 'Travels Outside the Empire: The Revision of Subaltern Historiography in Amitav Ghosh' for *South Asian Review* attributes this phrase to Amitav Ghosh, highlighting his views on Ghosh's style of writing.

5 Taken from Salman Rushdie's famous 'The Empire Writes Back with a Vengeance', which appeared first in 1982 in *The Times*.

6 From Norma Evenson's essay 'Review: *An Imperial Vision: Indian Architecture and Britain's Raj* by Thomas R. Metcalf; *The Indian Metropolis: A View toward the West* by Norma Evenson', which was published in the *Journal of the Society of Architectural Historians* in 1992.

7 Barbara Romanik in her essay 'Transforming the Colonial City: Science and the Practice of Dwelling in "The Calcutta Chromosome"' explicates the role of Calcutta as a multicultural city, especially through colonial intervention, becoming a site of immense potential for scientific enterprise.

8 Amitav Ghosh has often dissociated his work from labels of postcolonialism, and in T. Vijay Kumar's interview, he is cited as viewing the category as doubly disabling rather than enabling. The interview, '"Postcolonial describes you as a Negative": An Interview with Amitav Ghosh', was published online in June 2008.

WORKS CITED

Archer, John, rev. 1992. 'Review: *An Imperial Vision: Indian Architecture and Britain's Raj* by Thomas R. Metcalf; *The Indian Metropolis: A View toward the West* by Norma Evenson.' *Journal of the Society of Architectural Historians*, 51(1): 85–87.

Banerjee, Suparno. 2010. 'Other Tomorrows: Postcoloniality, Science Fiction and India.' Published PhD Thesis: Department of English, Louisiana State University and Agricultural and Mechanical College.

Bhabha, Homi K. 1994. *The Location of Culture*. New York and London: Routledge.

Dixon, Robert. 1996. 'Travelling in the West: The Writing of Amitav Ghosh.' *Journal of Commonwealth Literature*, 36: 3–24.

Foucault, Michel. 1976. *The History of Sexuality*. New York: Pantheon Books.

Gandhi, Leela. 2003. 'A Choice of Histories: Ghosh vs. Hegel in an Antique Land.' *New Literatures Review*, 40: 17–32.

Ghosh, Amitav. 1996. *The Calcutta Chromosome*. New Delhi: Ravi Dayal.

Ghosh, Amitav, and Damien Stankiewaicz. 2012. 'Anthropology and Fiction: An Interview with Amitav Ghosh.' *Cultural Anthropology*, 27(3): 535–541. http://www.jstor.org/stable/23252412 (accessed on 9 December 2020).

Hawley, John C. 2005. *Amitav Ghosh: Contemporary Writers in English*. New Delhi, India: Foundation.

Nandy, Ashis. 1983. *The Intimate Enemy: Loss and Recovery of Self Under Colonialism*. Delhi: Oxford University Press.

Rushdie, Salman. 1982. 'The Empire Writes Back with a Vengeance.' *The Times*, New York, 3 July.

Romanik, Barbara. 2005. 'Transforming the Colonial City: Science and the Practice of Dwelling in "The Calcutta Chromosome".' *Mosaic: An Interdisciplinary Critical Journal*, 38(3): 41–57. http://www.jstor.org/stable/44029669 (accessed on 3 December 2020).

Said, Edward W. 1978. *Orientalism*. New York: Pantheon Books.

McClintock, Scott. 2006. 'Travels Outside the Empire: The Revision of Subaltern Historiography in Amitav Ghosh.' *South Asian Review*, 27(2): 5–24. 10.1080/02759527.2006.11932439 (accessed on 3 December 2020).

Kumar, Vijay T. 2007. 'Postcolonial Describes You as a Negative.' *Interventions*, 9(1): 99–105. 10.1080/13698010601174203 (accessed on 3 December 2020).

Viswanathan, Gauri. 1995. 'Beyond Orientalism: Syncretism and the Politics of Knowledge.' *Stanford Humanities Review*, 5(1): 19–32.

Chapter 3

DECOLONISING ENCOUNTERS OF THE INDIAN KIND: READING THE POSTCOLONIAL 'OTHER' IN VANDANA SINGH'S *THE WOMAN WHO THOUGHT SHE WAS A PLANET AND OTHER STORIES*

Devapriya Sanyal

INTRODUCTION

By Editors

One of the immediate effects of postcolonial Indian SF's significant re-historicisation, not only its own history but that of the world's as well, is the relocation of the otherwise non-normative othered subjectivities and identities primarily bound to and within colonial subalternity as, or at least within, the locus of the centre. Through the narrative processes of these fictions, as India finds its own history outside the colonial imperial project and is rather unaffected by it, the identities of all subjects within that national marker also garner a rather fresh matrix of historical individualities. Thus, neither are these 'othered' beings bound by the violence of an ostensible superiority nor are they chained to a history that forces them into unparalleled servitude. This Other, within the contours of postcolonial Indian science fiction (SF), then finds itself in the limelight and sees its history as its own and not as one of inferiority, lack, violence and a darkened absence.

What this effectively implies is that the marginalised other, in essence, is not the 'other' anymore. There is, in fact, often, no presentation of this binary, since with a history untethered to the colonial incursion, there is no colonial marginalisation. There is, then, an ideal that allows a kind of equity where the Indian identity is able to find an existence at par with those of the coloniser's. This ultimately allows a future that is not spent in simply rebuilding or tackling the failures of doing so. Devapriya Sanyal's present chapter shows exactly this centring of the othered communities through postcolonial Indian SF. In fact, she argues, it is only within and through the possibilities presented by this (sub)genre of fantasy fiction, especially in its ability to find a new route of history, that such political statements are possible. Towards the same, Sanyal presents how Vandana Singh's stories, working within this framework, is able to centre not only colonially othered identities but those sidelined by normativities of gendered existences as well.

Having said that, one should keep in mind that these narratives are neither fantasising perfect utopias nor peddling jingoistic sentimentalities. What they do is show an alternative that acts perhaps as a reminder of not only that which is lost but that which could be but, more importantly, is not.

****

POSTCOLONIALISM AND SCIENCE FICTION

The emerging genre of postcolonial science fiction (SF)—of which Indian science fiction is a part—is a hybrid genre that reflects intriguing affinities between two genres: science fiction and postcolonial literature. As Erika Hoagland and Reema Sarwal write in the introduction to *Science Fiction, Imperialism and the Third World: Essays on Postcolonial Literature and Film* (edited by them) that both the genres have borrowed liberally from other genres, and in doing so have refashioned those very genres from which they have borrowed. Both continue to be used for polemical and political purposes, and both try to make sense of what the world means. While it has long been assumed by critics such as Darko Suvin and John Reid that SF is primarily produced by white male writers, one finds a curious tendency of the hybrid genre of postcolonial SF to hold up to light-sensitive and thoughtful portrayal of differences. Most often, it's how the Third World is imagined and portrayed. However, postcolonial writers have now taken to the genre to reimagine themselves and their world and create visions of other tomorrows. The erstwhile historical records drawn up by colonisers have become suspect and need revision if not outright rejection. The rewriting or revision of history along with the recovery of the subaltern subject[1] are an integral component of postcolonial studies, and it also serves as a mirror of science fiction's complex relationship with history.

Michelle Reid's comments on postcolonial SF become pertinent in this case. Pointing out the estranging capabilities of SF, she says it allows SF to debunk the history of the real world and create worlds unburdened by colonial oppression, where colonisation never happened or real-world power relations are reversed and re-examined. She argues that the theme of colonisation of other planets is critical in this respect, and that the use of the alien as a representation of the 'other' is a potent trope for examining politics of race, culture, nation and gender. In this regard, Anglophone Indian SF exists at the cusp of these two areas, and as such merits some exploration. The texts falling under this rubric are a response to the hybridisation of Indian culture that is speculative of what future society will look like. They are also in a way reflective of the rapid modernisation of India through technoscientific development.

ANGLOPHONE INDIAN SF AND VANDANA SINGH

Both Vandana Singh and Uppinder Mehan argue for speculative literature that not only allows postcolonial authors to imagine futures different from the hegemonic Western pattern but one that has also been successful in addressing issues of imperialism, postcolonialism and, most importantly, identity. Indian SF in particular helps to bring to the forefront the complex problem of Indian identity in a globalised world, while at the same time helping to untangle the complex knots of history by rewriting it often. Rewriting colonial histories and reinvesting colonial tropes with new meaning are familiar modes of wresting agency from the colonisers. Although postcolonial SF sometimes creates fantasies of escape, more often than not, these works genuinely question all ideologies of domination, including those of colonial, neocolonial and nativist origins. Jessica Langer writes, 'SF has always been a politically active form of literature.' So Indian writers in the genre are using that particular capacity to its fullest potential. They have begun to broaden the genre of SF, pulling it away from its Western roots and transforming it, thus helping SF to become a force for anticolonial or postcolonial resistance and change. It is in the light of such arguments that this paper intends to examine three of Singh's short stories from her collection *The Woman Who Thought She Was a Planet and Other Stories* to make the case that she is an Indian postcolonial SF writer. A reading of her stories yields several themes that she explores through the genre of speculative SF, which she calls 'imaginative literature'.[2]

The strategy of literalising otherness and the use of estrangement or defamiliarisation[3] are effective not only for Western audiences but for all readers. Such processes make readers confront issues that they would otherwise hesitate to acknowledge in the normative world. Indian readers, who operate in a highly traditional yet diverse society and often reject the slightest deviation from their own sociocultural norms, are an equally appropriate target for Singh's use of such frameworks of estrangement. Several interviews in which she talks about her fiction reveal one important thing: It is difficult to compartmentalise her work into neat boxes. And this is perhaps what makes her work unique.

Her use of SF strategies, such as spatio-temporal disjunctions and fluid identities, makes the reader confront these estrangements from a perspective that is different from and less constrained than a realistic narrative. This non-mimetic style of writing, which refracts the reality Singh has lived and the one she sees, allows her to speculate about different scientific and philosophical notions. However, alienation against the postcolonial subject is her most important concern. Most of the stories in her other collection *Ambiguity Machines: And Other Stories* are set on alien planets with humanoid, humans and aliens as the protagonists. They foreground the native/settler binary to engage with the discourse of alienation. More importantly, the social dynamics in India as brought about through Western influences demand that India's future be imagined through a medium that is an admixture of Western and Indian values. This is perhaps possible through the tropes as employed by science fiction that help liberate the texts from realism and yet provide them with logicality. Her writings are invested with tropes of post-coloniality, identity and nationhood. They engage in the dialectics of hybridity and indigenism that inform the debate on national identity. Across cultural currents and concerns with a global future (bordering on climate change and so on), her work uses Indian literary traditions, Indian history and an Indian scenario while dealing with the status of composite identities. Some of the issues she is dealing with are real and rising threats of religious fundamentalism, gender oppression and inequality, political hegemony, effects of industrialisation, conflicting ideas of nationhood as well as myths, superstitions, subalterns, knowledge, et cetera.

Singh, in a sense, creates the metaphor of worlds or times beyond normal perception, specifically to focus on the inner lives of her protagonists and to suggest that these worlds are as real as the outside world of daily interaction. Such exposition, however, is deeply influenced by her detached tone and is mostly narrated in the third person, while her language remains relatively simple and straightforward and is full of Indian cultural references that place the stories firmly in the Indian milieu. Thus, Singh's language and narrative style re-enforce her conceptual frameworks by creating discourses of alienation rather than drawing attention to themselves. Singh's works cannot just be described as postcolonial mimicry—a return gaze by the colonised people that displaces the coloniser's authority. Her characters arise out of an Indian society that has moved beyond the direct coloniser/colonised binary and, hence, mimicry of the powerful West is muted and intrinsic rather than being the main instrument of subversion.

A minute study of Singh's fiction reveals that her protagonists exist simultaneously in two worlds—social bindings and of personal desires—often coming into conflict and resulting in anxieties, most often, in a postcolonial Indian society. Singh uses SF to highlight these torn selves aggressively, which may be seen as critiques of the above. Sometimes these anxieties take the form of immigrants experiencing alienation because of conflicting allegiances, while at other times these anxieties come out as a tendency of the marginalised to look beyond the suppression of people by the newly founded postcolonial nation. And in still other instances, gender roles become the main point of focus. Singh uses images such as the alien, tropes such as dimensional and historical anomalies, and distortion of space and time to project her subjects' inner state of alienation.

Most of Singh's stories deal with individuals living in a discordant world. This discord is shown from multiple perspectives: economic discord between the rich and the poor, familial discord between husband and wife, gender discord between men and women, environment discord between man and society and sometimes communal discord between Hindus and Muslims. In several of her stories, such as 'Infinities', 'Are you Sannata 3159?', 'Ambiguity Machine', this is pronounced. But, surprisingly, it is also the protagonists' predicaments that allow them other levels of existence that the dominant order cannot see.

EXAMINING VANDANA SINGH'S WORLDS IN 'DELHI', 'THE TETRAHEDRON' AND 'THIRST'

In 'Delhi', Singh draws up the character of the protagonist, Aseem, to straddle two different worlds. He is educated and has a college degree but could very well be mistaken for a person from a lower class because of his dishevelled appearance. He has lost his parents and has no home to speak of. He wanders all over Delhi protecting people from what he calls 'a certain preoccupation in the eyes of some of his fellow citizens: the desire for the final anonymity that death brings' (Singh 2008). Much like Singh's other protagonists, Aseem too is special despite his unremarkable features; he can interact with the city's past and future. Although Aseem may not come across as a reliable narrator, his visions as one recognises in time are like the apparitions that appear and have connections across space and time.

Aseem's excursions serve as an excellent metaphor for the unrestricted power of humans, otherwise restricted by caste, creed and religion especially in a country like India. His kind nature and keenness to help others highlight an individual's capacity to transcend social drudgeries and limitations. Through this story, Singh also offers us a nostalgic history of Delhi that 'spoke of the places of her girlhood:

parathe-walon-ki-gali, the lane of the paratha makers … and Dariba Kalan, where after hundreds of years they still sell the best and purest silver in the world' (Singh 2008). In the end, the protagonist comes to terms with the fact of his alienation from the world, which is a sense that pervades all her stories. None of her protagonists makes an effort to discard their unusual forms, desires or beliefs to mingle with the rest of humanity. Aseem is an alienated young man with the power to see into and interact with the past and future of the city of Delhi.

Aseem's musings about his past and family, and his ability to see people, places and things across time and space, seem to hint at schizophrenia, thus making him an unreliable protagonist. However, his life on the streets constitutes a mission to look out for people like himself (which, he says, is reflected in their eyes) while chronicling his trans-temporal journeys.

Like Singh's other protagonists, Aseem's loneliness is emphasised through his mental and economic states, which make him an outsider in respectable society, while his education and knowledge make him unfit in Delhi's underbelly. The vision of an upper and a lower Delhi is a metaphor for the yawning divide between the rich and the poor, another trope that runs through several of her stories. Singh's portrayal of Delhi is a living entity—its needs alien, unfathomable. About Delhi, Singh writes in the short story thus: 'It is an entity in its own right, expanding every day, swallowing the surrounding countryside … spawning satellite children, infant towns that it will ultimately devour' (Singh 2008).

Such frameworks of alienation continue in different forms throughout Singh's other narratives as well. One of them, which finds a special place in her oeuvre, arises out of traditional domesticity and assigned gender roles. Some of the stories that play this up prodigiously are 'Thirst', 'The Tetrahedron', 'The Woman Who Thought She Was a Planet' and 'The Room on the Roof'. I will be exploring the short stories 'Thirst' and 'The Tetrahedron' in some detail in this paper.

In 'Thirst', for instance, Singh's protagonist is a middle-class housewife Susheela whose daily chores consist of routinely kneading paratha dough for her husband's breakfast, taking care of their young son and sundry other household chores. Through this story, Singh criticises the entrenched gender duties that the middle-class woman has to perform throughout her life—first as a dutiful daughter and then a grovelling wife, doubling up as a servile housekeeper—and silently bearing the drudgeries of domesticity and childbearing. In this story, the exalted feminine roles of the mother and the wife, too, are explored. Such designated social roles, which are often taken for granted in Indian society, are created to keep women subjugated and often result in split selves because of the estrangement from their inner selves.

Susheela is a character trapped in the role of a wife and mother in a middle-class family in small-town India. Her daily routines bespeak an existence in which she is expected to be a dutiful wife and a caring mother. She has no family, apart from a brother who sends an occasional postcard, and her husband's family is the only family that she can think of. While she is a respectable middle-class housewife and young mother, Singh depicts her as possessing some other kinds of qualities, often rebellious, as well. She has, for example, an insatiable craving for an unknown symbolised by the lake in the neighbouring park where her young son, Kishor, loves to visit. However, these kinds of odd cravings have to be hidden under the guise of ordinary duties, such as walking the child. '[T]he market was her excuse for surreptitious visits to the lake in the park with her boy (poor innocent boy) as chaperone and protector' (Singh 2008). Spawned by a snake and a human mother, Susheela is unhappy in her surroundings, especially in her relationship with her husband and her life with his family. Even while doing things the narrator says, Susheela felt like an alien. Neither her marriage nor her son's birth assuaged the feeling of emptiness in her. Susheela thus comes across as someone who feels the lack of connection in both public and private spheres. Designated gender roles assume that women would feel complete with marriage, domesticity and motherhood. However, Singh's portrayal of her protagonist as being unhappy or feeling alienated is in keeping with the way she questions stereotypical gender roles. The concept of the Indian family, which crushes individuals instead of relieving them of loneliness, comes under heavy criticism in this story. Susheela's mother-in-law constantly reminds Susheela of her 'otherness'—the fact that she is cursed. Instead of assuaging her loneliness and making her feel like a member of the family, her mother-in-law is constantly carping, even blaming her when Kishor knocks over a bucket of water and wets himself.

While in 'The Tetrahedron', Maya finds an escape from her dreary and challenging existence by walking into an alien object called Tetrahedron, Susheela, in 'Thirst', decides to enjoy the best of both the worlds. Singh makes Susheela a rebel with a cause. Even though confused in the beginning, a tryst with her snake kinfolks, which is nothing short of magical, makes Susheela a far more self-aware individual in the end. She consciously chooses to return to the lake soon but learns to lead a dual life successfully.

She realises she has a special gift when she is drawn to the neighbourhood lake. She not only changes her avatar but also, at last, finds happiness being with her reptilian kin. While the underwater kingdom promises freedom from her unhappy state in the human world, she decides to return to the latter for the sake of her young child who, she feels, will find it difficult to grow up without a mother. She strikes a compromise, depriving herself of the pleasure that was hers for the taking and willing to stay a while longer, for the sake of motherhood, in the human world that already seems like an alien place to her.

Through the characterisation of Susheela, Singh seems to be suggesting that the marginalised subsistence of someone like Susheela makes her privy to another existence that the dominant order cannot see. In fact, Singh seems to be celebrating this kind of liminal existence, perhaps even trying to tell her readers to be aware of the 'others' while also being inclusive of them. 'Thirst' especially deals with the concept of hybrid identities and the resultant anxieties caused by rejecting the Manichean binary, but it also explores immigrant identities and diasporic thinking, two major trends in the twenty-first–century Indian postcolonial discourse. It also involves an exploration of estrangement, as far as the concept of 'alien' figures goes.

In 'The Tetrahedron', as in 'Thirst', the protagonist, Maya, feels unhappy and displeased with her life. Born into a lower-middle-class family and expected to toe the line like any other girl—be an obedient daughter, marry, become wife, bear children, et cetera—she is forced to kill her ambitions and desires. Maya is engaged to Kartik, an accountant, with a bright future in a small firm. (According to Maya's family, it is a match made in heaven.) She is a university student and feels stifled at the prospect of getting married to a self-congratulating and dominating man. Her life takes an unusual turn with the appearance of the Tetrahedron in the middle of a busy thoroughfare in Delhi. It baffles not just the Indian government but also governments across the world, with the result that hordes of tourists, especially from foreign, descend on the city and are as baffled by the Indian way of life as they are by the Tetrahedron's presence.

By having the Tetrahedron descend on the Indian capital, something that baffles the international media as well as the US president, who is about to declare war on India for this, Singh attempts a writing back to the centre that postcolonial critics such as Bill Ashcroft et al. talked about. In most science fiction stories written by white authors, aliens inevitably end up in First World countries; one can recall H.G. Well's *The War of the Worlds* in this regard. Instead, Singh makes Delhi occupy the centre stage with her story and also uses it to a very different end, namely as a point of escape for Maya. In doing so, she not only counters the First World colonial discourse but also fills the lacunae in representations while instituting a new order by changing absence into presence.

Singh marries the narrative of the stifling Indian ways and mores to certain tropes of fantasy, as used in Science Fiction, which acts as nothing but a trap for women, as exhibited by Maya's family but here used as a means of relief and freedom for Maya. Designated social roles are created to keep women in their place and aid in patriarchal domination in economic, social and political spheres. The Tetrahedron, which comes to represent the 'other', could also be a metaphor for people like Maya, whose physical presence belies the depth of their wants and desires, and those who can be seen but are never heard. The narrative is one of oppression suffered at the hands of a traditional Indian family, which seems like malaise and appears as a background in many of Singh's stories.

As a postcolonial SF writer, Singh, through the presentations of these othered dualities within singularly realised selves, attempts to rewrite colonial histories and reinvest colonial tropes with new meanings, as reiterated earlier. It is a well-known mode of wresting agency from the colonisers. These tropes—which are made literal, as many critics have argued—make this wresting even more explicit. 'The Third World writers are using the genre to re-imagine themselves and their world to "set the record straight" by dismantling the stereotypes that science fiction in part has helped to support and in essence "strike back" at the empire' (Hoagland and Sarwal 2010). Her writings constantly emphasise the existence of other possibilities. They advocate socio-cultural acceptance, as in several of the stories examined here. Through cyborg identities, time travel, futuristic multiculturalism, et cetera, Singh express antipathy towards totalitarianism of any sort.

Singh's works not only speak back to the metropolitan centres from the position of the social, cultural and, often, gendered 'other' but also encourage domestic readers to confront disjunctions and disconnections in contemporary Indian society. Her narratives are steeped in Indian culture and philosophy, and Singh uses this cultural milieu as a source of inspiration as well as an object of examination.

NOTES

1 The concept of 'the Other' is a common element in both science fiction and postcolonial studies. The function of the 'Other', as Roberts puts it, is that 'encountering the Other forces us to encounter ourselves' (Roberts 2000).

2 In one of her interviews, Singh makes a case for 'imaginative literature', which, according to her, provides more scope to deal with the kind of questioning that she wishes to indulge in. In a way, while it answers the description of postcolonial literature, for Singh, imaginative literature, which is an admixture of science fiction and fantasy, provides a much wider scope to experiment with.

3 The term 'defamiliarisation' was first coined in 1917 by Russian formalist Viktor Shklovsky in his essay 'Art as Device'. Shklovsky invented the term as a means to 'distinguish poetic from practical language on the basis of the former's perceptibility'.

WORKS CITED

Hoagland, Ericka, and Reema Sarwal. 2010. *Science Fiction, Imperialism and the Third World: Essays on Postcolonial Literature and Film*. Jefferson, NC: McFarland.

Langer, Jessica. 2011. *Postcolonialism and Science Fiction*. London: Palgrave Macmillan,

Reid, Michelle. 2005. 'Postcolonial Science Fiction.' Science Fiction Foundation.

Roberts, Adam. 2000. *Science Fiction*. London: Routledge.

Shklovsky, Viktor. 2007. 'Art as Technique.' In *The Critical Tradition: Classic Texts and Contemporary Trends*, 3rd ed., edited by David H. Richter. Boston: Bedford.

Shohat, Ella. 1992. 'Notes on the "Post-Colonial".' *Social Text*, 31/32: 99–113.

Singh, Vandana. 2008. 'Science Fiction and the End of the World.' jeffvandermeer.com.

———. 2008. *The Woman Who Thought She Was a Planet*. New Delhi: Penguin Books and Zubaan.

———. 2018. *Ambiguity Machines and Other Stories*. Massachusetts: Small Beer Press.

Chapter 4

GREEN MEN: POWER, DYSTOPIA AND THE POLITICS OF GENRE IN BENGALI POSTCOLONIAL SF

Subhadeep Ray

INTRODUCTION

By Editors

Derek Attridge, in his rather interesting and thought-provoking book *The Singularity of Literature*, finds the 'other' not only within and as the presentations of the human but also as something that hits against the limits of the self. The creative writer, in Attridge's interrogation, is the one who:

> registers, whether consciously or unconsciously, both the possibilities offered by the accepted forms and materials of the time, and their impossibilities, the exclusions and prohibitions.... Out of the former emerges reworkings of existing models, out of the latter emerges the otherness (our emphasis) which makes these reworkings new works of literature. (Attridge 2004)

What this implies is that the 'other' always lurks outside of embrace and, as Attridge later shows, is allowed an entry into the self once the latter is open to accept it. Rather obviously, this 'other' is not necessarily a human but, for the lack of a better word, a framework of existence in opposition to (or, as Attridge puts it, in relation to) the self. In which case, if the self exists in the present-real, the 'other' exists in an epiphenomenal world accessible only through the application of imagination, especially since, as a conceptual position, imagination works in the manner of a bridge: between that which *is* and that which lies 'outside'.

Within such a theoretical framework, where does, then, the 'other' of SF or—more importantly, and for the purpose of the current volume—postcolonial Indian SF lie? Is it just the colonised and subjugated human who finds an othered identity within the pages of the genre without any relational junctions within them? Or, is there something greater that allows the postcolonial SF writer access to this 'othered' human? Is the access, in itself, an action within an acceptance of the 'other' through the modalities of imagination? If yes, how do the two effectively entangle with each other and form, as it were, a holistic whole and present not only a 'different' history of the colonised human but also the political possibilities of both its present and future? Finally, what does this imaginative act, which is, at the same time, reaching out and allowing in what it finds, do to the structures of the self?

These are a few questions that Subhadeep Ray's present chapter deals with. Ray reads the *Green Men* series and generic *kalpavigyan* to complicate not only the present renditions of the postcolonial Indian self but also the structures and processes of the reclamation of the othered Indian identity through the function of the imaginative dimension of SF.

****

Science fiction as a cultural idiom is extensively wide-ranging and polyvalent and, therefore, resists any specific definition. Set 'in other worlds', to use the title of Margaret Atwood's 2011 deliberation on the slippery nature of SF, the points of departures are as important as the sense of belongingness in this genre's examination of the unforeseen possibilities lurking in the real world, along with the establishment of some cognitive relation between what exists and what may happen. If Darko Suvin's (1979) seminal characterisation of SF—as distinguished from other imaginative works by 'the presence of scientific cognition as the sign or correlative of a method (way, approach, atmosphere, world-view, sensibility) identical to that of a modern philosophy of science'— provides a good starting point, the longing for or fear of the other world, from the SF perspective, is equally a matter of distribution and reception of any cultural product as mediated by the existing social divisions[1]. In the light of this generic flexibility within a complex network of power and knowledge, this chapter studies how the rise of Bengali SF during the colonial period, as both an offshoot of the introduction of Western science and an articulation of the nationalist aspiration to overcome foreign domination by the cultivation of scientific knowledge in the motherland, forms the backdrop of the postcolonial movement of Bengali SF, with an objective to contest the worldwide imperial aggression during the post-World Wars decades. This study closely follows a transformation from the nationalist-utopian outlook in colonial SF to the rejection of totalitarianism as a dystopia in the postcolonial SF and concentrates on a particular experiment of the 1960s, namely *Green Men*, to show how the poststructuralist aspects of this cultural production suggest an inventive, aesthetic reflection on multiple possibilities of a changing context. In respect of this argumentative pattern, the tension generated by the simultaneous promise and threat of modernity and science was part of the intellectual awakening in Bengal, both under the influence of and in confrontation with the Western education system in the nineteenth and early twentieth centuries when a number of Bengali literary works bordering on what is designated today as SF established the link between the colonial context and the evolving potential of the genre to logically explore an unknown world. The travel of a cluster of themes, motives and tropes broadly associated with Bengali SF, or *kalpavigyan*[2], across the border between the Raj and the Republic sets up an interesting dialectic of utopia and dystopia in terms of the genre's interactions with history and social power.

Any mapping of the tradition of Bengali SF, therefore, needs to consider the fluid, contradictory and overlapping attempts of Bengali enlightenment to conceive of a more liberating future as an outcome of its 'scientific temper' predicated on alternative modernity. The nineteenth-century Bengali embrace of the post-Newtonian natural science, as expressed in Raja Rammohun Roy's appeal to Lord Amherst in 1823 to 'promote a more liberal and enlightened system of instruction' by introducing 'mathematics, natural philosophy, chemistry and anatomy' (Tagore 1975)[3], initiated a series of intellectual communications that cannot be understood in terms of any simplistic binary between what Amartya Sen (2009) locates as two historically improbable entities: 'a unified West' and '"quintessentially eastern" priorities'. In this context, amongst numerous intersecting forces of colonial modernity, the discursive claims of early SF written in the nineteenth-century Bengal as 'claims made by real speakers for particular purposes in specific situations' (Altman 1999) are established by utopian speculations about a native regeneration in science and technology that would empower Indians to liberate themselves from the British rule. This seems to continue a project of constructing *Svapna Lobdho Bharatbarser Itihasa* (The History of India as It Appeared in a Dream), the title of Bhudev Mukhopadhyay's passionate combination of rationalism and nationalism in 1875.

Against the backdrop of colonial exploitations and conflicts, a specific stream of Bengali literature is thus found to seek humanist, futurist, nationalist, militant, feminist and socialist ideals[4] in an imagined motherland by applying kalpana, or imagination, which is 'an active process of the transformation of things' (Chattopadhyay 2016), from the perspective of *vigyan*, or *vishes gyan*, the specialised knowledge of nature[5]. Though it remains difficult to demarcate an exclusive territory for Bengali SF in its formative period, against the mutable and inconsistent networks of diverse creative threads, the blending of the elements of science and fantasy to predict a better future in the genre can be seen to subvert the near dystopia of foreign hegemony. By the mid-nineteenth century, the native mode of life was conceived to reach an impasse under the threat of 'a "monster" named *nabya*', meaning, 'specifically in this case, the "new things and customs"' that 'threw centuries-old traditions off-balance' (Chakraborti 2019). But this antipathy towards *paschimi* (Western) *nabya* evolved into a mythological narrative of the common descent into the kaliyuga, the apocalyptic fourth-era in the Hindu time cycle, when the Western-educated Bengali middleclass began to become victims of an unequal distribution of career opportunities in favour of their British compatriots[6] and could be projected as suffering for their evil association with English manners. On the contrary, 'as an alternative to the author's empirical environment, the literary apparatus' of Bengali SF 'reconfigures the historical moment so that it can be seen and responded to in a new light' (Moylan 2000). The simultaneous presence of the utopian science/speculative fiction and the kaliyuga narrative[7] helps one to perceive the ideological alternatives offered by the so-called Bengal Renaissance.

Patricia Kerslake (2007) observes that 'through an implicit comprehension of cultural, political and historical forces, SF has become an experiment in the quasi-predictive. And nowhere has that experiment been more enlightening than in the exploration of the notion of power formed within the construct of empire'. The postcolonial examination of SF written by colonial subjects as a way of creating a codified framework of alternative reality, where their human strengths and weakness would be realised, therefore, is of key importance. The very recent postcolonial extrapolations of the subcontinental tradition of SF, such as Suparno Banerjee's thesis, *Other Tomorrows: Postcoloniality, Science Fiction and India*[8], Tarun K. Saint's introduction to *The Gollancz Book of South Asian Science Fiction*, Bodhisattva Chattopadhyay's essays on 'non-Anglocentric' SF and research conducted by the *Kalpabiswa*[9], throw light on the genre's Bengali genealogy. Significantly, 'one of the earliest fictions written in English turns out to be a science fictional account of a future rebellion against the British rule' (Banerjee 2010). Kylas Chunder Dutt's *A Journal of Forty-Eight Hours of the Year 1945* was published in 1835, the same year Macaulay's *Minute* was published. What Saint (2019) refers to as the '[c]olonial era proto-SF' was practised in the English language by both Kylas Chunder and Shoshee Chunder Dutt, whose *The Republic of Orissa: A Page from the Annals of the 20th Century* (1845) is another anti-imperialist text, speculating a violent rebellion against the British force from the states of Bengal, Bihar and Orissa. 'The estrangement that takes place in these texts is temporal' and they create 'a nascent futuristic discourse about nationalism' (Banerjee 2010). This may be further noted that these proto-SFs had struck the colonial cultural hierarchy well before 'the (generally reported) first Indian novel in English, *Rajmohan's Wife*[10], was published' in 1864, and also 'the idea of the Indian novel in English' began to be 'developed and changed considerably since the mid-1880s' (Varughese 2017).

While the first Indian fiction about technological automation was also written in the Bengali language: Hemlal Dutt's '*Rahasya*'—Mystery—(1882), two seminal works of Bengali SF at its colonial phase are Jagadananda Roy's space-adventure story '*Shukra Bhraman*'—A Visit to the Venus—(1895) and Jagadish Chandra Bose's '*Niruddesher Kahini*'—The Tale of an Unknown World—(1896). They seem to carry forward what may be phrased, after Ernst Bloch, as 'the principle of hope', which is the principle of 'not-yet-being', marked by 'the tension oriented to the perfection in future' (Abensour 2012). Bose, especially, 'serves as one of the cornerstones of the Bangla (and Indian) imagination given his scientific achievements in the colonial period, alongside the figure of Rabindranath Tagore in the arts' (Chattopadhyay 2016). Emerging as one of the major twentieth-century scientists by overcoming colonial discriminations, Bose was also one of the first seekers of the freedom of choice in the study of science[11]. His practice of using apparently simple and native equipment for complex scientific experiments centrally contributed to an active utopia, sustained by modern (wo)men's 'will to change—to transform both themselves and their world' so that they can feel at home (Berman 1983)[12]. Bose's well-discussed tale '*Niruddesher Kahini*', later published as '*Palatak Tufan*'—Runaway Cyclone—(1922), tells of the power of a locally produced hair oil, a drop of which saves millions of lives in the tumultuous sea. Written for the promotion of a native industrial enterprise[13], the interplay between the theory of surface tension and advanced, experimental but less mechanical and more inclusive technology in Bose's narrative suggests what Raymond Williams (2005) explains in 'Utopia and Science Fiction' as a 'willing return to a "simpler", "more natural" way of life'. Bose's humanist outlook, therefore, combines the global with the local and shapes the future course of SF in the subcontinent, which is distinguished by 'a cosmopolitan, yet grounded perspective' and deserves an 'emphasis on the human and culture specific side of the story' (Saint 2019). An endless series of thought experiments in a more liberating world, thrown open by the aforementioned works, is important for the analysis of postcolonial writings that uses SF as a medium of critique of the imperial power. The SF movement of the 1960s is specifically marked by antagonism towards a despotic utopia by drawing inspiration from the enlightenment association of science and justice.

In an 1958 Bengali fantasy movie *Yamalaye Jibanta Manus*[14] (A Living Man in the Land of Yama), a living Bengali middle-aged widower is mistakenly brought to heaven by the messengers of the god of death. Arriving in heaven, the fellow questions the dharma of the omnipotent who, himself enjoying the eternal pleasure, lets human beings suffer an untimely death, disease, accidents, war, violence and, most importantly, hunger. The movie serves as a powerful commentary on the horror of nuclear explosions in the Second World War, and, as a balance between romantic comedy and dark humour, it remains a key clue to the reversal of cultural consciousness from a utopian mythos of future to a dystopian one. The first major post-Independence Bengali SF movement exemplifies an imaginative engagement with the global anti-imperialist struggle of the decades following the Second World War. The mid-twentieth–century Bengali SF is seen to estrange the imperial agents and expansionists, so they began to represent a monstrous anti-human from whom humans must maintain a safe distance. Confronting the imperial 'othering' of a vast segment of mankind as 'unfit' for 'civilisation', the call of suppressed humanism across all borders is held up. In the 1960s, the production and circulation of Bengali SF entered a new stage with the employment of mass media, though 'science fiction was never "popular" in the same way as other genres in India, even though it emerged from the same crucible of the mass cultural genre system and its periodicals and pulps' (Chattopadhyay et al. 2019). This is partly because, unlike the works of American futurologists, SF in India retains the goal set by its nineteenth-century predecessors of the genre, which is primarily 'a combination of "sentence and solas", i.e., aimed to offer instruction as much as entertainment' (ibid.). In these terms, the production of *Green Men* in 1966[15] was part of a larger project initiated in 1963 by the release of a Bengali SF magazine *Ashchorjo!* (Amazing!)[16] by Adrish Bardhan. The *Aschorjo!* team, which includes Premendra Mitra, Satyajit Ray, Khitindranarayan Bhattacharya, Dilip Roychaudhury, Ranen Ghosh and Bardhan himself, established the first SF cine-club of India in 1966 and arranged for the broadcast of two audio stories, *Mahakashchari Bangali*—The Bengali Space Traveller—(1965) and *Sabuj Manush*—Green Men[17], by the Kolkata radio for two consecutive years. This movement in the Bengali vernacular, which may be compared and contrasted with the post-war wave of SF in the US under the leadership of John Campbell, was meant to explore the field of cultural production in relation to organised fandom well-trained in appreciating a 'supra-educational project' (Chattopadhyay et al. 2019) and to display SF's dual roles of celebrating the 'myth of technological mastery and transcendence, and deflating it' (Vint 2014).

The inventiveness of the movement organised by the *Ashchorjo!* team can be understood in the light of Jacques Derrida's (1992) observation on *discourse* 'presenting itself as an invention'. Derrida suggests that discourse 'will have to have its invention evaluated, recognised, and legitimised by someone else, by another', or 'the other as a member of a social community or of an institution'. Derrida proceeds to explain: '[N]ever does an invention take place, without an inaugural event. Nor is there any invention without an advent', by which Derrida means 'the inauguration for the future' of possibilities. Therefore, a creative act is always accomplished at a point of historical and structural juncture, and it has to look back and forth while reinventing both the generic inheritance and generic advent. *Green Men*, particularly, incorporates an inventive process of creation by being programmed as a *baroarigolpo*, or community story. The title *Green Men* is given by a pioneering author of Bengali speculative fiction Premendra Mitra, whose first SF, 'Mosha' ('The Mosquito'), was published in 1945[18]. There are four episodes in *Green Men*, each organised around the icon of an alien monster, or a devilish post-human species with unidentified origin in the guise of homo sapiens. All episodes are written by separate authors and read by the authors concerned during radio broadcasts, without any consultation amongst themselves. The author of one episode situates his story on a set of assumptions about a series of possibilities thrown open by the other three episodes by being a part of a community of performers. The creative spirit of none of the four creators, namely Premendra Mitra, Adrish Bardhan, Dilip Roychowdhury and Satyajit Ray, is enfolded by another's work, but each of their contributions is acknowledged by its power of communication to both an implied predecessor and an implied successor. The *Green Men* narrative seizes the opportunities offered by science fiction for cross-fertilisation of travelogue, epistolary fiction, detective thriller, gothic and horror story. It is also a philosophical narrative on human survival and ecology. In 'marking itself generically', the 'text unmarks itself' (Derrida 1992). But, it also maintains a specific historical framework, for how the 'other' is seen is depended on where one stands 'on the social angle at which' one learns and on the way one's 'personal paradigms allow' one 'to perceive' (Kerslake 2007). The entire project is further left open for multiple renditions and receptions, that is, to inaugurate another cultural process[19].

According to Derrida, the institution of literature 'can, at a certain historical conjuncture, serve strategic purposes' to 'proffer the chance of a productive and important intervention' (Attridge 1992). Derrida emphasises the literary capacity to live history upon 'the possibility of meaning, upon the past, present, or promised future of meaning and truth' (Derrida 1992), a quality that science fiction exhibits perhaps better than any other type of genre fiction. For instance, the 'green man' icon is derived from modern European and American tales about aliens, such as Edgar Rice Burrough's Mars-travel series and Mack Reynolds's post-Second World War SF *The Case of the Little Green Men* (1951) in which a private detective is in search of green-skinned aliens hidden amongst the people. The fantasy of an evil stranger with a green complexion, however, has a rich European tradition that can be traced back to Celtic and Middle English chivalric romance, most powerfully represented by the Arthurian legend *Sir Gawain and the Green Knight*, which intricately combines two medieval plots of beheading the enemy and exchange of victory in a war[20].

In contrast, the 'green men' in Bengali postcolonial work are members of an evil species, secretly present everywhere around the world and work as agents of human destruction by instilling hatred in common men and women. The composition appropriates a typical trope of horror fiction in which the 'most "challenging" monster cannot be [readily] distinguished by sight; indeed, its menace is generated by that very fact' (Kerslake 2007). The *Green Men* was written against the mid-twentieth–century backdrop of famine, bloodshed, communal disharmony, the Second World War, the holocaust and ethnic cleansing that used excuses and alibis derived from a wide network of pseudoscience. The period also witnessed mass movements for economic and political freedom of colonies and civil rights and struggles for the liberation of coloured people, working class, women, differently abled and other marginalised people. The *Green Men* could thus conceive of a strange villain with vile manifestations, threatening to take control of the world and turn humanity into its prey. The four encounters with 'green men' told in four different voices, creating an identifiable rational atmosphere, construct an unprecedented experience in the Bengali cultural tradition; and it serves to define SF by its very feel, as Margaret Atwood (2011) writes, 'Thus: looks like science fiction, has the tastes of science fiction—it IS science fiction!'

Raffaella Baccolini and Tom Moylan analyse:

> Unlike the 'typical' utopian narrative with a visitor's guided journey through a utopian society which leads to a comparative response that indicts the visitor's own society, the dystopian text usually begins directly in the terrible new world; and yet, even without a dislocating move to an elsewhere, the element of textual estrangement remains in effect since the focus is frequently on a character who questions the dystopian society. (Baccolini and Moylan 2003)

This orientation is established in the opening episode of *Green Men* by Premendra Mitra, whose narrative evokes an uncanny terror of international scale: 'If I had I wouldn't have had the chance to write this story. It seems those who set eyes on them, those who get to know the secret of green men for themselves, are obliterated from the earth' (Mitra et al. 2019). The narrator is a Bengali scientist committed to making the world aware of the danger of the green men and their dangerous scheme. He happens to meet a Flemish-Algerian stranger Herman Gill during an academic conference in Belgium. Gill shows a bunch of typed documents to the narrator in a hotel room, and the latter finds in the documents a long list of accidents, ecological disasters and civil wars. When Gill claims that a common enemy known as *sabuj manush* (green men) has been organising all these calamities and urges the narrator to help him by informing the Indian state authority about the threat of the green men, the narrator laughs him away. But during their conversation, an onlooker, who is a co-boarder in the same hotel, lurks in the vicinity, and being apprehensive about the third person's presence, Gill slips away with all his papers. After a couple of days, the narrator reports that 'the local newspaper ran a photograph of a man who had drowned in the sea. Just the face of the dead man, but it seemed to be Herman Gill' (ibid.). The third person, too, disappears. In Derrida's (1992) words, the story 'gathers together the corpus' of a set of signifiers around the icon of the green men, but the 'axiom of non-closure or non-fulfilment enfolds within itself the condition for the possibility and the impossibility of taxonomy', which is explored in the next episodes of the *Green Men* series.

The second episode, authored by Bardhan, is located in India, as a sort of confirmation of Gill's speculations (in the first episode) about the range of green men's activities, and told in the form of a long letter from a medical representative Ramakanta Bhakta to the editor of a newspaper. The theme of travelogue seems to interconnect two distinct generic forms in the first two episodes, and, as explained earlier in Derridean terms, the indeterminate nature of this project of telling and retelling the entire narrative matches with the sudden attack of the green men. During a trip to Mysore, Bhakta does not notice, while being completely engrossed in the story of the flying saucer, that a man in suit and gloves has boarded the train and entered the same compartment. But he feels a little annoyed by the intervention of a fellow passenger who mysteriously questions the narrator why he is amused by the prospect of the arrival of aliens in flying saucers: '[N]ow I sat up straight, "how did you know I was thinking of flying saucers?"' The stranger's ability to read someone else's mind arouses fear and suspicion, but the situation turns grave as Bhakta's gaze follows the man:

'But the hand? Entirely green. A light green, like newly sprouted grass'. The mysterious man's conduct suddenly changes as he becomes aware that he is being followed: '[H]e saw me staring at him with bulging eyes, he recoiled in shock. Slipping his hand into his glove in a flash, he said with a wry smile, "I burnt my hand, so I put some lotion on it"' (Mitra et al. 2019). After a few seconds, the person with a strange complexion is nowhere around, but his suitcase is found lying on the opposite seat. Inside the suitcase, Bhakta finds documents about a species of aliens with the power of telepathy and extraordinary physical features, such as greenish skin and abnormally long arms that stretches beneath the knees. Bhakta expresses his intention to handover the suitcase to the state administration, but the editor receives information about his death due to a bus accident, and no such suitcase is found around the place of the accident.

The first two episodes thus speculate about the terrifying rule of a global empire of killers that is both estranged and cognitively connected to reality through a sequel of experiences. The third episode of *Green Men*, by Roychowdhury, intensifies the sinister vision of the world, and its narrative movement characterises SF in terms of its search for 'ways to explore and to go where others will not, might not, dare not go' (Moylan 2000). The green men's scheme of mass slaughter is delivered in a more organised form in the third tale. A Bengali researcher working for some pharmaceutical company in New York encounters his two mysterious supervisors who seem to be a mirror image of each other: They both have two long arms and copper green complexion. It is significant that the narrative of *Green Men* reconstructs a new standard of normative physicality to contrast the cosmopolitan human 'self' with an evil 'other' designated by 'abnormal' features. Now, the Bengali scientist is informed that the project he is engaged in is meant to invent a clinical medicine that would wipe out racial violence, but just before reaching his target, the tale takes a dramatic turn: 'I was summoned. Reviewing the results of my research, Dr Serkovitch said, "I'm putting compound number 300 into production"' (Mitra et al. 2019). As his boss is not ready to wait for the result of the clinical test of a certain compound, the narrator decides to go to the testing centre, but he is prevented from reaching there by the police: '"Disappear", one of them told me, "Riots have broken out. You look like an Indian, these mad dogs won't spare you"' (ibid.). The episode ends with the accidental death of a young lady secretary of the office as two supervisors run away with all the documents and research products.

The narrative preoccupations of two major post-Second World War Anglo-American works *Nineteen Eighty-Four* (1949) by George Orwell and *Earth Abides* (1949) by George R. Stewart with dystopic and apocalyptic visions, respectively, of the world set a trend for perceptive SF of the following decades. However, the Bengali take on the interface between dystopia and SF, such as in *Green Men*, views a warring and an exploitative world through the lens of nineteenth- and early twentieth-century humanism that seems to not allow early postcolonial works to lose trust in the regenerative capacity of human justice and responsibility. In a study on the science fantasy of Sukumar Ray and Leela Majumdar[21], Debjani Sengupta (2019) notices that '[a]lthough emerging from a dissemination of imperial sciences, the Bangla *kalpavigyan* stories of Ray and Majumdar produce "rich imaginative possibilities for empire's anti-thesis"', and this anti-thesis is primarily constructed on the identity of the scientific explorer/inventor as 'the savior and not an exploiter of the world'. The final episode of *Green Men*, told by Satyajit Ray, begins with a tactical admission by the narrator, here a Bengali botanist, that he is not sure whether his tale can be called a 'green men story'. To use Sen's (2009) observations on the nature of justice, in Ray's narrative, reasoning moves 'from the observation of a tragedy to the diagnosis of injustice'.

The narrator of the closing episode of *Green Men* has had a long-term association with another scientist philosopher Bhandarkar, who was a pupil of Tagore at Shantiniketan. Bhandarkar arrives at the narrator's personal greenhouse after attending some conference abroad and claims that he has come across some new ideas about human beings and has abandoned his earlier humanist stand. Bhandarkar's concepts are, however, drawn from the late nineteenth-century 'development of physical anthropology and of "ethnology" as disciplines concerned with differences between races' (Brantlinger 1985). The politics of anthropological poetics, particularly in the form of social Darwinism[22], contributed centrally to the imperial hegemony, Tagore being the most prolific voice opposing this empire building. In a series of arguments spelt out by Bhandarkar in the tale, heritage, environment and fate are seen to regulate existential capacity. He, therefore, rejects all the fuggy ideas of liberty and equality and proposes to spread the concept of 'survival of the fittest' and establish totalitarian governance of some extremely strong being who would streamline mankind according to the fixed master-slave hierarchy. The similarities between this set of arguments and the cultural logic of the mid-twentieth–century Fascism are obvious enough, and they relate to John Stuart Mill's use of the term 'dystopia' in 1866 'to describe a situation or a government that would be the "worst imaginable"' (Dasgupta 2012). The ruler's utopia is based on such a wish for occupying and brutalising the world—as is reflected in Bhandarkar's retort: 'If the strong can use their power to obliterate the weak, that will be best for society. The power I'm talking about will soon be felt by people on earth—by you too. The days of those who believe in the nebulous, unreal axiom of universal brotherhood are numbered' (Mitra et al. 2019). Significantly, the narrator's immediate worry about the fate of Bhandarkar's students suggests an awareness of the manifest injustice whose roots must be eradicated to save humanity and the environment with all its plurality[23]. Amidst the narrator's vehement protest against his inhuman proposals, Bhandarkar leaves the place, but his hand is cut by a cactus tree. All plants of the greenhouse instantly turn pale, and there is a drop of green blood on a cactus leaf.

The truth of invention is established by the inconclusive nature of the green men project that looks forward to an ongoing battle between the imperialist 'green-blooded' species and the responsible red-blooded human beings across socio-historical and geographical borders in the near future. Thus, Bengali postcolonial SF, with a rich cultural heritage rooted in Enlightenment thought, becomes a powerful cultural weapon in the fight for decolonisation, which demands both reasoned scrutiny of the authoritarian frenzy and a creative pull that reminds us of the limit of totalitarianism. Experiments in a work such as *Green Men* shed light on the overlapping areas of postcolonial politics and the study of genre fiction in the context of the subcontinent.

NOTES

1 This chapter uses some of the overall concepts of John Rieder's *Science Fiction and the Mass Cultural System* (WUP, 2017).

2 The term *kalpavigyan* is used here to mean, as Bodhisattva Chattopadhyay explains, 'a type of literary production that draws upon the natural sciences or the scientific method for at least a part of its narrative argument' (Chattopadhyay 2016).

3 The diffusion of Western knowledge became possible with the founding of the Hindu College in 1817, in which Rammohun Roy played a central role, and he was annoyed by the founding of the Sanskrit College, meant for the cultivation of Orientalist knowledge, in 1824. Ishwar Chandra Vidyasagar later modernised the curriculum of the Sanskrit College.

4 A significant 1905 Bengali feminist utopian SF is *Sultana's Dream* (1905) by Begum Rokeya Sakhawat Hossain.

5 On the other hand, the non-fictional writings of the same time involve an ideological retreat into the past in an effort to trace the origin of modern science and technology in precolonial India, as most powerfully represented in *A History of Hindu Chemistry* (1902–1908) by the chemist and social activist Sir Prafulla Chandra Ray.

6 See Sumit Sarkar's *Writing Social History* (OUP, 1998).

7 The main nineteenth-century medium of kaliyuga myth was, as Aritra Chakraborti shows, Bengali chapbooks, which utilised one major

product of modernity, printing, to disseminate conservative resistance to modernity (Chakraborti 2019).

8 This chapter would draw upon Suparno Banerjee's doctoral dissertation of 2010, which was followed by his book *Indian Science Fiction: Patterns, History and Hybridity* (UWP, 2020).

9 A Bengali web magazine engaged in publishing speculative and science fictions and conducting research in this field.

10 The novel is by Bankimchandra Chattopadhyay.

11 As Christin Hoene points out, for Bose, 'interdisciplinarity is crucial in order to attain what he variously calls "the comprehensiveness of truth"' in science (Hoene 2020).

12 One may see Subhadeep Ray's *Bengal Renaissance & Scientific Temper* (Bluerose Publishers, 2019).

13 The tale was awarded the *Kuntalin* prize, named after a Bengali oil product.

14 This dark comedy was directed by Prafulla Chakraborty and produced by Ananta Singh.

15 *Sabuj Manush* was transmitted on the radio at 8 pm on 16 February 1966.

16 The title, as Arunava Sinha notes in his translation of *Sabuj Manush*, 'may have been inspired by the English science fiction magazine *Amazing Stories*'.

17 The textual quotations used in this chapter are translated by Arunava Sinha; his translation uses the Bengali text of *sabuj manush* by *Kalpabiswa* (2019) as the source text.

18 'The Mosquito' is also the first story of the famous Ghanada Series.

19 *Green Men* was printed in the radio magazine *Betar Yagat*, followed by a number of literary creations around the same icon in the SF-magazine *Fantastic*, a book published by *Fantastic* in 1983 and a reworking of the primary composition in the form of a single radio drama broadcast in 1982.

20 The influence of romance on science fiction and speculative fiction has been widely analysed in the European context.

21 Sukumar Ray and Leela Majumdar, founders of modern Bengali children's literature, are Satyajit Ray's father and aunt, respectively.

22 A doctrine principally proposed by the English sociologist Herbert Spencer, not Charles Darwin as is popularly believed.

23 The removal of manifest injustice remains a continuous preoccupation in Ray's art, for example, in his 1980 speculative film *Hirak Rajar Deshe* (In the Land of King Hirak), there is a call to the toiling mass to remove the unjust king from the throne.

WORKS CITED

Abensour, Miguel. 2012. 'Utopia: Future and/or Alterity?' In *The Politics of the (Im)Possible: Utopia and Dystopia Reconsidered*, edited by Barnita Bagchi, 23–46. New Delhi, Thousand Oaks and London: Sage.

Altman, Rick. 1999. *Film/Genre*. London: British Film Institute.

Attridge, Derek, ed. 1992. 'Introduction'. In *Acts of Literature*, by Jacques Derrida. New York and London: Routledge.

———. 2004. *The Singularity of Literature*. London: Routledge.

Atwood, Margaret. 2011. *In Other Worlds: SF and the Human Imagination*. New York, USA: Nan A. Talese/Doubleday.

Baccolini, Raffaella, and Tom Moylan. 2003. *Dark Horizons: Science Fiction and Dystopian Imagination*. New York and London: Routledge.

Banerjee, Suparno. 2010. 'Other Tomorrows: Postcoloniality, Science Fiction and India'. PhD diss, LSU. https://digitalcommons.lsu.edu/gradschool_dissertations/3181(accessed on 20 February 2021).

Berman, Marshall. 1983. *All That Is Solid Melts into Air*. London and New York: Verso.

Brantlinger, Patrick. 1985. 'Victorians and Africans: The Genealogy of the Myth of the Dark Continent'. *Critical Inquiry*, 12(1): 166–203.

Chakraborti, Aritra. 2019. 'A Series of Unfortunate Events: Natural Calamities in 19th-Century Bengali Chapbooks'. In *Indian Genre Fiction*, edited by Bodhisattva Chattopadhyay, Aakriti Mandhwani and Anwesha Maity, 57–72. London and New York: Routledge.

Chattopadhyay, Bodhisattva, Aakriti Mandhwani and Anwesha Maity. 2019. 'Introduction'. In *Indian Genre Fiction*, edited by Bodhisattva Chattopadhyay, Aakriti Mandhwani and Anwesha Maity, 1–14. London and New York: Routledge.

Chattopadhyay, Bodhisattva. 2016. 'On the Mythologerm: Kalpavigyan and the Question of Imperial Science'. *Science Fiction Studies*, 43(3): 435–458. http://www.jstor.org/stable/10.5621/sciefictstud.43.3.0435 (accessed on 6 February 2017).

Dasgupta, Subhoranjan. 2012. 'Dystopia, Utopia, and Akhtaruzzaman Elias's Novel *Khowabnama*'. In *The Politics of the (Im)Possible: Utopia and Dystopia Reconsidered*, edited by Barnita Bagchi. New Delhi, Thousand Oaks and London: Sage.

Derrida, Jacques. 1992. *Acts of Literature*, edited by Derek Attridge. New York and London: Routledge.

Hoene, Christin. 2020. 'Jagadish Chandra Bose and the Anticolonial Politics of Science Fiction'. *The Journal of Commonwealth Literature*. https://journals.sagepub.com/doi/full/10.1177/0021989420966772 (accessed on 9 March 2021).

Kerslake, Patricia. 2007. *Science Fiction and Empire*. Liverpool: LUP.

Mitra, Premendra, Adrish Bardhan, Dilip Roychowdhury and Satyajit Ray. 2019. 'Sabuj Manush'. In *Sabuj Manus: Kalpavigyaner Golposankalan*, [Greenmen: Selected SF Stories] by Premendra Mitra, Adrish Bardhan, Dilip Roychowdhury, Satyajit Ray and others, edited by Adrish Bardhan, Santu Bag and Dip Ghosh, 21–38. Kolkata: Fantastic and Kalpabiswa Publications.

Moylan, Tom. 2000. *Scraps of the Untainted Sky: Science Fiction, Utopia, Dystopia*. Boulder, USA: Westview Press.

Saint, Tarun K, ed. 2019. 'Introduction'. In *The Gollancz Book of South Asian Science Fiction*. Gurugram: Hachette.

Sen, Amartya. 2009. *The Idea of Justice*. New Delhi: Penguin Books.

Sengupta, Debjani. 2019. 'Explorers of Subversive Knowledge: The Science Fantasy of Leela Majumdar and Sukumar Ray'. In *Indian Genre Fiction*, edited by Bodhisattva Chattopadhyay, Aakriti Mandhwani and Anwesha Maity, 73–85. London and New York: Routledge.

Suvin, Darko. 1979. *Metamorphoses of Science Fiction: On the Poetics and History of a Literary Genre*. New Haven and London: YUP.

Tagore, Saumendranath. 1975. *Rammohun Roy: His Role in Indian Renaissance*. Kolkata: The Asiatic Society.

Varughese, E. Dawson. 2017. *Genre Fiction of New India: Post-Millennial Receptions of 'Weird' Narratives*. London and New York: Routledge.

Vint, Sherryl. 2014. *Science Fiction*. London, New Delhi, New York and Sidney: Bloomsbury.

Williams, Raymond. 2005. *Culture and Materialism*. New York and London: Verso.

Chapter 5

E PUR SI MUOVE: TOWARDS A DECOLONIAL SCHOLARSHIP OF *KALPAVIGYAN* LITERATURE

Rajarshi Roy

INTRODUCTION

By Editors

Thus far, the present volume has dealt with two rather central concerns of the postcolonial Indian SF: re-historicisation with a view to salvaging historical identity from the chains of coloniality and an ontological renegotiation of conceptual otherness found in the discursive presentations of the relationship between the Indian nation and its colonisers. The next step, and a quite obvious one at that, is the interrogation of the possibilities of the entanglement of these two ideas and seeing any potentialities of such an entanglement. One of the key aspects of Rajarshi Roy's present chapter does the very same and shows that the re-historicisation along with the renegotiation of the othered Indian self within the Bengali tradition of *kalpavigyan* allows a possibility of not just finding an Indian voice back but also decolonise it. For Roy, *kalpavigyan* is not merely science fiction but something more: something that, with the addition of kalpana (imagination), allows not only decentralisation of Western concepts of science but also initiates the Nehruvian vision of an Indian scientific paradigm.

Along with the previous chapters in this volume, there is, then, a display of a trend that postcolonial Indian SF seems to revel in. First, there is a rejection of identity, both historical and national, that is granted by their past colonised status. Then, there is a moment of redrawing of this identity that has been for a very long time othered. The postcolonial Indian SF, through its deviations and variations, does so through its centring of the imaginative within the contours of its SF narratives. This is not to say that Western SF narratives are not imaginative. They certainly are. Where the former differs, however, is in disallowing its imaginative 'reaching out' to be curtailed by the rigidities of either Western science or the scientific method. As Roy notes in this chapter as well, there is a definite opening up of the very notion of science in postcolonial Indian SF which allows it to initiate requisite processes of decolonisation. It is this that allows this genre to perhaps embrace another.

****

In the Kolkata Bookfair 2020, the genre of science fiction was the trump card of Bengali fiction publishers. Major young adult publishers, such as Patra Bharati, Deb Sahitya Kutir and Kishor Bharati, have invested heavily in established *kalpavigyan* writers such as Anish Deb, Himadrikishore Dasgupta and others. Most notably, one can cite the example of *Kalpabiswa*, which has, of late, taken the plunge of producing and supporting various forms of *kalpavigyan* writing ranging from Futurist speculative fiction to steampunk. All these publishers have, in a sense, allowed science fiction, or at least a part of it in and as *kalpavigyan*, to evolve from a genre entrenched deep into the matrices of a niche audience to something so extensive that has taken up the project of the political and political writing. In such a scenario, this chapter tries to locate this methodological political through the decolonisation of the scholarship attributed to the genre of Bangla *kalpavigyan* writings of Satyajit Ray (cited in translations), Premendra Mitra and Taradas Bandopadhyay. The essay does this by placing these authors within a larger ambit of scholarship attributed to science-fiction writing from India and the rather infantile treatment given to the classical Indian method of scientific enquiry that had not been considered in detail by postcolonial scholars.

For the longest period, the act of science-fiction writing in Bangla has either been a product of translating works from other languages or simply writings designed to fit in with the intellectual development of young adults and instil in them a sentiment of scientific curiosity. It is only with the advent of *kalpavigyan,* however, that the authors of this genre have finally found the supporting rudiments of a 'collective project' behind them. Adrish Bardhan, the legendary Bengali *kalpavigyan* writer and translator, has, in his definitive analysis of the concept of *kalpavigyan*, stated that the genre is not about its fidelity to the strictures of scientific laws or adherence to a realism dictated by science. Instead, he lays stress on the term 'kalpana' to be intrinsic to the formative bases of the genre. In translating science fiction as *kalpavigyan* literature, Bardhan had, in a way, identified a method for *kalpavigyan* writing (Bal 1996). This is an important intervention that Bardhan makes, especially, as will be shown later, in its contemporaneity with Nehru's demands for scientific temper and the practicable navigation of various scientific possibilities.

Before beginning, it is important to note that while contemporary scholars of Indian science-fiction literature have considered the *kalpavigyan* genre by translating it as science fiction, it is only superficially so. This triviality of translation is revealed by the simple fact that neither the genre itself nor the acknowledgement of the term *kalpavigyan* is a pan-Indian phenomenon. While science-fiction writers from other regions of the country, such as Siddharth Narlikar, have collaborated with *kalpavigyan* writers, the former group considers their work as science fiction rather than *kalpavigyan*. Even anthologies produced in collaboration between these two groups of writers have been marketed as science fiction and not *kalpavigyan*. As a matter of fact, the tendency to translate the word *kalpavigyan* as science fiction is a fairly recent one. While it is understandable that such a strategy offers a large body of texts to a scholar of Indian science fiction, it is important to realise that the *kalpavigyan* phenomenon is something that originated in West Bengal and stayed integral to children's literature in the region. In this context, one must mention how even in Bangladesh the term 'science fiction' has often been replaced with '*baigyanik kalpakahini*' (scientific fantasy narratives) by authors such as Muhammed Zafar Iqbal. The present chapter, however, seeks to deal only with the *kalpavigyan* genre and not with Indian science fiction or '*baigyanik kalpakahini*'. This chapter argues how the existence of *kalpavigyan* is in terms of its political project and its periodisation intrinsically related to the Nehruvian argument in favour of a scientific temper. The contiguity of *kalpavigyan* to the Nehruvian project offers to 'de-link' the genre in question from the larger ambit of Indian science fiction and pre-Independence Indian science-fiction writing. However, this does not in any way discredit the possibility that pre-Independence Indian science-fiction writing may have been an origin point for the subsequent birth of *kalpavigyan* after Independence. Eminent *kalpavigyan* writer Mitra has, in his introduction to his anthology, *Premendra Mitrar Bigyan Nirbhar Galpo* (1964), written about a distinct genre of '*bigyan nirbhar galpo*' (scientific narratives) and how the new phrase *kalpavigyan* in 1964 rapidly captured public attention. However, Mitra states that the new phrase may or may not be a literal translation of the phrase 'science fiction'. Thus, the possibility of *kalpavigyan* as being a separate genre from science fiction, despite sharing similar origin points in the case of India, has not yet been explored. Such neglect, then, delegitimises the historical chronology of the *kalpavigyan* text, prejudicing it in favour of the much-popularised Nehruvian vision of scientific temper and progress. In such a scenario, this chapter tries to consider the question of the *kalpavigyan* genre as something historical and opposed to mythological, thereby decolonising it and, as has been mentioned, delinking it with the larger science-fiction writing in India.

Even in terms of trying to posit itself by way of the causal sphere of scientific laws, the question metamorphoses into a distinct one: if *kalpavigyan* is, in fact, a fictional way out of the endlessly signifying circuit of scientific thought? Can such a form of fiction writing absolutely deny its inheritance of a non-Western/nativist mode of scientific enquiry? Simply put, despite defining *kalpavigyan* as being in opposition to the Western model of science-fiction writing, why is it that science-fiction theorists consider this genre as 'postcolonial' instead of calling it an authentic agent of the project of post-Independence decolonisation?

Kalpavigyan tells us that its representative fictions are largely 'parables' of application of scientific knowledge to an end or an ultimate that is yet unknown at the time of its theorisation. Interestingly, such a model of 'scientific breakthrough' is also to be noted in how new scientific knowledge and 'breakthroughs' have faced criticism from institutions of science and technology. Thus, when in vitro fertilisation (IVF) was first successfully carried out by Dr Subhash Mukhopadhyay in India by using his home refrigerator, the 'fire' had been stolen, in a Promethean sense, from the order of medical verifiability. The act of using a commonplace domestic apparatus (the proper term here should perhaps be non-sterile) made it more of a parable of scientific application. Though he made history with the application of such technology, it led to his ex-communication from the medical fraternity and ultimately to his suicide. What is interesting, however, is that Dr Mukhopadhyay's fate is not very different from that of either Acharya Jagadish Chandra Bose during the early phase of his career or Satyajit Ray's Professor Shonku in the short story 'Shonku and the UFO' where Professor Shonku is forced to abandon his work fearing infringement of Dr Carboni's findings on alien life.

History provides a decisive analogue in the relation between the sciences and their application as technology. The presence of the Greek word 'techne' in the formulation of the concept of 'technology' defines how the spirit of application is largely more human in comparison to the spirit of episteme that is linked with the discourse of the sciences. Even the primary question of the logical position of technology is essentially related to the Greek word 'aletheia', which means an act of revealing or disclosure. Dissemination, subsequent to the application of scientific truth, is at its kernel more of an ethic of technology than the sciences wherein technology forever acts as an instrument of science. The very basis of the Greek word 'techne' is a definitive validation of that, as Martin Heidegger himself defines it in his 'technology lectures'. He defines 'techne' as a brute force that humans have to learn to subsequently make sense of their 'thrownness' that nature forces them into with its unknown, untrammelled and unharnessed infinite potentialities, as characterised by another Greek term that he refers to—'dike'. Technology is in more ways perhaps an experience of mankind's own impulses that they have tried making sense of with the help of nature. They are conscious of the presence of history, from the very ability of its 'application' (Heidegger 2013). The *kalpavigyan* authors, too, in the wake of Nehru's clarion call for progress, involved themselves in an act of revealing the scientific to the popular imagination. The *kalpavigyan* authors would thus effectively induce a much needed 'turn' in the general populace's interactions with science. The 'turn' witnessed was a necessary one. Especially since one cannot deny the political implication of this turn when Nehru took it upon himself to formulate an 'ideology of science' that could be utilised to liberate the modern nation from the 'incubus of custom', deprivation and backwardness (Arnold 2013). Nehru perhaps had his sights set on a form of 'state science' that would include the creation of a responsible techno-industrial nexus, which would be controlled by state policymaking. *Kalpavigyan* continued in its project of raising scientific awareness and induced a popular social interaction with the sciences in Bangla, in which speculative inventions and scientific ethics commanded an equal presence.

This theoretical framework allows the political delinking of *kalpavigyan* from the Indian science fiction of pre-Independence existential space. The writers of *kalpavigyan* fiction, in terms of their own historical presence in the Nehruvian era, have shown a defined sense of political awareness in shifting from the motive of popularising the sciences to fictive speculations about technological discoveries (the best example being the adventures of Professor Shonku), scientific ethics (as seen in the 'Sabuj Manush' series) or even geopolitical ramifications of technological discoveries (noticeable in the *kalpavigyan* works of Ray and Mitra). The argument for such a form of delinking espoused by *kalpavigyan* and the science-fiction genre has been given an interesting resolution in a review essay titled 'Professor Natboltu Chakra: Amriter Sandhan na Samay Noshto' by Riju Ganguly in the Adrish Bardhan special issue of the *Kalpabiswa* webzine. The central point put forward by the essay is that the exemplary texts of the genre have to often take recourse to *obigyan* (non-science) and *opobigyan* (pseudoscience) in order to devise a fictional narrative that would be a sugar-coated tablet (in Adrish Bardhan's own words) for children and young adult readers. While an informed reader of science fiction might consider this to be a rudimentary invocation of Darko Suvin's model of the novum, the science-fiction scholar should perhaps identify this as a transgression from the canonical science-fiction model. There is, here, a shift from the scientific to an order predominantly interested in the implications of science, technology and its relation to the discourse of progress.

Similarly, the science-fiction writer is too involved in speculating about diverse ways to make sense of the obscure nexus that nature does well to hide behind the absolutist laws of natural sciences. Such a mode of speculative writing justifies how, in most cases, the technologies utilised in such fiction is centred on the outcome than on the property bases of material resources. This distinction finds an interesting fictional treatment in two of Professor Shonku's adventures, namely 'Hypnojen' and 'Swarnaparnee' (published in translation as 'The Tree with the Golden Leaves'). 'Hypnojen' narrates the invention of a hypnotic drug by the fictional Norwegian adventurer/scientist Alexander Krag, which he seeks to utilise in the following way:

> The mission was essentially this—to establish himself as the singular ruler of the world. The rest of the world would live under his thumb. All the treasures of each and every museum, library and art gallery of this planet would belong to him alone. And this would be made possible with the help of this hypnojen. (Ray 2015)

In 'Swarnaparnee', we find Professor Shonku discovering a new drug called the Miracurall pill that can cure all the diseases known to man except the common cold. The following excerpt gives us an idea about how Shonku sees himself as the inventor of the drug:

> The statement [of being awarded automatic patent rights for his drug] left me with mixed feelings. It doesn't feel bad to admit that Miracurall belongs to me alone, yet it is also true that because this drug can't be reproduced and released in the market, millions of dying people will be deprived of this medicine. (Ray and Majumdar 2020)

Both these excerpts hint at two distinct features of the 'obscure nexus' between natural sciences and human need. First, it iterates the primacy of the causal logic that links the scientific experiment and the outcome event, which is understandable via the ends that both these drugs seek to actualise. Second, both these fictional events also argue for a possible case for the 'application' of technology. Such an argument is something that can be understood to be a typical feature of *kalpavigyan* literature at large. This dissension point is better understood, perhaps, in terms of the fact that pre-Independence Bengali and Indian science-fiction literature are, in most cases, examples of future writing (at least the best examples are). A scholar of science fiction specialising in the Indian examples of the genre must realise that while *kalpavigyan* literature has argued for possible political implications of technological application, Indian science fiction has, on the other hand, been keen on futuristic narratives. Therefore, Indian authors, who identified themselves as science-fiction writers, have cast off the political implications of scientific imagination. *Kalpavigyan* authors, however, have delinked their own scientific speculations from such futurist writing and have posited their work firmly in real-time. In doing so, they have kicked off the project of de-colonial scientific writing. The 'Sabuj Manush' series and the adventure series of Professor Shonku are brilliant examples of such a mode of de-colonial thought. Simply put, *kalpavigyan* literature has remained the strongest vanguard of the Nehruvian vision of scientific temper and technological progress. The project of *kalpavigyan* is thus subsumed ever so gracefully or perhaps cannibalised completely within the progressive rationalist discourse of the Nehruvian Non-Alignment Movement. It would be, in essence, inaccurate to formulate a single historiographical arc for such literature coming out of colonised India and those that came out of recently independent India. The split in this historiographical gradient effectively grants these two literary alignments their respective and individually separate historic specificities. The older colonial texts are, as argued by scholars, indeed products of the 'imperial sciences' and the larger project of the colonising power to introduce European scientific pedagogy to Indian universities of the time. Post-Independence, the project moved into the arena of 'scientific application', working in tandem with Nehru's vision of 'scientific temper'. In doing so, there arose a contemporaneous conspicuous shift in the political subtext of these works from the order of 'dissemination' and 'popularisation' to the ambit of 'rational application'. Having said that, this shift must be navigated cautiously, for this allows a possible hypothesis where the category of 'postcolonial Bengali science fiction' does not make much sense. Instead, it is safer if this genre remains '*kalpavigyan* literature' (in keeping with Adrish Bardhan's comment) without being translated as science-fiction literature.

However, such a position has its own sense of complications. Bodhisattva Chattopadhyay has offered us two distinct implications of the term *kalpavigyan*:

> The first half of the neologism has its own set of tensions. The word kalpa is a unit of time in Dharmic cosmology. [Though] its meaning differs in Hindu and Buddhist cosmology .... Bardhan, however, seems to have derived its usage in the term kalpana from a second definition which, as a word in common parlance across many Indian languages, means imagination, commonly understood. (Chattopadhyay 2016)

The first implication of a cosmological presence in the term is foreclosed already within the secular scientific projects at play around the historic origin of *kalpavigyan* literature and by the fact that *kalpavigyan*, since its birth, has not, till date, engaged with the *dharmic* implications of time. While the cosmological implications of kalpa can be found in Bengali horror fantasy fictions dealing with tantric practices, such narratives require a separate space for analysis. The second implication, however, becomes more interesting and important as it resonates with Nehru's demand, in his speech at the 47th Annual Science Congress, for a scientific approach to be the primary 'temper' in the face of new knowledge and imagination. He also exalts the scientific approach as 'a way of life, a process of thinking' and calls it to be the only method of acting and associating with the citizenry. He had argued:

> It is the scientific approach, the adventurous and yet critical temper of science, the search for truth and new knowledge, the refusal to accept anything without testing and trial, the capacity to change previous conclusions in the face of new evidence, the reliance on observed fact and not on pre-conceived theory, the hard discipline of the mind—all this is necessary, not merely for the application of science but for life itself and the solution of its many problems. The scientific approach and temper are, or should be, a way of life, a process of thinking, a method of acting and associating with our fellowmen. (Mahanti 2016)

It is quite interesting to note how Nehru's exhortation of the scientific temper is in close resonance with Bardhan's definition of 'kalpana'. Both these discourses offer clear-cut references to the presence of a 'method'. If the method in Bardhan's definition of 'kalpana' is one of adherence to the imaginary instead of fidelity to scientific laws, the Nehruvian defence of 'scientific temper' is about a national identity that is divorced from all forms of mystifying agents and is based on 'scientific approach'. Neither of these two 'methodologies' acknowledges a contingency of the method to the cosmological order. The parallels between these two claims have to be read as reasons as to why the scientific method should, in the first place, be sanitised from the 'cosmological mode' to be truly empirical and authentic. Simply put, *kalpavigyan* literature, in terms of its historical chronology to the Nehruvian project, acts as a rational testimony to the same. As a result, in *kalpavigyan* literature of the age, all the events that carry a remembrance of the mythical and religious are conscientiously erased and replaced with citations to classical scientific learning from various civilisations. Even though these citations are sometimes fictional and, at their worst, wrongly attributed, it brings about assurance of a debt that scientific rationalism owes to the historical. Such examples are rife in Professor Shonku's adventures. The most pertinent example is from the short story 'Swarnaparnee', where he insists how the key herb ingredient in his medicine Miracurall is actually cited in the *Charak Samhita*, a Sanskrit text on Ayurveda (traditional Indian medicine). While the citation in the *Charak Samhita* is obviously not available, the author's desire to provide a historical validity to the invention is commendable. Similarly, in 'Shonku's Golden Opportunity', the protagonists try to recreate an experiment on alchemy from a Spanish manuscript on the subject by a fictional mage Manuel Saavedra. However, the best example of such a project has to be from Mitra's yet untranslated short story 'Karal Karkat' (roughly translated as 'The Cursed Crabs'), which provides a fictional history about how a Bengali doctor posted in the Indo-China accidentally develops an effective vaccine against pox (*basanta rog*) while being imprisoned by Cambodian pirates. The brilliant short story narrates how the protagonist accidentally injects himself the poxvirus that then begins to spread like wild contagion throughout the island of his imprisonment and ultimately kills all its crabs, which had earlier infested the region and literally fed on the pirates and other prisoners.

Another interesting observation that needs to be talked about in the context of *kalpavigyan* literature is the use of language to describe inventions. Certain examples from *kalpavigyan* literature utilise the concept of nomenclature in a way that strongly relates to the outcome that the application of the invention seeks to achieve. Simply put, the presence of a method in such fiction is hinted at by invoking a causal relationship between the end that the protagonist-inventor wishes to achieve and its perfect assonance with the actual end achieved. Adrish Bardhan's definition of *kalpavigyan* is thus vindicated in terms of its validity, as we realise that imagination vis-à-vis the event that the author tries to formulate are perfectly bound in terms of a method and its intended outcome. As an example, we can cite 'Professor Shonku O Frankenstein' in which Professor Shonku effortlessly combines brain surgery with lab notes from Victor Frankenstein. The very fact that there remains a shift in such fictional models of science (dare I say 'fantastic science') from the actual 'hypothesis to theory' to the 'outcome centred' model highlights an important lesson on the distinction between the Enlightenment and the classical Indian philosophy of scientific enquiry, that of the centrality of the act of naming or nomenclature in Indian scientific philosophy. This is known as the theory of effability and is particularly central to the Nyaya school of thought in Indian philosophy (Sarukkai 2005). This becomes relevant when we consider Shonku's other primary inventions, namely the Miracurall pills and the Annihilin pistol. While the Miracurall pills are effective in combatting any disease known to man, the Annihilin pistol is a contraption that disintegrates its target. The source words for naming such devices—Miracurall for a miracle cure for all and Annihilin to annihilate—in fact, show how the axiom of effability almost becomes the principle behind the potency of all of Professor Shonku's inventions. On a grander scale, the language used in *kalpavigyan* literature itself performs the role of a technological instrument par excellence wherein scientific truths and theories of an order are largely demystified from their world of formula and hypothesis and conjured up, or even 'de-territorialised' (Deleuze et al. 1983), fundamentally in a distinct plane that has little to do with science. Simply put, the all-pervasive presence of such a language acts at a metatextual level inside the plot of a *kalpavigyan* text wherein scientific knowledge are no more than signifiers of a world that lies beyond its subsequent successful applicability. The distinctive functioning of language, inside and outside of a science-fiction novel, thus makes technology no more than a habitual metaphor of its functioning and plot progression.

The possibility of such a subtle de-territorialisation is one of the primary reasons for the (improbable) existence *of kalpavigyan* as a rather typical postcolonial Indian science fiction. The genre, in a sense divorced from the colonial demands of science and science fiction, can answer the 'cosmopolitan claims' of the Nehruvian brand of 'scientific temper' and its insistence on a rationale devoid of the cosmological blight. Having said that, there is no denying that such a claim inadvertently brings up a troublesome question vis-à-vis the representation of colonial modernity in *kalpavigyan* literature. In other words, the question if this reading of *kalpavigyan* suffers from the inadequacy of not acknowledging colonial India's interactions with the sciences looms large.

I would suggest that such a strategy of considering Indian SF as a postcolonial text is inconsistent with the 'analogical' model. While the arguments in favour of the 'mythologerm' are (perhaps) consistent, one cannot evade the presence of a historical sanitisation that is a part of the discourse (academic or commercial) that translates *kalpavigyan* simply as Indian science fiction. Such an act of mythic extrapolation with the scholarship of *kalpavigyan* is a mild case of mauvaise foi perpetrated under the 'cause' of the postcolonial project that drowns the authenticity of the genre in the pitch-dark umbra left by colonial modernity. Darko Suvin's comment on the dissonance between this 'extrapolation' and the 'analogic model' vindicates this argument further:

> The analogic model of SF is based on analogy rather than extrapolation. Its figures may but do not have to be anthropomorphic or its localities geomorphic. The objects, figures and up to a point the relationships from which this indirectly modelled world starts can be quite fantastic (in the sense of empirically unverifiable) as long as they are logically, philosophically and mutually consistent. The analytic model can thus comprehend the extrapolative one, but is not bound to the extrapolative horizon. (Suvin 1979)

There is an urgent need for a slight correction to Suvin's model of science fiction. It is necessary to posit here the relevance of the core argument for a decolonial scholarship, as stated by Anibal Quijano, and referred to by Walter Mignolo, in 'Epistemic Disobedience and the Decolonial Option. A Manifesto'.

> The critique of the European paradigm of rationality/modernity is indispensable even more, urgent. But it is doubtful if the criticism consists of a simple negation of all its categories; of the dissolution of reality in discourse; of the pure negation of the idea and the perspective of totality in cognition. It is necessary to extricate oneself from all the linkages between rationality/modernity and coloniality, first of all, and definitely from all power which is not constituted by free decisions made by free people. It is the instrumentalisation of the reasons for power, of colonial power in the first place, which produced distorted paradigms of knowledge and spoiled the liberating promises of modernity. The alternative, then, is clear: the destruction of the coloniality of world power. (Quijano 2007)

What this implies is that the argument for considering *kalpavigyan* in the same historic vein as that of colonial Indian science-fiction literature would ultimately present a false proposition that the 'imperial sciences' and its pedagogy continued unhindered in the then recently independent nation as well. Nehru's lecture on 'The Spirit of Science' furthermore defines his intellectualism to be central in positing a new 'sociology of science' and its relation to the independent republic. In his 1950 lecture, presented at the opening of the Fuel Research Institute at Digwadih, Nehru conjectured as to how the question of science has become something 'glib' in the minds of the Indian citizenry, where even the industrialists are only wont to see science as merely a 'handmaiden to make their work easier'. Nehru goes on to posit a new form of scientific rationalism that he believed to be a necessary spirit of the age whose basis lies in a form of rational enquiry and not on any cosmological given (Nehru 1967).

Nehru's conceptualisation of the scientific spirit is important, for it not only defines the contextual relevance for a separate 'sociology of the science' for the nation (as opposed to that of the Raj) but he also inaugurates a context that allows for a reimagination of the sciences that is distinct from the hitherto Imperial sciences project that remained contingent on the Enlightenment in Europe. Nehru, thus, kicked off the earliest possible project of what Samir Amin later defines as 'de-linking' (Amin 2006), which not only proved to be important in fashioning a new form of sovereign selfhood in the Third World but also influenced Quijano, Mignolo and several others to consider the Bandung Conference as relevant to the project of decoloniality.

Interesting examples of such a form of the decolonial project are available in some of the stories of Professor Shonku in which the protagonists navigate the classical scientific studies of alchemy ('Professor Shonku's Golden Opportunity'), flying ('The Unicorn Expedition') and the moving image ('Professor Shonku and the Box of Baghdad'). All these narratives are bound by the concept of radical 'de-linking' from the classical bases of such studies. However, the best example of such a form of 'progressive' decolonial project of *kalpavigyan* is to be noticed in Taradas Bandopadhyay's yet untranslated short story '*Alokborsho*' ('Light Year'). The story is about a group of researchers travelling through outer space in their Parivrajak-1 spacecraft. The entire narrative has been shrewdly set in a future time in an alternate civilisation where no geopolitical boundaries exist and the entire earthly civilisation rallies behind the 'cult of identity' of a single patriarch. The whole of the social order of science has been effaced in favour of a technocratic society, which is, in turn, 'de-linked' from the erstwhile political habitus through the agency of the patriarch called Sayantandeb. An excerpt from the story will render clarity to such 'epistemic de-linking':

> হালকা ছাইরঙা ইউনিফর্ম পরে নিলেন কনিষ্ক দেশাই | শার্টের বুকের কাছে আগুনরঙা মনোগ্রাম অধিনায়ক : পরিব্রাজক ১ | দেয়ালে আঁটা ড্রেসারের খোপ থেকে সৌর-বিশ্ব সময়ের হাতঘড়ি টা বের করে পড়তে পড়তে নজরে পড়ল ড্রেসারের ওপরে রাখা স্বাবিংশ শতাব্দীর মহামানব সায়ান্তনদেবের বাঁধানো ছবিটার ওপর | এই মহাকাশযানের প্রতি কক্ষে সায়ান্তনদেবের একটি করে ছবি রয়েছে | থাকবেই তো , থাকবারই কথা | সমস্ত পশ্চিমী সভ্যতা চার-পাঁচশো বছরের জীবনচর্যায় যা সার্থক করতে পারে নি , যিনি তাই করেছিলেন | এর চিন্তার প্রভাবেই স্বাবিংশ শতকের মাঝামাঝি সমগ্র পৃথিবী তে মুছে যায় রাজনৈতিক সীমারেখা , মুছে যায় সাদা কালোর ভেদ | আজ যে পৃথিবীতে কেবল একটি মাত্র রাষ্ট্র , একটি জাতি মানুষ জাতি , সে সায়ান্তানদেবেরই অলৌকিক ব্যক্তিত্বের ফলে |
>
> রামধনু রঙের ঝিনুকের খোলা দিয়ে বাঁধানো ত্রিমাত্রিক ছবির ভেতর থেকে আশ্চর্য্য দীপ্ত চোখে সায়ন্তনদেব তাকিয়ে আছেন |

প্রবাদে পরিণত ছবির এই মানুষটি | যীশু, বুদ্ধ, মোসেসের সাথে মানুষ একে এক আসনে বসিয়েছে | যেকোনো শিশুকে অবশ্যপাঠ্য হিসেবে প্রাথমিক শিক্ষাস্তরে সায়ান্তানদেবের বক্তৃতাগুলি পড়তে হয় - "জাগো মানুষ, মনের ভেতর তাকিয়ে দেখ - সেখানে জাতি নেই , বর্ণের বিদ্বেষ নেই , ধনীর শোষণ নেই , সাধারণ পৃথিবীর মানবকৃত খণ্ডিতকরণ নেই | পৃথিবীতে আছে শুধু মানুষজাতি , আর পৃথিবী রয়েছে সবাইকে ধরে , তাতেই সকলের বন্ধনহীন উত্তরাধিকার |[1] (Bandopadhyay 1963)

The readers should note the term 'Western civilisation' ('*paschimi savyata*' in the original text) and its usage in the foregoing excerpt. In the same excerpt, the author credits the patriarch for an ideological solution to the questions of caste, race and social hegemony. In other words, the author seems to argue for a form of historic 'de-linking' that tries to tackle the question of subjugation as a product of Western civilisation. However, even when considering such a possible train of thought, one must think about the concept of 'progress analogue' that has been evoked earlier in this chapter. Just as Nehru's postulations on the question of 'scientific temper' are perhaps, at their very core, corrections to what he considered to be 'glib' evaluations of the sciences by the techno-industrial nexus, Sayantandeb's views too are, at best, 'corrections' made by 'de-linking' the context of human progress from the paradigm of the geopolitical order at the cost of what the author calls 'Western civilisation'. The readers are thus made aware of how the context of progress in *kalpavigyan* literature is also a major dialectical force affected by the question of 'de-linking'. The dialectical nature of such a model of 'progress' in *kalpavigyan* literature is, furthermore, interestingly affirmed in other popular works of *kalpavigyan*, with the best example being Ray's short story 'Sabuj Manush', which was written for the state radio broadcast station Akashwani Kolkata. Ray's short story narrates a short conversation between a professor of philosophy, Narayan Bhandarkar, and the narrator who is a botanist. The very climactic conversation is a distinct example of the epistemic 'de-linking' talked about earlier in this chapter. Bhandarkar, who has just returned from a conference at Uppsala, seems to have his understanding of universal peace and equality turned on its head. Likewise, he fails to see any point of peace between the weak and the powerful, the affluent and the poor, the scholar and the rake, and so on. The conference brings Bhandarkar in contact with an eminent intellectual, discoursing with whom over the period of the conference leads him to a realisation that the project of universal humanism has no rational basis. On the other hand, the reality of discrimination is based on a triad formed by heredity, environment and chance (Ray 2019). What Bhandarkar seems to suggest in this rather controversial outburst that could perhaps be a characteristic of the project of such an epistemic 'de-linking' that Samir Amin calls for: 'De-linking is a rejection of subjugation to the logic of the world capitalist system and the imperative passive adaptation with the conditions of integration with world system' (Amin 2006).

Racist at its worst, decolonial at its best, the context of progress in Bangla *kalpavigyan* literature is indeed dialectical in its nature. Both Bhandarkar's diatribe and Sayantandeb's call to action are the means to the end of the project of decolonisation that *kalpavigyan* literature writers considered to be the genre's subtext. Right from Nehru's passionate argument in favour of 'scientific temper' to the Indian Right's insistence on cosmological excuses in lieu of scientific explanations, *kalpavigyan* and its authors continue their Galilean task of delinking popular non-science and pseudoscience from rational thought.

And yet it moves.

NOTE

1 Kanishk Desai slipped his pale-ash grey uniform on. The shirt had his designation in the team stitched on a pale fire monogram: 'Captain: Parivrajak-1'. He was wearing his solar battery wristwatch as he gazed into the framed portrait of Sayantandeb on the dresser. Sayantandeb, the patriarch of the twenty-second century! His portrait could be found in all the rooms in the spacecraft. It was obvious for he had achieved what 500 years of Western civilisation could not. It was only his praxis that made an erasure of all forms of repressive political hegemony possible in the middle of the twenty-second century; as a result, racial discrimination was now a historian's fancy. The whole world was now a single World State, a single race of humans. Such was Sayantandeb's gravitas.
Kanishk absent-mindedly kept on gazing at the picture, as colours of the rainbow played on the 3D portrait of Sayantandeb.
The man in the portrait was one you would find in parables perhaps, thought Kanishk. Jesus, Buddha, Moses … Sayantandeb. One would find his lectures in the compulsory readings in school: Wake Up, Introspect! There is no race, no colour, no conflict between creeds, no exploitation … no man-made boundaries. The citizens of the world shall inherit this universe with their lives and generations to come. [Translations mine]

WORKS CITED

Amin, S. 2006. 'Does the Rise of China Challenge the Imperialist Order?' In *Beyond US Hegemony: Assessing the Prospects for a Multipolar World*, translated by P. Camiller, 25–48. London and New York: Zed Books.

Arnold, D. 2013. 'Nehruvian Science and Postcolonial India.' *Isis*, 104(2): 360–370.

Bal, R. 1996. *Banglay Bigyan Charcha*. Kolkata: Somila.

Bandopadhyay, T. 1963. 'Alok Borsho.' In *Chhotogalpo*, 213–221. Kolkata: Mitra and Ghosh Publishers.

Chattopadhyay, B. 2016. 'On the Mythologerm: Kalpavigyan and the Question of Imperial Science.' *Science Fiction Studies*, 43(3): 435–458.

Deleuze, G., F. Guattari and R. Brinkley. 1983. 'What is Minor Literature?' *Mississippi Review*, 11(3): 13–33.

Ganguly, R. 2017. 'Professor Natboltu Chakra: Amriter Sandhan na Samay Noshto'. kalpabiswa.com/article//প্রফেসর-নাটবল্টু-চক্র-অম/ (accessed on 13 May 2021).

Heidegger, M. 2013. 'Science and Reflection.' In *The Question Concerning Technology and Other Essays*, translated by R. Lovitt, 155–182. New York: HarperCollins.

Mahanti, S. 2016. 'Nehru's Vision of Scientific Temper.' *Journal of Scientific Temper*, 4 (3&4): 154–156.

Mignolo, W. 2011. 'Epistemic Disobedience and the Decolonial Option: A Manifesto.' *TRANSMODERNITY: Journal of Peripheral Cultural Production of the Luso-Hispanic World*, 1(2): 44–66.

Mitra, P. 2009. 'Karal Karkat.' In *Bhootshikari Mejo Karta Ebong*, 187–199. Kolkata: Dey's Publishing.

Nehru, J. 1967. 'The Spirit of Science.' In *Jawaharlal Nehru's Speeches, Volume II*, 362–366. New Delhi: Publications Division, Ministry of Information and Broadcasting, Government of India.

Quijano, A. 2007. 'Colonial Modernity/ Rationality.' *Cultural Studies*, 21(2–3): 168–178.

Ray, Satyajit. 2015. 'Hypnojen.' In *The Mystery of Munroe Island and Other Stories*, translated by Indrani Majumdar, 31–69. Gurgaon: Puffin Books.

———. 2019. 'Sabuj Manush: Chaturtha Adhyay.' In *Sabuj Manush*, edited by Adrish Bardhan, Santu Bag and Dip Ghosh, 34–37. Kolkata: Fantastic and Kalpabiswa Publications.

Ray, Satyajit and Indrani Majumdar. 2020. 'The Tree with the Golden Leaves.' In *The Final Adventures of Professor Shonku*, translated by Indrani Majumdar, 186–243. Gurgaon: Puffin Books.

Sarukkai, S. 2005. 'Knowledge, Truth and Language.' In *Indian Philosophy and Philosophy of Science*, 209–250. New Delhi: Project of History of Indian Science, Philosophy and Culture.

Suvin, D. 1979. 'SF and the Genological Jungle.' In *Metamorphosis of Science Fiction: On the Poetics and History of a Literary Genre*, 16–36. New Haven and London: Yale University Press.

Chapter 6

ACTOR-NETWORK THEORY AND THE POSTCOLONIAL: A READING OF AMITAV GHOSH'S *THE CALCUTTA CHROMOSOME*

Sayan Parial

INTRODUCTION

By Editors

One of the immediate implications of postcolonial Indian SF's delinking of the procedures of imagination from the boundaries of Western science is a rejection of science itself. For, science, as it is performed in current times, is primarily a Western entity. It begins with Western philosophical traditions and is bolstered by the West's (historical and conceptual) emergence from a very typical form of rationality: Reason. Science, in other words, is the West's ontic realisation of an ontological ProtoScience, where the latter is characterised by a primal desire that the human has to find, and episteme with which they can evaluate and manipulate nature, where nature includes objects of all kinds and found all over the cosmos. This effectively means that an Indian version of Science is something very different entirely. As a note of caution, to say that there is an Indian version of science neither delegitimises the Indian realisation of ProtoScience as uncomplicated quackery nor puts it in a subversive relationship to science. The idea here, instead, is to show that the Indian actualisation of ProtoScience is just different from the west. One could, for the lack of a better word and in full knowledge of its linguistic incongruities, call the totality of this Indian epistemology (where this totality includes all the diverse manifestations of ProtoScience within the Indian nation throughout its space and history) *vigyan*.

What postcolonial Indian SF is allied imaginatively to, then, is *vigyan*. This not only changes the way history is presented (thus bringing in re-historicisations) in and through this genre but also the way the Indian identity finds its roots outside situations of coloniality. For, if science cannot be wrenched out of the West's historical evolution, something that science, in turn, contributes to as well, neither can *vigyan* be taken out of India's historical location: one that is fundamentally outside the West's influence. For *vigyan*, as already established earlier, is a whole in itself. Thus, within the discursive contours of postcolonial Indian SF, as Sayan Parial shows in this chapter, there is not only a simultaneous rejection of Western scientific imperialism but also a fleshing out of a primarily Indian realisation of ProtoScience. Thus, Parial's chapter reads Amitav Ghosh's *The Calcutta Chromosome* to present the methodologies of re-historicisation (that Jaya Yadav speaks of in her chapter) through an acknowledgement of a different modality of ProtoScience itself.

****

Amitav Ghosh's science-fiction novel *The Calcutta Chromosome* explores the notion of connectivity between assorted human/non-human, sociopolitical, cultural, technological entities and offers a new interpretive practice to dismantle the authority of Western science and the attendant hierarchical power structure within the domain of knowledge production. This exploration is done by binding together history and fiction and weaving the plot alongside the original diary entries and letters of the historical Ronald Ross during his research of the malaria pathogen. Effectively then, this hypertextual narrative, within fictional narratology, holds together rich and poor, Indian and diaspora, Egyptian and American, a self-made man and a nineteenth-century lab assistant, colonial science and native counterscience, a chromosome and a human body, human and machine interfaces and finally the colonial spaces of the lab, hospitals, railroads, country clubs, colonial mansions with the native's project of transmigration of the soul to show that the discovery of malaria pathogen does not rely upon the individual authority of Western science but emerges out of associative performances of heterogeneous sociopolitical, cultural, ideological, scientific and technological entities. This interrogative matrix, channelled through Ghosh's use of genre science fiction to trace the workings of these heterogeneous agents, paves away several discursive trajectories to question the epistemological biases within Western modern science, which deliberately negates the 'other' influencing factors and homogenisation in the creation of knowledge. To thus investigate the human/non-human 'other' and their influences, this chapter attempts a postcolonial reading of *The Calcutta Chromosome* in conjunction with Bruno Latour, Michel Callon and John Law's actor-network theory (ANT) and rethinks the social world by calling into question the ontological dualism such as the social and natural, subject and object, human and non-human within the discourse of social theory.

These categorical divisions hinder a dialogic negotiation between the social world and the material world. This novel points at this epistemological crisis by exposing the segregation of the non-human 'other' from the social world and tries to bridge the gap between the social and the material world. The dialogic interaction between the social and material can construct a productive cultural trajectory, where social sciences meet with science fiction to formulate an evolving epistemology. Even Ghosh's science fiction *The Calcutta Chromosome*, being an imaginative assemblage of the self and the world, the subject and the object, the spirit and the matter, provides a resourceful network to trace the association of subaltern bodies, those who have always been treated as non-humans within the rational discourse of humanist philosophy, the agency of non-human or material artefacts and the Western science behind the revolutionary invention of malaria pathogen. In such a scheme of things, this paper proceeds with a postcritical enquiry to deconstruct modern Western science for its nature to essentialise itself as a self-contained field of thought, and manifests, one by one, the role of the supercomputer Ava, the chromosome or the malaria parasite, the laboratory, the cyborg subaltern bodies and the colonial city Calcutta in *The Calcutta Chromosome*.

The novel starts with the character Antar, an Egyptian, working in the office of the International Water Council, New York, with Ava, a supercomputer that works like a digital archive to unravel all lost connections in the process of a huge scientific project of a native cabal headed by Mangala. Antar's life revolves around his computer as it has been programmed to work hard to extract lost information for different projects. It is only when Ava gets hold of a parallel narrative of the history of the discovery of the Malaria pathogen through an unearthing of Murugan's ID that all other narrative strands of the novel rush headlong in the form of letters from Ronald Ross, Cunningham, Phulboni's story about Laakhan, the connection between Urmila and Romen Haldar, and so on. This electronic archive, as a potential mediator, reconfigures the historiographic practices by deriving silent subaltern narratives and registers cultural memory within cyberspace as digital texts. Ava being an actor or mediator is in constant negotiation with a human actor, Antar, in excavating the missing threads of a parallel history of malaria research and in assuming a posthuman future, where the notion of the human as autonomous, individual, coherent and self-contained agent is newly conceptualised as an emergent entity evolved out of enmeshment with technology. Ava is also programmed with a localised interface to respond in the Arabic dialect. Antar sometimes recognises in Ava's language 'the authorship of a long-forgotten relative in an unusual expression or characteristic turn of phrase' (Ghosh 2008). Ava 'refigures the possibility of cultural history' and imagines 'how to read the silence of the vernacular within the archive of modernity' (Frangos 2013). As such, both Ava and Antar become actors or actants, as they have the ability or agency to act, modify and customise social affairs by creating a heterogeneous web of networks among themselves. According to actor-network theorists, the social world is made of networks of 'actors' or 'actants'. An actor or an actant can be a network in its own right. ANT theorists claim that one should follow the actor's own ways and begin 'one's [our] travels by the traces left behind by their activity of forming and dismantling groups' (Latour 2005). It is important to mention that no single actor, be it human or non-human, has complete control over any social phenomenon. Anything can be a useful mediator in a network because the production of knowledge involves various elements that associatively create a performative space where the human agency works with the material world. ANT does not prioritise non-humans or de-humanise humans, rather it deconstructs the system that sets humans as standard agents to measure agency. ANT, thus, negates the notions of exclusionism and passivity that exist in the social theories and adds non-human bodies to the sociological, anthropological and scientific studies. In a similar way, in *The Calcutta Chromosome*, Ava, being 'not simply the hapless bearers of symbolic projection', shows a conglomeration of set human–non-human agencies that destabilise traditional stability of humanism and go beyond human-centrism to include technology to recover subaltern agency (ibid.).

The malaria parasite itself, as Nelson (2003) writes, becomes 'not a thing in itself but a series of interconnections'. The Anopheles mosquito carries the virus and injects it into the human blood. The virus takes shelter in the liver and hides from the immune system. It then forms cysts that burst and make way for parasites to feed on the host's haemoglobin. The parasite can reside in human bodies for years. For instance, when Antar is busy collecting traces of Murugan, he runs the same kind of fever. The parasites can transform the body, and in the process, they get mutated. Even in Mangala's experiment, when the donor's traits meet with the recipient's bodily features through the pigeon's blood, categories like sex, gender, race, religion get subverted, thus evolving anew postcolonial human. Mangala's transformation into el-Magari, Mrs Aratounian and Tara, and, similarly, Laakhan's transformation into Romen Haldar and Lucky suggest how a 'Western and Indian become so intermixed and self-transforming that the old binaries cannot express the extent of their interdependency and the complexity of their relationship' (Romanik 2005). These postcolonial new humans are the production of assimilation between human and non-human forms of life, like the parasite or the pigeon's blood. This involvement of human and non-human actors interrogates the very idea of subjectivity and calls for an inclusive view of life. It is important to realise, before representing a holistic worldview, that human thought processes do not reflect the whole reality but only a fraction of it, rendering the human existence as an untethered vector within a smorgasbord of often conflicting moments and movements of knowledge and ignorance. But, within this chaos and uncertainty, there is, towards the stabilisation of Being, a necessity of an orientation towards order. It is this order, however ephemeral and, at times, myopic, that the novel moves forward towards. Even within (and through) scientific performances towards possible comprehension, there is no conclusive experimental proof of truth or falsity. An act of reason is only a perception of the mind, not a universal truth. So, to grab the wholeness, it is necessary to trace all the interconnections, fusions and interdependencies involved in the production of knowledge. This novel achieves wholeness and, for the lack of a better concept, order, by focusing on this interconnectivity by not just referring to the discovery but assuming various meanings to conceptualise life.

Interestingly, the Calcutta chromosome differs from the scientific conceptualisation of the term chromosome, as mentioned by Murugan:

> For the sake of argument let's call it a chromosome: though the whole point of this is that if it is really a chromosome, it's only so by extension, so to speak—by analogy. Because what we're talking about here is an item that is to the standard Mendelian pantheon of twenty-three chromosomes what Ganesh is to the gods; that is, different, non-standard, unique—which is exactly why it eludes standard techniques of research. And which is why I call it the Calcutta chromosome. (Ghosh 2008)

The Calcutta chromosome resists any definition and acts as a counter-intuitive non-human trope, which claims to dethrone Western scientific legitimacy that has turned its back on myth and tradition. It does not exist in a particular scientific site, but it takes its shape out of an action that is 'dislocal', and at the same time, it is 'distributed, variegated, multiple, dislocated and remains a puzzle for the analysts as well as for the actors' (Latour 2005). It can only be perceived by the scientists outside the dominant discourse of Western science. Mangala represents this subaltern agency, which plays its part silently for the malaria research to extend the research towards transmigration of the soul. She attempts to go beyond the traditional conceptualisation of humans as beings only and forges associations, on multiple levels, between Eastern spiritualism, which is outside of the Brahminical patriarchy of Vedic tradition and much closer to the peripheral Gnostic tradition of Indian folk culture, and Western science, even as either act on the 'human'. This association leads to other associations between actors, like laboratories, chromosome or malaria parasites, pigeons, human bodies, technologies and all other material or immaterial artefacts. These actors are working and creating symbiotic alliances and networks with each other as the 'action' (scientific invention) is distributed to them.

In *The Calcutta Chromosome*, the laboratory is a space of experiment where disordered, heterogeneous human and non-human actants collide and translate their interest to work with each other in the production of scientific facts. Mangala being a lab worker uses Ross as an agent to manoeuvre Western technology for the project of transmigration of the soul. Mangala's team finds a curious connection between malaria and the syphilis pathogen with which syphilis bodies can be cured. She creates these bodies in human laboratories and holds control over those modified bodies. In a broader sense, the colonies can be seen as laboratories of modernity. Colonial modern science has always used the colonised bodies as mice and guinea pigs for experimentation and discredited any contribution by the natives by positing totalitarian models of Western science. Ghosh, in his novel, de-romanticises Ronald Ross's invention of malaria pathogen by emphasising the matters of concern that are involved in the scientific process. The ANT highlights the matters of concern rather than a matter of fact, as the former leads to uncertainty, disorder, controversy and towards argument as well. There is some difference, according to ANT theorists, between 'matter of fact' and 'matter of concern'. Sociologists care about social facts, natural scientists care about natural facts, and some facts are universalised. 'Matter of fact' is a coherent, stable entity, but 'matter of concern' advocates against this stability. The universalisation of socio-scientific facts is a myth as, for instance, a virus can call into question all established facts by spreading mysteriously into our way of life. The matters of concern consist of several social factors that are relevant to put forward while discussing any scientific activity or any social affair. According to Bruno Latour, the laboratory is something 'highly social' and 'their science is only strong ('real') if they can mobilize the highest number of associations, linkages, resources, and allies' (Nelson 2003). Latour, in his first work, *Laboratory Life* (1979), a collaboration with Steve Woolgar and the product of two years of participant observation in an American laboratory, observes a different image in science labs, where the prevalent ordered, coherent, logical image of laboratories do not exist. Rather, he finds the laboratory as a sterile inhuman place consisting of a disordered array of different entities, influences and observations with which scientists struggle to produce order. In other words, scientific facts emerge out of the long and laborious process that is very messy and disordered. But the 'scientific practice is often presentist, proceeding by the erasure of incorrect assumptions, rival hypotheses, and wrong turns' (Luckhurst 2006). In his work *The Pasteurization of France* (1988), Latour similarly problematises the authoritarian status of Louis Pasteur as the inventor of microbial transmission of disease in the mid-nineteenth century. He is presented as an actor acting as an assembler of different elements and interests from, even, beyond the world of the laboratory. He creates a web of interconnections, as Luckhurst says, between farmers, army doctors, Louis Bonaparte, hygienists, newspapers, French nationalism, the bureaucrats of the Second Empire, cows, industrialists, popular and specialist journals, transport experts and the French Academy as well as the microbes themselves (2006). Latour focuses on a heterogenous list of his interests to prevent the 'mad cow disease', including the beef market, several entities in the laboratory, politicians, vegetarians, public confidence, farmers and Nobel prize-winning French scientists (Luckhurst 2006). Thus, science is socialised and produced through a series of associations: 'We are never confronted with science, technology, and society, but with a gamut of weaker and stronger associations' (Latour 2003). There is, thus, no such thing as 'pure' science, as all scientific inventions emerge out of their alliances with social factors. Ghosh's novel, in the same vein, 'follows all the multifarious actants networking away in the lab—the room itself, but also the larger post-colonial laboratory in which he and his readers live' (Nelson 2003). In effect, the novel neither embraces the ostensible 'uniqueness' of Western science nor celebrates native science as the only influencing factor. It does not go for a 'determination of action' or any 'calculative abilities of individuals'; rather, there is a movement towards a 'third space' where with an 'under-determination of action' a series of transactions and interconnections between colonial science and native science takes place (Latour 2005). In this economy of connected commerce, the lab becomes not only a non-human actor but a network of diverse, assorted sociopolitical actors and techno-scientific artefacts as well in its revelation, at least in spatial coordinates, of Ghosh's presentation of an 'un-worlded' inclusivity, and adds non-human actors in the discussion.

Even the human body changes. In fact, there is no unique human body in *The Calcutta Chromosome*. These bodies are cyborgs, as they diminish the boundaries between human and machine, organic and inorganic, and even blur the animal-human barrier by manufacturing miscegenated bodies as DNA crosses over from pigeons to humans, mosquitoes to humans and, finally, humans to humans. Antar's life, on one hand, is very much mediated by Ava. He works with it the whole day and lives under its surveillance. Murugan gains its presence in cyberspace as well. In either of these cases, the human body is 'networked, wired and altered through insertion into the machinic universe' (Nayar 2009). On the other hand, Abdul Kadir and Laakhan are sent to the laboratory by the native cabal to create new humans. The bodies of Maria and Tara are connected to Urmila and Sonali, and they all are connected to Mangala. At the end of the novel, Antar inscribes all the digital codes into his body from Murugan. The transportation of 'souls' is done by the transmission of computer code or the malarial pathogen. So, the singularity of individual humans in modern Western epistemology and ontology takes a back seat in the face of postcolonial cyborgisation. Ghosh weaves a trajectory with the foreign modes of existence to define the 'self' that is, somehow, reverberating Rimbaud's famous words: 'je est un autre' (self is other or somebody else).

Finally, the colonial city Calcutta is an actant as well as a network of sociopolitical, economic and technological structures with all its laboratories, hospitals, railway stations and colonial mansions. The characters in Ghosh's novel 'redefine as well as reassert the categories of colonizer and colonized, British and Indian, powerful and powerless', in exercising 'science, dwelling, walking, and moving in the city' (Romanik 2005). Mangala and Laakhan bring change by redefining the binaries coloniser-colonised, self-other, subject-object and the modes of mobility within the dominant milieu of colonised Calcutta. These colonised characters, at least insofar as their historical location is concerned, learn the technology of the colonisers and use it to subvert their authority. Laakhan and the technology of railways, for example, work together to project Laakhan as one with technoscience. This transference of identity claims synthesis or hybridity. In fact, the colonial city itself as a network becomes a contact zone of opposing binaries. The city is also a site of construction where enterprises are made, but tiny material details that are involved in the construction are never recognised by the official narratives. We tend to see the whole or a 'final product', as the lack of 'empirical requirement' within conventional epistemologies distracts our vision to see 'what it is for a thing to emerge out of inexistence' (Latour 2005).The reason behind the exclusion of material or immaterial influences cannot be justified by simply levelling the tag of 'incommensurability' to the objects, as the data regarding their contribution is available; but what lacks is a will to put them on discourse to view 'collective' as an entanglement of human–non-human interactions.

Ghosh, in *The Calcutta Chromosome*, projects a world where the supercomputer Ava, the chromosome, the laboratory, the city Calcutta, the humans and all the material artefacts with agency and shared responsibility influence a groundbreaking scientific project in the history of human civilisation. Having said that, this assertion stirs up doubts within social theories regarding the prevalent conceptualisation of the social world as a place for humans only and threatens the very conviction of modern science as it assigns recognition to only humans for any scientific invention. For instance, 'if, ultimately, truth or error in science and technology depends (at least in part) upon the actions of objects, then it makes no sense to leave them out of the explanation or to pretend that they matter and make a difference only in some instances' (Dolwick 2009). Within the field of Western philosophy, ontology is the study of being and epistemology is the study of knowledge. These two concepts are relational, as in, to know how knowledge is produced it is necessary to know what there *is*. Social theorists have shown little agreement regarding their epistemological and ontological analysis as they interpret their objects of study in their own ways. So, this methodological pluralism does not vouchsafe 'social' as a universal object of study with a myriad of perspectives, rather it talks about how different theorists are producing a heterogeneous, ambivalent, inconsistent version of 'social'. The inculcation of heterogeneity is posited by social theorists such as Georges Bataille, who first, with his heterological thinking, reviewed the 'social' as something ambivalent in nature and analysed the 'difference' by posing threat to the homogeneity of modern science that negates the unaccepted realities or the 'waste' of society that are also contributing factors for forming a civilisation. Zygmunt Bauman, similarly, sees 'social' as a disordered and chaotic hub that consists of interactions and intersubjectivities. Gilles Deleuze and Felix Guattari, too, find 'social' as rhizome—a web of interconnected roots without any point of origin—that amalgamates the human, things and ideas (ibid.). These theorists have presented their versions of 'social' instead of focusing on 'social' as a single entity or something that is universally defined. Despite these social thinkers' emphasis on heterogeneity, interconnections, association within social theories, the inclination towards material objects or artefacts, somewhere, is lacking in the conceptualisation of 'social'. Sometimes, these objects are mentioned with a sense of passivity. One of the problems of social theories is that it does not include the non-humans like animals, machines, environment, et cetera, into the social discourses; rather, they are interested in the pure form of humans. The emphasis on 'purity' or 'universality' has become a non-existent entity in today's hybrid world. In response to the dearth of framework to include and analyse the non-humans, a group of social theorists (Bruno Latour, Michael Callon and John Law) suggests the methodology of ANT that will incorporate heterogeneous elements and refuse the human-centric dimension of sociological enquiry. They ask:

> What is a society? What does the word 'social' mean? Why are some activities said to have a 'social dimension'? How can one demonstrate the presence of 'social factors' at work? When is a study of society, or other social aggregates, a good study? How can the path of a society be altered? (Latour 2005)

According to Latour, there are two ways of answering these questions. One of the ways talks about the specific phenomenon called 'society', 'social order', 'social practice', 'social dimension' or 'social structure' (ibid.). It is the traditional way of seeing sociology, one that represents society as a homogenous entity, where social dimensions are prefixed, where an institutionalised social context exists and where everything under its umbrella is shown as framed by its social order. The other way of seeing the doubts sheds light on the elements that are assembled in the process of constructing a society. Here, the homogenous order of society is challenged by an alternative lens of viewing society as an association of diverse elements, including sociopolitical institutions, environmental entities, repressive state apparatuses, material artefacts, et cetera. Even in its broadest sense, the term 'social' means association; it is derived from the Latin word 'socius', meaning a companion or associate, with the root 'sequi' meaning 'to follow' (Dolwick 2009). So, it includes anything that is associated together. It means, without any specificity, that the term consists of humans, non-human entities and all material or immaterial artefacts. According to this etymological meaning of 'social', a social world is made of heterogeneous networks and assemblages between humans, groups, environment, ideas, institutions, and so forth. Sociologists often face uncertainty while defining the parameters of the social world, as the word/concept 'social' itself has varied meanings. Latour says, 'social scientists have too often confused their role of analyst with some sort of political call for discipline and emancipation' (Latour 2005). To have a perception of the social world or any social affair as a whole, one must look for heterogeneity instead of purity and chaos in place of order because 'if the social is to be assembled, every hand is needed' (ibid.). Even in Ghosh's world, Ava, chromosome, laboratory, Calcutta work collaboratively with humans in the malarial research programme. So, the approach to purify the subject from the object is illusory, as reality is the outcome of incessant hybridisation of natural, social and technological entities. Ghosh, in this novel, does not provide any 'master vocabulary' or 'common currency' to trace the actors by imposing the role of intermediaries that can only transport meaning not transform, but he holds the actors as mediators that can translate, transform or modify meanings.

In *The Calcutta Chromosome*, Ghosh explores not only the agency of the non-humans but also unmasks the segregation of the colonised bodies by the European scientists. These bodies are dehumanised into animals and othered, just as the non-human entities from humanist discourses. In traditional humanism, a human is regarded as the centre of the universe. Humanism essentialises the autonomy and rationality of humans and sets a standard measure to define what it means to be human. Gradually, the humanist perspective becomes a weapon for the West to divide and rank people based on race, class and creed. Postmodern critics such as Michel Foucault, Jean Francois Lyotard and others criticise the Western humanist notion of universalisation of human nature to even justify the imperialism and oppression of the colonised natives (Davies 2001). Eurocentric humanism has always denied the recognition and agency of those who have suffered the violence of colonialism and hallmarked them as non-humans or less than humans. The exclusivism of the philosophy of humanism has not only produced ontological divisions but also censored many peripheral narratives and the contributions of those 'others'. Ghosh, through his novel, has weaponised the genre of science fiction, which is a Western invention, to see the 'other' and to demystify the colonial singularity and the epistemological biases within imperial humanist discourses by exposing the interdependencies and connections between the East and the West, human and the non-human, nature and culture, subject and object behind the evolution of the social world. Ghosh's intensification of postcolonial concerns within a Western genre of science fiction—to debunk the legitimacy of Western science by, on one hand, employing human–non-human symbiosis and, on the other, by formulating a digital habitat to bring into light native counterscience—shows his objective towards forming an inclusive space or, in other words, a hybrid space of new possibilities to reimagine the indigenous past. Ghosh creates a nexus between history and science fiction and revisits the subaltern by making his novel a multidimensional space, where the notion of imagination is grounded in the logical discourse of science and an ethical futuristic trajectory is packaged with entertainment and the anxieties of the past, present and future.

The novel's narratological organisation is designed to transgress the barriers within social theories and to offer a new interpretive practice in a manner of postcritical tradition to conceptualise humans as a category evolved out of the association between heterogeneous human and non-human entities. It is also designed to problematise individualised colonial historiography to bring the history of native counterscience in dialogue with Western modern science. Ghosh's world embodies a postcritical domain to think about connectivity that can be unfolded through the framework of ANT. Rita Felski, one of the founders of the school of postcritique, finds ANT offering a new direction within social theories to ruminate on the concept of interrelatedness or connectivity as it aims to 're-describe' the style of thinking and to 'de-essentialize the practice of suspicious reading by disinvesting it of presumptions of inherent rigor or intrinsic radicalism—thereby freeing up literary studies to embrace a wider range of affective styles and modes of argument' (2016). Latour himself, in his essay 'Why is Critique Running out of Steam', points out the limitations of the dominant mode of critical thinking within the 'hermeneutics of suspicion' to destabilise the power structure. He favours decoding the activities of actors by distancing himself from the sociological criticism that claims to explain the actors better than the actors themselves. He prefers the phrase 'sociology of associations' as, according to him, the sociological school is limiting in the sense that these schools try to explain social objects with predetermined dualisms. Every social object, even a chromosome or a computer or any sociopolitical, economic, cultural, environmental, technoscientific entity, is also the outcome of networks of association. *The Calcutta Chromosome* maps out a productive and dynamic space, where there is no division between centre and periphery, no point of origin; rather, there is a web of interconnections between human and non-human entities that are involved in the production of scientific knowledge. It is important to see science and technology in terms of what is social or cultural.

Some 'thinkers have answered C. Wright Mills's famous call to develop a "sociological imagination" by exploring science fiction writing as valuable source material for sociological thinking' (Gerlach and Hamilton 2003). Science fiction writers, such as Ghosh with their literature of 'cognitive estrangement', utilise the literary space as a medium for sociological enquiry by fictionalising the present with certain futuristic assumptions and by delving deep into the critical explorations of socio-economic and sociocultural realities. ANT as a social theory focuses on a world that is not a place of categorical divisions but a place that consists of strange but productive hybrids, what Latour calls 'risky attachments' or 'tangled objects'. Latour calls this process of hybridisation 'scientifiction'. Interestingly, the term 'scientifiction'[1] was first coined by Hugo Gernsback in the magazine *Amazing Stories*, which later became science fiction. Latour's ANT posits a fertile trajectory to theorise science fiction. Ghosh's science fiction *The Calcutta Chromosome* incorporates the Latourian sense of an evolving world of strange but fertile conglomerations. This sense of productivity within a hybrid world leads the novel towards investigating the construction of sociocultural epistemologies. Knowledge is productive as it is self-contradictory. The deliberate use of unreliable narrators in this novel manufactures an unattainable truth. The mystery that pervaded throughout the novel is unknown even to the author and the reader as they both share the same episteme. Once knowledge is produced, it is ready to be changed. There is no fixed destination as every destination is a point of departure. The focus should be on the heterogeneous network that produces a set of knowledge. *The Calcutta Chromosome* becomes, as Hubert Zapf (2007) says, a 'laborator[y] of human self-exploration' and 'imaginative biotope' that critiques the limits of knowledge and culture. The novel follows the actors with futuristic assumptions instead of pointing towards a certain conclusion. This uncertainty leads to postcritical readings with much emphasis on the association and interconnectedness between actors that form new epistemologies at the expense of opposing ontologies.

NOTE

1 'Scientifiction', according to Gernsback (1926), is 'a charming romance intermingled with scientific fact and prophetic vision.'

WORKS CITED

Davies, Tony. 2001. *Humanism*. London and New York: Routledge.

Dolwick, Jim S. 2009. '"The Social" and Beyond: Introducing Actor-Network Theory.' *Journal of Maritime Archaeology*, 4(1): 21–49.

Felski, Rita. 2016. 'Comparison and Translation: A Perspective from Actor-Network Theory.' *Comparative Literature Studies*, 53(4): 747–765.

Frangos, Mike. 2013. 'The End of Literature: Machine Reading and Amitav Ghosh's *The Calcutta Chromosome*.' *DHQ: Digital Humanities Quarterly*, 7(1): 1–27.

Gernsback, Hugh. 1926. 'A New Sort of Magazine.' *Amazing Stories: The Magazine of Scientifiction*, 1(1): 3.

Ghosh, Amitav. 2008. *The Calcutta Chromosome: A Novel of Fevers, Delirium, and Discovery*. Gurgaon: Penguin Books.

Gerlach, Neil, and Sheryl N. Hamilton. 2003. 'Introduction: A History of Social Science Fiction.' *Science Fiction Studies*, 30(2): 161–173.

Latour, Bruno, and Steve Woolgar. 1979. *Laboratory Life: The Construction of Scientific Facts*. Princeton, New Jersey: Princeton University Press.

Latour, Bruno. 1993. *The Pasteurization of France*. Translated by Alan Sheridan and John Law. London and New York: Harvard University Press.

Latour, Bruno. 2003. *Science in Action: How to Follow Scientists and Engineers through Society*. Cambridge, Massachusetts: Harvard University Press.

———. 2004. 'Why Has Critique Run out of Steam? From Matters of Fact to Matters of Concern.' *Critical Inquiry*, 30(2): 225–248.

———. 2005. *Reassembling the Social: An Introduction to Actor-Network-Theory*. New York: Oxford University Press.

Luckhurst, Roger. 2006. 'Bruno Latour's Scientifiction: Networks, Assemblages, and Tangled Objects.' *Science Fiction Studies*, 33(1): 4–17.

Nayar, Pramod K. 2009. 'The Informational Economy and its Body in Amitav Ghosh's *The Calcutta Chromosome*.' *Kunapipi*, 31(2): 52–69.

Nelson, Diane M. 2003. 'A Social Science Fiction of Fevers, Delirium and Discovery: "The Calcutta Chromosome", the Colonial Laboratory, and the Postcolonial New Human.' *Science Fiction Studies*, 30(2): 246–266.

Romanik, Barbara. 2005. 'Transforming the Colonial City: Science and the Practice of Dwelling in "The Calcutta Chromosome".' *Mosaic: An Interdisciplinary Critical Journal*, 38(3): 41–57.

Zapf, Hubert. 2007. 'New Directions in American Literary Studies: Ecocriticism and the Function of Literature as Cultural Ecology.' In *English Studies Today: Recent Developments and New Directions*, edited by Ansgar Nünning and Jürgen Schlaeger, 139–164. Trier: WVT.

Book II

WORLDS

Chapter 7*

THE DAY AFTER TOMORROW IN BENGALURU: ENVIRONMENT, GLOBAL CLIMATE CHANGE AND DYSTOPIA(S)

Sami Ahmad Khan

INTRODUCTION

By Editors

Amitav Ghosh argues that the climate crisis is both a crisis of culture and imagination. According to him, climate change has an inordinately smaller presence in literary fiction since the unnaturalness of ecological catastrophes goes against the ethos of the modern novel: the quality of verisimilitude and representation of everyday ordinariness. In such a case, how does one represent climate change in a meaningful and holistic manner and not simply as a sensational, apocalyptic event? In this chapter, Sami Ahmad Khan uses global climate change, and its interlocking with science, technology, economics, politics, et cetera, as an entry point to explore the dynamics of dystopic and utopic projections that emerge in science or speculative fictional narratives in India. It focuses on three short stories: S.B. Divya's 'Microbiota', Zac O'Yeah's 'Bluru' and Lavanya Lakshminarayan's 'The Ten-Percent Thief', all set in Bengaluru, an urban centre that has become synonymous with India's technological and commercial progress. These stories represent three different forms of engagement with eco-dystopias and demonstrate how the phenomenon of global climate change is intricately bound with economical and sociopolitical developments, all within a postcolonial matrix. Khan argues that each of these stories uses a 'novum', 'a scientifically plausible

* Acknowledgement: This chapter is a part of a project that has received funding from the European Union's Horizon 2020 research and innovation programme under the Marie Skłodowska-Curie grant agreement No 101023313.

innovation that catalyses an imaginary historical transformation' (Csicsery-Ronay Jr.) to throw light on a broad spectrum of issues ranging from ecological problems such as air pollution, water scarcity, overpopulation, environmental disasters, et cetera, to sociocultural and political ones including surveillance, caste system, global terror and economic instability. The responses to the eco-dystopia found in these narratives range from hope to satire to rebellion, thereby demonstrating the engagement of India's contemporary Anglophonic SF with what Khan calls the 'home-ecology-economy trilectic'. By projecting a bleak futuristic urban landscape ravished by ecological and sociopolitical developments, these stories ultimately draw attention to the present moments and their many nuances. This chapter brings out the unique trope of hybridisation of environmental apocalypses with elements from sociopolitical dystopias and how this produces a novel form of representation of global climate change, transforming it from a merely biophysical phenomenon to one that truly impacts every sphere of our lived existence.

****

> Everybody's got cancer nowadays in town. I have a week more to live according to my astrologer, so luckily, you got here before my untimely demise.
>
> —O'Yeah (2018)

> Tomorrow, there will be consequences. Today, there is hope.
>
> —Lakshminarayan (2020)

Our planet is dying—and our fictional futures with it.

As of 2020+, the Global South is ravaged by apocalypses waiting in the shadows; its notional and tangible spaces reel under the onslaught of the present (e.g., environmental degradation) and future (e.g., ecological disasters) threats; and it becomes one site where 'real' (climatic) phenomena fuse with 'speculative' (literary/cinematic) manifestations that reorient contemporary reality. As technoscientific tsunamis of metaphorical dimensionalities pummel our world, our popular imagination gets lacerated by 'eco-dystopias' and ecological catastrophes. In a world already taxed by excessive pollution, bourgeoning population, acute depletion of resources, exploitative systems of governance (and modes of production), et cetera, the visible sociopolitical fault lines gain prominence—'identities' come even more alive.

There is nothing permanent except (global climate) change. This global climate change (GCC) emanates from—and precipitates—

interlocking epistemes of science, technology, economics, environment, ecology, ethics, culture, et cetera, and contours humanity's engagement with itself and the planet it inhabits. No wonder this 'change' has been the subject of rigorous academic scrutiny. GCC's intersections with 'ethical responses' (see O'Hara and Abelsohn 2011), 'economics' (see Stern 2008), 'geopolitics' (see Hommel and Murphy 2013), 'global governance' (see Saran 2009) and ecology (see Stableford 2005) bear testimony to its rhizomatic, *gestalten* being.

Zooming in further amplifies our problems: global cartographic projections, market forces and national counterpoints emerge. GCC becomes a thorny issue for India, especially since the nation 'does not want any constraints on its development prospects' yet aspires to be 'seen as an emerging global power that requires a leadership role on key global issues like climate change' (Kapur et al. 2009). Balancing the two demands becomes a difficult act for a nation struggling with climatic actors. As I argue elsewhere, many regions are routinely flooded during the monsoons. The NITI Aayog predicts 'severe water scarcity for hundreds of millions of people' in India by 2030 and 'air pollution is now the third-highest cause of death among all health risks' (CSE), so there is a clear reason why '*2012* (2009) begins at the fictional Naga Deng Copper Mine, and *The Day After Tomorrow* (2004) premiers with a UN conference on global warming in Delhi' (*Star Warriors* 196).

Dori Griffin argues that 'within the last five years, several authors have suggested that speculative disaster fiction is a symptom of troubled times; near-future dystopias proliferate when the present seems particularly grim (Heffernan 2015; Hughes 2013; Määttä 2015)' (Griffin 2019). The material realities of such 'zero world(s)' are bound to influence India's cultural production, too, notably its speculative fiction, which encodes environmental and sociopolitical concerns. To cite three examples of short stories from Bangla, Marathi and English: J.C. Bose's 'Palatak Toofan' (1921), Jayant Narlikar's 'Ice Age Cometh' (1993) and Kenneth Doyle's 'Rain' (1993) foreground, inter alia, environmental degradation. Moreover, GCC is bound to reify dystopian polities in its wake; literary representations, consequently, fuse ecological catastrophes with socio-economic disparities with élan. To cite examples from a recent novel, (short) films and a short story is reflective: Prayaag Akbar's *Leila* (2017) projects an India of the near future where the groundwater has almost dropped to nil (88); *Carbon* (2017) projects a Delhi NCR of 2067 CE as a soot-ridden shell of its former glory; *Hope* (2017) is set in a dark, post-apocalyptic future that faces an acute shortage of resources and energy; and Manjula Padmanabhan's 'Sharing Air' (2004) is set when/where the atmosphere has become so thin that stars often 'show in the daylight' (89).

These eco-dystopias become about *our today*. Sakshi Dogra and Shweta Khilnani note that while Amitav Ghosh 'views the merger' of SF and climate fiction as an 'ethical violation' since the alternate/ future settings of SF negate the 'nowness' of the challenge; however, Vandana Singh believes the 'novum' as fundamentally imbricated in our times, which generates a 'significant engagement with the present-day' rather than postponing the issues at hand (Dogra and Khilnani 2020). This chapter tilts towards Singh's assessment and pursues its objective by (loosely) playing with (Trexler's) eco-dystopias and (Moylan's) critical utopias. Griffin finds eco-dystopia as emerging from 'utopic literary tradition' where '*utopias* offer fictional times or places that are unchangingly perfect'; '*anti-utopias* show an elsewhere or else when that is nihilistic and without the possibility of change'; and '*critical dystopias* function as "anticipatory machines" and tools of transformative critique, warning of the possible future consequences of present actions' (Moylan 2000, 160–199). These critical dystopias 'suggest strategies for resistance or change and offer the hope that action is not useless (Elphick 2014, 171; Sisk 1997, 6; Stillman 2003, 15)' (Griffin 2019). Hollie Johnson notes that 'eco' for Trexler can be about our '*oîkos*', our home/household, that is, a 'space/ place/time of dwelling'; about our 'economy', referring to 'the material circumstances of everyday life and social relationships'; and about our 'ecology', including 'environmental factors, such as geography and climate, in shaping the dystopian society' (Johnson 2019).

The intersection of home, economy and ecology, especially vis-à-vis emergent technologies, future projections and unequal societies, that too in order to spur the present reader to urgent remedial intervention, is often explored by science fiction, justifying this chapter's choice of this particular genre/mode. It then selects a spatio-temporal location (India/2020) and a specific format and language (short story in English) to interrogate how eco-dystopias are structured and operationalised.[1] Now, Samuel Delany finds SF to be a narrative convention that employs the 'future' to present distortions of the 'present' (quoted in *Seven Beauties* 78). For contemporary Anglophonic SF in India, the city becomes a contested space as its narratives extrapolate (and interrogate) past(s) and future(s). One can mention three metropolitan cities in India's recent SF: the Mumbai of Varun T. Mathew's *The Black Dwarves of the Good Little Bay* (2019) projects an 'invasion of the sea' owing to the 'melting of the polar ice caps and the rise of ocean levels across the globe' in the country's near future; it also attributes severe atmospheric changes in Mumbai to 'decades of environmental degradation and the chemical reconfigurations' (Mathew 2019). Set in 2089 CE, Anil Menon's 'Shit Flower' (2019) traces overpopulation by ascertaining how 'twenty million people, and at least as many non-people, can and will produce an ocean worth of biosolids on a daily basis.'

Kolkata, too, finds its future selves subversive: if Ruchir Joshi's *The Last Jet-Engine Laugh* (2001) makes the city brave a water crisis in 2030 CE, then Vandana Singh's 'With Fate Conspire' (2019) drowns the city as 'the river overflowed … sea came over the land'; cities across the world share the same fate since 'everywhere cities are flooded or consumed by fire. Everything is dying'. A parched, dystopian Delhi is in the middle of a post-CBRN (Chemical, Biological, Radiological and Nuclear) warfare reconstruction in Shovon Chowdhury's *The Competent Authority* (2013), and the capital city is plagued by a water crisis, hazardous air quality, gated communities and surveillance state in Samit Basu's *Chosen Spirits* (2020).

This chapter, however, focusses on representations of a fourth city, one central to a neoliberal, globalised India's technocapitalist imagination; it studies the portrayal(s) of Bengaluru, the Silicon Valley of India, and maps its fictional futures via an environment/dystopia *dispositif* when placed within a postcolonial matrix. The choice of this city is again intentional. T.G. Shenoy finds that the 'fictional futures' of Bengaluru occupy a unique place in India's popular imagination: 'Delhi is power, Mumbai is money and glamour, but Bengaluru is technology, though it is as much about art and history, a cosmopolitan city that refuses to be tied down' by 'regionalism or parochialism'; it is, in essence, 'futuristic while being rooted in the past'. Now, this city appears even in Elizabeth Bear's novella *In the House of Aryaman, a Lonely Signal Burns* (2018), a murder mystery set in a Bengaluru of the future, and in Shalini Srinivasan's 'Road: A Fairy Tale' (2019), which Shenoy opines *is* about 'urban decay' and 'environmental degradation' in Bengaluru since 'the Road is Sampige Road and Sludge is the Vrishabhavathi' (email).

This chapter adopts the novum to interrogate the eco-dystopias of/in Bengaluru, which have been published in the last three years (2018–2020). The novum is 'a scientifically plausible innovation that catalyses an imaginary historical transformation' (Csicsery-Ronay Jr. 2005), and when viewed in the light of the assertion that 'ecological issues are situated at a complex intersection of politics, economy, technology and culture' (Heise 2006), it acts as a node through which cultural, ecological, environmental and sociopolitical projections of/onto Bengaluru can *excavate* extrapolations.[2] These three stories—'Microbiota', 'Bluru' and 'The Ten-Percent Thief'—manifest three diverging nodes of how India's contemporary Anglophonic fiction engages with eco-dystopias, which not only project 'failed sociopolitical structures' but also futures where 'the environment has been damaged, perhaps irreparably—usually by human population growth, pollution, new technologies, and the unchecked cycle of production and consumption' (Griffin 2019).

LOVE, LIES AND CRISPR: 'MICROBIOTA AND THE MASSES: A LOVE STORY'

Divya's 'Microbiota' features 'a sickly biologist' who has 'shut herself off from the world and its deadly pollutants to research her beloved microbiota in peace—until a chance encounter drives her to venture out into an unliveable Bengaluru' (Divya 2019). Moena Sivaram is a genius researcher who has isolated herself for the past five years. She rarely steps out and her limited encounters with the outside world are necessitated by a desire to keep her immediate (artificial) environment sanitised. Her 'friends' and 'children', thus, are the flora, bacteria and biomes that surround her and exist within her.

Moena's bubble is burst when Rahul Madhavan, a field applications engineer, drops by to conduct repairs of a faulty 'Smart Window', and the recluse finds herself falling for a (metaphorical) 'outsider'. Against her better judgement (and the alarmed advice of a friend, Professor Das) Moena applies for an internship at Hariharan Ecological Group (HEG) to meet Rahul again, which she manages to, albeit under a false identity. During this meet, Rahul launches into an ardent speech on 'water pollution, remediation, plant and bacterial seeding' and Moena feels her academic, insular approach to research being swayed by Rahul's hands-on engagement with 'community effort and citizen science, of working with the earth and not against it'.

According to Bodhisattva Chattopadhyay, a lot of SF produced over 'the past two decades concerns climate change, population growth and technological developments'; he adds that SF 'authors do not try to predict what society will be like; rather, they extend the tendencies they see here and now into the future' ('Science Fiction'). Moena—as Meena—develops her own vision of the future as she volunteers for the HEG and is tasked with 'collecting soil and water samples for analysis' from Agara Lake, which is 'rife with industrial metals, plastics, and animal waste'. When she steps out and draws 'her first breath of raw city air in five years', she notices the dust in the air, the 'black exhaust' spewed by diesel trucks and the 'decaying refuse and putrid sewage' that makes her gag. The banks of the lake are slime-ridden, and 'white-foam' floats in 'Rorschach' blotches and make Moena wonder how the 'state of the world had got so rotten'.

As Moena falls deeper in her research— and in love with Rahul—she also finds newer ideas and specimens to make Bengaluru better. She had written a thesis on 'fresh water bioremediation' and now intends to use her skill set for the betterment of a local lake. However, these foreign bacteria infiltrate her 'cultivated sanctum' one day and attack Moena's body, resulting in skin rashes, runny rose and headaches. Galvanised into action, Moena utilises CRISPR technology to engineer bacteria that become 'oxygen-devouring microbeasts' that attack plastics; she finds a way to 'improve the breakdown of the polycarbonates' using enzyme sequences from a fungus (*Geotrichum candidum*, which is a member of the human microbiome) and by splicing it with a gram-negative bacterium (*Flavobacterium*). She decants 'half of her custom bacterial solution into a sterile test tube' and gets ready to take a leap of faith. If novum is that 'historical innovation or novelty in an SF text from which the most important distinctions between the world of the tale from the world of the reader stem' (Csicsery-Ronay Jr. 2005), then this splicing becomes the novum, which then leads to a transformation. There are also other contenders such as the Smart Windows but the efficacious CRISPR-based gene editor and its solution look more promising. When dumped into the Agara Lake (the other half she uses on her home), the 'single-celled lovelies' manage to 'digest the iron and polycarbonates in the water' and 'then make their way into the locals'; this may lead to a cascade effect that would soon infect the 'sewage runoff and restore the water to liveable purity'. Interestingly, while SF is full of horror stories that start right here, this particular experiment succeeds. Moena records her findings in a paper, which are corroborated independently by Rahul: he has the 'HEG do the lab analysis' on samples from the lake and the results are promising. The story ends with Moena/Meena and Rahul getting comfortable with their real identities and bonding over how they want to change the world. Rahul moves in with Moena and is welcomed 'home'. Tomorrow can be better—if we work towards it.

While 'a kind of GM rice' originally meant to 'combat global malnutrition and hunger' in Rajat Chaudhuri's *The Butterfly Effect* 'takes over ecosystems' and 'causes death, ageing and forgetfulness in humans' (*Star Warriors* 156), Moena's unleashing an 'unverified, unpublished' treatment for the city's ecosystem does more good than harm. Divya, when asked about CRISPR and whether the exigencies of a love story forced a happy ending that deviated from the more commonly used strain of 'warning SF', replies that she finds genetic engineering to be a 'tool' that 'has the potential to do as much good as harm and has already done some of both'; she adds that she 'prefer[s] to write realistic depictions of the future with a healthy dose of optimism', and she 'specifically wanted to demonstrate that we have people working today in environmental remediation using bacteria' (email 2021).

The home is safe, so is the economy and ecology. Rather than being reified, class, too, is transcended with Rahul and Moena, perhaps an extension of Divya's claim that she does not see a Bengaluru of the near future 'falling into a political dystopia any time soon', though the environmental concerns of pollution and climate change are likely to get worse without immediate remedial action (email). However, the next story manifests another node of the eco-dystopian imagination: home may be (relatively) safe but the economy and ecology slowly begin to bear the brunt of vikas.

INCREDIBLE INDIA: SATIRE, SURVEILLANCE AND HYBRIDITY IN 'BLURU'

Zac O'Yeah's satirical 'Bluru' is set in a dystopian Bengaluru (often shortened to Bluru). Fusing concerns of GCC, overpopulation, pollution, caste and class conflicts, et cetera, 'Bluru' focuses on Herman Barsk, a former Swedish police officer, who visits Bengaluru along with his Indian wife, Kumkum, for a week-long holiday. Barsk exits the Bluru airport, which is 'guarded by heavily armed soldiers behind sandbags' as if to manifest an existential threat to the state, and then proceeds to spray himself with an 'anti-sunshine gel' (O'Yeah 2018). The city itself is an environmental wreck: 'the sun never shines' as hazardous levels of 'vehicular pollution' blocks the sun; 'smoggy fog' hangs so low one could touch it; this also prevents raindrops from reaching the surface and precipitates a shortage of clean air and water. 'The micro-waved air' feels like 'sucking at the exhaust of a garbage truck', forcing one to 'chew' and spit out 'the airborne crud' before 'swallowing the oxygen into your lungs'.

Suparno Banerjee argues that 'the exploitative nature of capitalist and neocolonial forces is also often expressed through the tropes of natural disasters'; he continues on how 'estranging devices of futurity' are utilised to reflect the 'ideologies of the present' and 'political, economic and environmental hopes and anxieties', which also leads to these futures evolving their own mechanics of operation between India and the West, a stage where hybridity and synthesis are most common (Banerjee 2020). Such hybridity is manifested more clearly after the couple is met by Hari Majestic (a detective from O'Yeah's oeuvre), an old acquaintance Barsk was trying to reach. Hari's assistant electronicappaswamy had hacked into Barsk's itinerary and prompted Hari to welcome the couple in India. After an exchange of pleasantries, the trio decides to dine in Gandhi Nagar: 'lunch-time is still on'. However, reaching there appears to be a problem: The infamous Bengaluru traffic finds itself indicted in a comic extrapolation. While 'thousands of taxi drivers' stand with their vehicles—some 'over 200 years old' occupying the road as 'medieval ruins'—outside the airport, there has been a gridlock in the city centre for over two decades now; the road leading to the city centre is such that 'people have been living in their cars, getting married, having kids' (reminiscent of *Doctor Who*'s 'Gridlock').

Sophia David avers that 'climate change sits outside inherited modes of thinking' as it 'renders previous modes for defining these as obsolete' and makes one 'rethink *a priori* knowledge, terms and habits' (265). Since the trio cannot travel via road, and any other mode of public transport seems unavailable, they decide to 'levitate' to their destination using yogic techniques. Interestingly, the yogic levitation rails are 'Made in China'—hybridisation at work again. As Barsk moves towards his lunch rendezvous, he sees 'fly-unders and fly-overs and fly-betweens crammed with cars, buses, cows, elephants, monkeys, demonstrations, riots, and what to him looked like civil wars judging by the sounds of booming bazookas and nozzle flares he could make out through the haze'. The story ends in the middle of this sojourn, just as Barsk has a profound (orientalist?) realisation about the country he is visiting. Tomorrow isn't really better; thus, we must work towards it.

This satirical take on climate change, hazardous air quality, overpopulation, traffic and pollution, et cetera, projects a dystopian Bengaluru in a state of stochastic chaos. As Johnson avers, 'the ecodystopian novel [and the short story by extension] does not simply use a post-apocalyptic of environmentally-ravaged setting as a backdrop' as it also focusses on the 'consequences of this environmental precarity' as 'central to the functioning of the dystopian society and central to the narrative' (Johnson 2019). While environmental degradation in Bengaluru and shortage of resources—and space—form the butt of the critique, the story simultaneously refracts sociopolitical concerns that plague contemporary India. From global terror (the airport is guarded by 'armed soldiers behind sandbags') to caste (Barsk's wife comes from an 'upper-caste family and was always right'), one can see the tongue-in-cheek linkages that mirror current realities.

Class finds its own presence: the 'rich have already evacuated' to the 'cool moon', which promises 'chill-out clubhouses, freezing-cold gym … and free ice cubes'. Luna has been terraformed and the powerful are attracted towards 'look[ing] down on the rest of the world'; this becomes the novum, especially as a 'rationally explicable material phenomenon, the result of an invention or discovery, whose unexpected appearance elicits a wholesome change in the perception of reality' (*Seven Beauties* 6). Moreover, the smog that has become metaphorically 'reified' can give this novum competition, according to Banerjee's take on synthesis. After all, 'climate change asks for authorial innovation, demanding plotlines and characterizations that participate in the global, networked, and controversial nature of climate change' (Trexler and Johns-Putra 2011). The economic instabilities also appear in this future after 'a spate of demonetizations', a clear reference to India's 2016 demonetisation that rendered eighty-six per cent of currency useless (see Tharoor 2017).

A critique of AI and surveillance state also creeps in: Barsk's credit card is shredded by an ATM since its 'sentiments' have been hurt (in an age of hurt sentiments and lynched bodies). Barsk has also not filed his KYC (know your customer) paperwork: without a valid social security number (he might be an illegal immigrant, after all!), he is neither able to withdraw money nor make telephone calls (divesting him of his purchasing power *and* his ability to communicate). With hints of Shovon Chowdhury's inimitable *The Competent Authority* (2013), this is another satire that cuts deep and not just (as) an eco-dystopia. The next (last) story presents disruptions of home, economy and ecology alike. Have we arrived at the point of no return?

RESISTANCE IS NATURAL: CROSSING THE CARNATIC MERIDIAN IN 'THE TEN-PERCENT THIEF'

Multi/transnational corporations—be they of the Umbrella kind (*Resident Evil*), the Weyland-Yutani kind (*Alien*), the LexCorp kind (*Superman*) or the Tyrell kind (*Blade Runner*)—are often primary antagonists in a lot of SF. Lavanya Lakshminarayan's 'The Ten-Percent Thief' adds another name to the table: Bell Corporation.

The story is set in Apex City that exists across a 'crater that was once Bengaluru' (Lakshminarayan 2020). Bengaluru has been, perhaps, wiped out by CBRN warfare egged on by a scarcity of natural resources. In its wake, Apex City—run by the Bell Corporation—has come into being; this city reminds one of the automated, capitalism-primed domed city in Shiv Ramdas's *Domechild* (2013), which divided the world into outside and inside. Apex City, however, is divided *internally* by a shield wall: a shabby, penury-ridden dystopia for the 'analogs' and the climate-controlled, ostensibly utopian sector meant for the 'virtuals'. The differences between the haves and the have-nots are extremely pronounced: (pod) homes, (hypercapitalist) economy and (fractured) ecology are all deformed. The zero world appears here: the seeds of Apex City could be traced back to when the 'ruins of an erstwhile civilization' necessitated a 'new order of governance', which was promptly supplied by the Bell Corporation. Not only did it believe 'itself to be the perfect solution', it seemed 'optimal—even utopian—for a world divided along social and communal lines, faced with the threat of dwindling resources and hostile climate'.

When asked how environment and dystopia hybridise, Lakshminarayan 'hopes for a future where we collectively direct our technology towards solving environmental crises', an effort 'where the efficacy of a solution is not gated on purchasing power'; this, however, 'is not helped by government legislations and corporate policies that actively de-prioritise the need to preserve the environment or enable solutions that can help repair the damage done' (email 2021). The story extends this line of reasoning: the analogue section of town is dilapidated, polluted and overcrowded; scrap metal and junkyards litter the place and its word-picture is captured by a 'solitary child' as he 'sits on a merry-go-round made from the ancient remains of a satellite dish'. However, on the other hand, the 'virtuals' section across the Carnatic Meridian is climate-controlled, where 'thousands of employees are ensconced in bio-mat and frosted-glass spirals, absorbed in HoloTech experiences'. Despite a dedicated 'Museum of Analog History', aesthetics (and not just politics) finds itself being contoured by the dominant paradigms: 'on their eastern walls, a well-known artist directs a crowd of analogs towards the completion of a mural' that 'reflects their past and celebrates their present'.

A metaphorical wall also cleaves the society apart: the top one per cent own and control everything. The top twenty per cent constitute the upper class and have the privilege of accessing the arboretum, among other things. The middle class is the next seventy per cent, who are allowed 'Hyper Reality gardens, [and] the occasional houseplant', an illusion of power. The lowest are the ten per cent, *les damnés de la terre*, who are barely 'given the right to breathe'. While the virtuals are protected by a 'SunShield Umbrella which orbits the Apex City' and provides climatic conditions 'optimised for human performance', the analogue side is 'exposed to heat waves and dust storms'. It is here that sociopolitical dystopia(s) fuse with ecological catastrophes and where home, economy and ecology intersect. Janet Fiskio opines that to 'engage with GCC as a phenomenon of meaning and politics, rather than merely a biophysical problem, requires engagement with the texts and images that reproduce these axiological narratives' (13). The story draws upon epistemes of hypercapitalism, cyberpunk, ecological dystopia, acute sociopolitical differences, mass exploitation and environmental degradation, et cetera.

The unnamed protagonist of the story is an exile who belongs to the lowliest ten per cent of society. She is a Robin Hood (Nayaka) for the analogues, stealing from the rich (virtuals) and giving it to the poor (analogues). The identity of the narrator remains a closely guarded secret, especially since her acts of 'subversion' range from stealing precious life-saving medical technology from the Bell Corporation during a cholera epidemic to securing 'holo-watches', which processes 'a thousand bottles of [potable] water'. She is 'discreet', 'invisible' and relies on 'dead drops', 'paper money' and 'safe capsules buried underground' to escape 'raid-bots'. However, the sword of Damocles hangs over her: a 'vegetable farm' looms large ahead, and Nayaka is aware of how she could be 'harvested' at any time (hints of *Soylent Green*), alongside other 'non-performing assets' of a society that swears by order and utility.

One day Nayaka impersonates a gardener to cross the Carnatic Median to execute a heist. She makes her way across this technologised marvel and teleports to the estate of Sheila Prakash, a 'HoloTech Mogul'. She comes across 'clear blue skies overhead and verdant meadows', a holographic simulation that, arguably, exists alongside (real) trees that curve 'on either side of her, all along the city's borders'; while the analogues 'have no conception of a tree', here, in the virtual side, 'thousands of trees flower in desolation'. This dovetails with how 'in many contemporary eco-dystopias, technological means both a movement away from and simultaneously into or towards nature—away from nature-as-nature-as-garden, a constructed, mediated, still essential to our definitions of urban space' (Hughes and Wheeler 2013). The protagonist is given the task of bringing 'all trees to flower by 3.49 p.m.', and she 'powers up her jetpack' and heads into the canopies with a 'sap-scanner, pruning shears and InstaBlossom compounds'. She locates a blind spot in the 'PanoptiCam' and steals 'three buds' and an InstaBlossom sachet. Nayaka returns to her own impoverished sector and plants a tree at the 'confluence of alleyways at its heart'; she drops a bud into a 'shallow pit', uses InstaBlossom and 'sacrifices a bottle of water'. A 'sapling plunges into the earth' and a tree 'shoots upwards with a shriek, reaching for the sky', and the tree is greeted with gasps of wonder as it flowers. The resistance gets a new symbol, and the analogues get a reason to fight. Nature becomes worth nurturing, and our day after tomorrow can be better than our tomorrow if the walls are pulled down.

With home, economy and ecology seriously compromised, Apex City creates a dystopia for many, at the expense of creating a utopia for a few. When asked how strains of predatory capitalism infect social justice and political-economic equality, Lakshminayaran says, '[H]istorically, we have perpetuated systems that have resulted in the uneven distribution of rights and opportunities across the human race. The fallout is our present reality, where socio-political divides and economic rifts continue to grow unchecked'; she further emphasises how 'climate crisis, unsustainable population growth' and 'the lack of access to healthcare brought to light by the COVID-19 pandemic' necessitate a re-examination of our world so that 'the disparities dividing the human race' can be resolved by their projections 'into the future' (email 2021).

CONCLUSION

Darko Suvin locates SF's 'specific modality of existence' as 'a feedback oscillation' that swings between the reader's/writer's reality and the world of the text 'in order to understand the plot-events' and then return to the reader's/writer's reality 'to see it afresh from the new perspective gained' (Suvin 1979). Griffin also finds that 'designing an effective visual metaphor to facilitate useful individual encounters with the complex and overwhelming problem of species and biosphere survival remains both challenging and necessary' (Griffin 2019). Bengaluru's literary projections of/in these futures become vantage points and zones of divergence from which one can receive 'feedback' (Csicsery-Ronay Jr. 2008) in/about our present times, a message that fundamentally changes the way we approach our present.

This *today* is shaped by how the nodes of home, economy and ecology within select eco-dystopias exhibit multiple modalities of engagement. Each writer evolves specific mechanics despite being influenced by a larger megatext. Divya, for example, asserts that her 'story is set 10 years in the future' and 'Bengaluru is not intended to be a metaphor, though it can certainly stand in for many modern cities'; she attributes the (postcolonial?) choice of this locale to her not finding 'enough non-Western settings' for SF, and that she 'had recently visited family [in Bengaluru] so the sensory details were still vivid' (email 2021). Lakshminarayan, on the other hand, harbours a sentiment that views Bengaluru as 'an international technoscientific hub, and it works as a global metaphor for technocracy'; she also adds that while 'technology is not evil as it can be an enabler and a powerful leveller, but we are currently passive consumers in a top-down, capitalist system that uses its soft power to contribute to profitability' (email 2021).

Evidently, in India's (contemporary) Anglophonic SF, the home-economy-ecology trialectic ranges from deploying scientific progress and well-intentioned human bonding to prevent the eco-dystopia from happening in the first place (as in 'Microbiota'), to consciously satirise a (mutated economy-ecology) tomorrow to make the eco-dystopia less palatable in the popular imagination ('Bluru'), to actively resist the eco-dystopia by underscoring its deleterious impact on home-economy-ecology via horrifying visions of the future ('The Ten-Percent Thief'). These projections negotiate the interpolation of sociopolitical and economic anxieties within environmental concerns; they also explore how human behaviour and organisation exists in a feedback loop with ecological and environmental realities.

Here, India becomes a site and sight where semantic elements from sociopolitical dystopias hybridise with those of environmental apocalypses in a syntax that generates impulses of resistance in our today(s). Contemporary cultural production, thus, operates as per a *dulce et utile* philosophy that warns as well as gives hope, that frightens as well and reli(e)ves, especially since 'ecocatastrophe[s] cannot be postponed' (Stableford 2005). Perhaps, our fictional futures are coming alive, and our planet with them.

NOTES

1 Now, this chapter, being aware of how climate change narratives are no longer speculative, focuses on their mimetic components to assess how the epistemic frameworks of GCC and dystopia fuse in literary representations of a major Indian city, especially those published during the last couple of years. It neither delves into the history of climate change narratives in India nor into the science fiction versus climate fiction versus dystopia debate. Rather, it fuses all three to view how these literary visions of tomorrow can act as harbingers of better (lived) tomorrows.

2 Though eco-dystopias generally do not focus 'on a *single* cataclysmic event triggered by nuclear disasters … but on the consequences of everyday human behaviors enacted repeatedly over protracted periods of time' (Griffin 2019, emphasis added), this chapter still utilises the novum to identify how disruptions in India's future evolve out of a play between the semantics/syntax of SF/climate fiction/dystopia in order to indict the present.

WORKS CITED

Akbar, Prayaag. 2017. *Leila.* New Delhi: Simon and Schuster.

Banerjee, Suparno. 2020. *Indian Science Fiction: Patterns, History and Hybridity.* Cardiff: University of Wales Press.

Basu, Samit. 2020. *Chosen Spirits*. New Delhi: Simon and Schuster.

Bear, Elizabeth. 2018. *In the House of Aryaman, a Lonely Signal Burns*. NA: Sobbing Squonk Press.

Bose, J.C. 2013. 'Runaway Cyclone' (Palatak Toofan). Translated by Bodhisattva Chattopadhyay. http://strangehorizons.com/fiction/runaway-cyclone/ (accessed on 12 March 2021).

Carbon: The Story of Tomorrow. 2017. Dir. Ramiz Ilham Khan.

Chattopadhyay, Bodhisattva. 2016. 'On the Mythologerm: Kalpavigyan and the Question of Imperial Science.' *Science Fiction Studies*, 43(3): 435–458.

Chattopadhyay, Bodhisattva. 2020. 'Science Fiction about the Future May Provide Solutions to Today's Crises.' *Sciencenorway*. https://partner.sciencenorway.no/climate-science-fiction-and-fantasy-society-and-culture/science-fiction-about-the-future-may-provide-solutions-to-todays-crises/1680746 (accessed on 21 March 2021).

Chaudhuri, Rajat. 2018. *The Butterfly Effect*. New Delhi: Olive Turtle.

Chowdhury, Shovon. 2013. *The Competent Authority*. New Delhi: Aleph.

Csicsery-Ronay Jr., Istvan. 2003. 'Marxist Theory and Science Fiction.' In *The Cambridge Companion to Science Fiction*, edited by Edward James and Farah Mendlesohn, 113–124. Cambridge: Cambridge University Press.

———. 2005. 'Science Fiction/Criticism.' In *A Companion to Science Fiction*, edited by David Seed, 43–59. New York: Blackwell.

———. 2008. *The Seven Beauties of Science Fiction*. Middletown: Wesleyan University Press.

David, Sophia. 2016. 'Eco Fiction: Bringing Climate Change into the Imagination.' PhD Diss., University of Exeter. https://ore.exeter.ac.uk/repository/bitstream/handle/10871/24331/DavidS.pdf?sequence=1

Divya, S.B. 2019. 'Microbiota and the Masses: A Love Story.' In *Contingency Plans for the Apocalypse and Other Possible Situations*, 27–57. Gurugram: Hachette.

Divya, S.B. Email communication. 15 March 2021.

Dogra, Sakshi, and Shweta Khilnani, eds. 2020. 'Introduction: Jayant V. Narlikar.' In *Imagining Worlds, Mapping Possibilities: Select Science Fiction Stories*, 115–118. New Delhi: Worldview.

Doyle, Kenneth. 1993. 'Rain.' In *It Happened Tomorrow*, edited by Bal Phondke, 242–250. New Delhi: National Book Trust.

Griffin, Dori. 2019. 'Visualizing Eco-dystopia.' In *Design and Culture*, 10(3): 271–298.

Heise, Ursula K. 2006. 'The Hitchhiker's Guide to Ecocriticism.' *PMLA*, 21(2): 503–516.

Hommel, D., and Alexander B. Murphy. 2013. 'Rethinking Geopolitics in an Era of Climate Change.' *GeoJournal*, 78(3): 507–524.

Hope. 2018. Dir. Partha Sarathi Manna.

Hughes, Rowland, and Pat Wheeler. 2013. 'Introduction Eco-dystopias: Nature and the Dystopian Imagination.' *Critical Survey*, 25(2): 1–6.

Johnson, Hollie. 2019. 'What is the "Eco" in "Ecodystopia"?' *The Ecocidal Imagination*. www.drholliejohnson.com (accessed on 15 March 2021).

Joshi, Ruchir. 2001. *The Last Jet-Engine Laugh*. New Delhi: HarperCollins.

Kapur, Devesh, Radhika Khosla and Pratap Bhanu Mehta. 2009. 'Climate Change: India's Options.' *Economic and Political Weekly*, 44(31): 34–42.

Khan, Sami Ahmad. 2021. *Star Warriors of the Modern Raj: Materiality, Mythology and Technology of Indian Science Fiction*. Cardiff: University of Wales Press.

Lakshminarayan, Lavanya. 2020. 'The Ten-Percent Thief'. *Analog/Virtual*, 1–6. Gurugram: Hachette.

Lakshminarayan, Lavanya. Email communication. 15 March 2021.

Mathew, Varun Thomas. 2019. *The Black Dwarves of Good Little Bay*. Gurugram: Hachette.

Menon, Anil. 2019. 'Shit Flower.' In *The Gollancz Book of South Asian Science Fiction*, 51–73. Gurugram: Hachette.

Narlikar, Jayant. 1993. 'The Ice Age Cometh.' In *It Happened Tomorrow*, edited by Bal Phondke, 1–20. New Delhi: National Book Trust.

O'Hara, Dennis P., and Alan Abelsohn. 2011. 'Ethical Responses to Climate Change.' In *Ethics and the Environment*, 16(1): 25–50.

O'Yeah, Zac. 2018. 'Bluru.' In *Strange Worlds! Strange Times!*, edited by Vinayak Varma, 41–54. New Delhi: Talking Cub.

Padmanabhan, Manjula. 2004. 'Sharing Air.' In *Kleptomania: Ten Stories*, 83–90. New Delhi: Penguin.

Saran, Shyam. 2009. 'Global Governance and Climate Change.' *Global Governance*, 15(4): 457–460

Shalini, Srinivasan. 2019. 'The Road: A Fairytale.' *Strange Horizons*. http://strangehorizons.com/fiction/road-a-fairytale/ (accessed 15 March 2021)

Shenoy, T.G. Email communication. 15 March 2021.

Shiv, Ramdas. 2013. *Domechild*. New Delhi: Penguin.

Singh, Vandana. 2019. 'With Fate Conspire.' In *Ambiguity Machines and Other Stories*, 1–24. Easthampton: Small Beer Press.

Srinivasan, Shalini. 2019. 'The Road: A Fairytale.' *Strange Horizons*. http://strangehorizons.com/fiction/road-a-fairytale/ (accessed on 15 March 2021).

Stableford, Brian. 2005. 'Science Fiction and Ecology.' In *A Companion to Science Fiction*, edited by David Seed, 127–141. Oxford: Blackwell.

Stern, Nicholas. 2008. 'The Economics of Climate Change.' *The American Economic Review*, 98(2): 1–37.

Suvin, Darko. 1979. *Metamorphoses of Science Fiction: On the Poetics and History of a Literary Genre*. New Haven: Yale University Press.

Tharoor, Shashi. 2017. 'India's Demonetization Disaster.' *Horizons: Journal of International Relations and Sustainable Development*, 9: 208–223.

Trexler, Adam, and Adeline Johns-Putra. 2011. 'Climate Change in Literature and Literary Criticism.' *WIREs Climate Change*, 2(2): 185–200.

Chapter 8

'THE SEA EATS PEOPLE': CAPITALOCENIC DYSTOPIA IN RIMI B. CHATTERJEE'S 'ARISUDAN'

Indrani Das Gupta and Shraddha A. Singh

INTRODUCTION

By Editors

While one of the characteristics of postcolonial Indian SF is its involvement with and reworking, as it were, of its history; another, in opposition to the first one, is the imagining of a future through that history. What is interesting to note is that this future, more often than not, working through the present Indian sociopolitical and existential contexts, is a dystopia where governments, capitalist conglomerates, ecological destructions and/or unchecked adherence to structures of dominance, whether political, religious or social, have destroyed any hope of founding a long-lasting successful 'modern' nation. While, in its earlier characteristic deployment, postcolonial Indian SF manages to step outside the controlling discursivities of the West, in its second avatar (here second has been used merely in a relational way), it shows how the promises offered by the freedom from its colonial past have been, in the wake of unmitigated human folly, completely squandered. Decolonisation of the Indian past, after all, does not guarantee a different present or a better future.

Indrani Das Gupta and Shraddha A. Singh's paper reads Rimi B. Chatterjee's novella 'Arisudan' as a representative narrative of this second form of postcolonial Indian SF to show how the Indian nation, despite the possibilities presented by a decolonised past, fails to live up to the ostensible freedom. They show how Chatterjee's novella, through the presentation of this dystopic future, comments on not only the failures of the Indian nation in its governmental capacities but also its social and ecological ones. Doom, in a sense, will strike the nation from all fronts if present methods of existential interactions are not modified.

What needs a special note, however, is that even as such novels present a rather scathing critique of the present Indian situation, it raises a rather poignant question to the past, especially this decolonised one as well. What is, for example, the need for this decolonisation if it does not lead to a fundamental restructuring of the way the Indian nation chooses to persist? Further, do such re-historicisations have, in themselves and not just in a theoretical space, a potential to change the way the nation currently is or is this stepping out of colonial history a mere exercise in abstraction?

****

Rimi B. Chatterjee's novella 'Arisudan' (2021), published in the online periodical *Mithila Review: The Journal of International Science Fiction and Fantasy*, is set against the backdrop of rising sea levels, rapid climatic change, accounts of oil capitalism, and proliferating narratives about global ecological and human devastation. Intersecting various fictional strategies and representations of apocalyptic write scenarios, and involving textual techniques drawn from fiction (or cli-fi), risk fictions and dystopian narratives, 'Arisudan' portrays a world where both philosophical reflection and activism are required to manifest an alternate future, and where harmony between the worlds of human and non-human and nature and technology are not analogous to control and exploitation. Instead, this alternate vision realigns the superior position of humans vis-à-vis other species and objects to enable the growth of an ecologically rich sustainable future. This sustainable future includes the critique of the inscription of anthropocentrism as well as patriarchal order in the microcosm of Arisudan to enunciate a value system that can challenge the precarious conditions engendered by neoliberal practices in the context of the escalating climate crisis.

An instance of climate fiction (cli-fi)[1], 'Arisudan' deals with the depletion of global ecological resources in the wake of increasing financial speculation, swelling global capital information networks, growing data accumulation, and rising digital and artificial programming popularised in pioneering novels such as William Gibson's *The Neuromancer* (1984). Chatterjee's novella describes an episode from one of her forthcoming novels tentatively titled *Antisense*. Set in a not-so-distant future, 'Arisudan' depicts a world where extensive human activities, by humans functioning as geological agents, have potentially destroyed the ecosphere as we know it, leading to a state where the 'sea apparently eats people'. This phrase, spoken by the protagonist Perzan's deceased brother, Kersi, and recollected as a memory by Perzan in a dream, locates the structure of the novella as an exemplar of ecological disaster narratives widely represented in contemporary popular novels such as Robin Cook's *Contagion* (1987), Maggie Gee's *The Ice People* (1998), Margaret Atwood's *The MaddAddam Trilogy* (2003–2013), Ian McEwan's *Solar* (2010) and Paolo Bacigalupi's *The Ship Breaker Trilogy* (2010–2017).

The dream sequence that begins Chatterjee's novella shows Perzan as a nine-year-old boy discussing with Kersi a series of disastrous events such as the Mumbai terrorist attacks of 2008 and the explosion of the submarine INS Sindhurakshak in 2013. This dream connects with other nightmarish visions that include the sinking of many coastal cities in 2032, including Mumbai, due to a climate catastrophe. Perzan, we learn, is presently a naval commanding officer under the administration of Indosphere, a term identifiable with the postcolonial Indian nation-state. He is also, after having lost his family as well as the city of Mumbai that he grew up in, a 'climate refugee'. This tragic disaster is followed by other similar climate crises across the globe, and Perzan now finds himself alone in the AI-enabled submarine Arisudan, with limited supplies, waiting for further instructions from Delhi, the capital of Indosphere.

However, even before the series of climate disasters strike across the globe, the narrator informs the readers that around the year 2022, the political governance of Indosphere fell apart as a result of a deadly pandemic, with riots and state-orchestrated violence emerging as a common occurrence in the experiential world of that time. This ironically parallels our contemporary existence. Amidst this terrible scenario of economic meltdowns and concurrent administrative policies to stop people from protesting and Indosphere's bureaucratic class employing other co-related ineffectual measures and policies, we see a heightened degree of confluence emerging between industrial, political, sociocultural, health and military sectors. Ramdhun Corporation, a multinational industrial capitalist organisation, starts taking charge of Indosphere's sociocultural and politico-economic order. By the year 2024, the Ramdhun New Deal has been signed between the political class of Indosphere and the stakeholders at Ramdhun, primarily to end critical voices against the failures of the administrative class of Indosphere. The key terms of the agreement are never made apparent to the common public and by the time the environmental disasters take place across the globe, Ramdhun Corporation has already spread its powerful tentacles to a point where exceptionalism and merit emerge as the new proviso to distinguish and marginalise certain sections of society. Meanwhile, Perzan's crew, including his friend and colleague Carlton Caron, leave the safety of the submarine to rescue any surviving members of their families uprooted due to environmental devastation and political malpractices, and thus offer a counterchallenge to Ramdhun's military and financial power in the global arena. Perzan is left behind to metaphorically hold the fort by remaining cooped up inside the submarine. The story ends with only Carlton surviving the adventure to the military might of Ramdhun Corporation while Perzan remains safe inside the AI-powered submarine, Arisudan, in the depths of the sea.

Chatterjee's fascinating novella registers the interface of environmental destruction, technological futures of AI and a state of precarity that engenders a rethink of the politics of the postcolonial state and also foregrounds the ideas of planetary imagination. In dramatising the contrasting visions of refuge and danger; the precarious existence of vulnerable citizens such as Carlton, Perzan, the crew members of Indosphere's navy and their families versus the privileged status of the capitalist regime of Ramdhun; the memories of lost home and family versus instances of politico-ethical corruption; and evolutionary capitalist paradigm amidst a series of climatic upheavals; Chatterjee's novella dwells upon the theoretical frameworks of capitalocene and ecoprecarity, the politics of nation-state and transnationalism and the ever-evolving scenarios of globalisation and militarised capitalist corporations. The novella's genre-bending and genre-mashing elements create a hybrid zone that draws from science-fictional imaginaries, adventure stories, thriller genres and journalistic reportage. However, this hybridity fails to break free of the bondage identified as an idiom of the capital.

The environmental catastrophe depicted in the novella follows Franklin Ginn's observation that not all ecological fictions are an illustration of 'politically regressive and postpolitical distractions' (2015). Instead, this story functions as a chronicle about activism and protest against Capitalocene networks and their intersection with gendered meritocratic assumptions of contemporary society. Taking this postulation as the starting point, questions such as what caused the 'sea to eat people' arise. Moreover, who are these climate refugees, or *climies*, emerging in the wake of complete devastation of global cities, such as Mumbai, Vishakhapatnam, Singapore and the upper reaches of Indosphere, that occurs due to rising sea levels? How do we place these refugees within the political space of the postcolonial Indian nation-state or the transnational linkages? This brings us to the key critical problem of whether any plan of action has been initiated by the political classes or nation-states in the wake of such destruction. With the capitalist oligarchy Ramdhun Corporation emerging as the dominant voice within the sociopolitical public sphere, what happens to the role of governance and the ethics of care? Where indeed does the responsibility and response-ability lie?

With such questions emerging from an engagement with the narrative, the novella positions itself as necessitating the need to participate in determined action against the rise of capitalistic oligarchies while exploring the scope of building towards a sustainable ecologically rich future. There is a more vital call to perform, which is to open the chapters of Indian and global histories for exploration and critical enquiry. Reading Chatterjee's novella as an illustration of navigating risks and the ongoing catastrophes, by focussing on the cautionary aspects of this apocalyptic cli-fi, demands that the readers reflect upon and re-examine the emergence of such scenarios that led to conditions of ecoprecarity. In doing so, the current chapter focuses on how 'Arisudan' fits into the wider Indian science-fiction imaginaries vis-à-vis global representations of cli-fi apocalyptic narratives.

INTERSECTIONS OF PRECARITY AND CAPITALOCENE

The series of disasters that frame the plotline of this novel dramatises the political and sociocultural failures of governance and the seduction of global capitalist monopoly, thus directing us to states of precarity. The concept of precarity, according to Johan Höglund (2020), emerged in the wake of the Second World War, the Great Depression and the present-day neoliberal job deregulations. Höglund identifies precarity as the lack of security in all sectors of life, making the 'precariat' especially vulnerable to environmental and political crises. Without denying the history of precarity linked with deregulation policies in the neoliberal global job economy or its linkages with colonialism, Höglund recognises the crucial link of precarity with the climate crisis in the Anthropocene era. Anthropocene,[2] according to Dipesh Chakrabarty, is identified by the disastrous consequences, such as rising sea levels and devastation of ecological biodiversity that global warming has on the biosphere as a result of humans' propensity to enact as geological agents and thus eventually transforming the course of the planet (2009). Höglund specifies that the urgency to investigate precarity has exacerbated with the increasing climate crisis accelerated by anthropogenic tendencies.

However, as studies by Malm and Hornborg (2014), Patel and Moore (2017) and Höglund show, climate crisis cannot be defined as the handiwork of the human species cogitated as a single monolithic unit. Höglund claims that defining the escalating climate crisis in anthropogenic terms has resulted in the negation of differences between the materiality of human cultures and practices (2020). Elaborating further, Höglund propounds that the origins of escalating climate disruptions lie in the 'capitalist (fossil fuel) economy enabled by colonisation and first established in Europe during the early modern period' (ibid.). This is corroborated in Jason Moore's (2015 and 2016) analysis of vulnerable conditions occasioned by the rise of technocentric empires. Moore in his study registers the need to include other frameworks to rethink the climate crisis. This leads us to read environmental degradations as an instance of Capitalocene. In defining the politics of Capitalocene, Christian Parenti (2016) discusses the role of the modern state to be the producer of environmental changes, with power, value and nature forging a nexus with each other. Read in the context of the politics of the postcolonial state where ecoprecarity[3] is an outcome of Capitalocene energies, this chapter examines 'Arisudan' as an illustration of Indian science-fiction imaginaries grappling with issues of planetary imagination linked to local, global and glocal realities.

'ARISUDAN'

Chatterjee's novella initiates its narrative trajectory using two common techniques: a dream sequence and the strategy of *in medias res*. The combination of these two techniques elaborates on the dystopic representation of our current geopolitical era. The paradigm of *in medias res* describes a moment in history, which includes a historiographical timeline of events in the past and events yet to take place. Beginning the story using the approach of 'in the middle' or in the thick of things allows this novella to showcase the climate crisis as one far from being over and to maintain a fast-paced narrative driven towards an accelerating future that seems to be doomed. While suggesting that there are no easy solutions, the *in medias res* approach locates the readers trapped in a world characterised by disasters and mapped by Rachel Greenwald Smith (2009) as 'disasters of the present'. The series of disasters that frame the novella is further corroborated by the dream sequence that opens the narrative. Perzan's dream is neither projected as an illusion nor as an escape from mundane reality. Even before we comprehend the sequence of events as underscored in the dreamscape, we soon realise that planetary transformations are changing at a faster pace beyond the scope of human imagination. Perzan's dream oscillates between scenarios of past climatic, social and cultural disasters, and the current environmental disaster of rising sea levels and local and global violence, suggesting that movement, progress, evolution and development, key terms in colonial and postcolonial historiographies, are here understood as being devoid of meaning. When everything including human achievements and geographical spaces seems to be submerged literally and metaphorically in the novella, the only probable solution is to rely on the imagination of the machine: the AI-enabled submarine, Arisudan, renamed by Perzan as Anahita. This dream-like narrative oscillates between the past and the present scenarios, portraying the contemporary world of Arisudan as part of the nightmarish dystopic vision, where even dreams deny an outlet to one's psychological and physical fears. Even as Arisudan extends a sanctuary to Perzan and performs the role of a confidant to Perzan's fluctuating emotions symptomatic of a changing dystopic world, for Carlton and the rest of the naval crew, Arisudan signals the collusive forces of neoliberal capitalist regimes and the postcolonial nation. It is emblematic of the risk that humanity inhabits, and yet it inaugurates the ethico-political framework of transforming global, social and planetary imaginations.

In *World at Risk* (2009), Ulrich Beck assesses the threats to humanity and deliberates on what he envisaged as a 'risk society' based on the innovations and technofixes that provide tools for development, but at the same time, without being monitored, run the risk of causing sociopolitical as well as climate calamities. While Beck's exploration of risk is cast in terms of 'the anticipation of catastrophe' (ibid.), Chatterjee's novella examines risk as the denominating factor of the present. Here, risk is no longer anticipated as an aspect of the future but is very much an idiom of the here and the now. The key idea that Beck's evocation of risk society embodies is that techno-futures and other related technological innovations become a risk to the survival of the world when it is no longer monitored in the way it ought to be. 'Arisudan' perpetuates this sense of risk and engenders a state of uncertainty, envisaging an intricate complex web of imaginative innovations to play out as the narrative progresses (Mayer 2014). These narrative complexities intensify as human and environmental disasters are experienced in this failed technocratic state.

The postulation of the failed postcolonial state vis-à-vis the rise of Ramdhun Corporation leads us to explore what kind of a state presently exists, if at all. With the transmission of power from the democratic postcolonial state to an industrial-military complex, the 'services' performed by the state are translated, we argue, in terms of the energies of the Capitalocene. Jason Moore's classification of Capitalocene as 'a way of organizing nature—as a multispecies, situated, capitalist world-ecology' (2016), explores how capitalistic networks have shaped and designed ecological perspectives and fashioned our social and political lives. In 'Arisudan', Chatterjee brings to the fore the hold capitalists have on not just the global economy and politics but also nature. They toy with the environment as and when they please, based on their whims and fancies, and wreak havoc in the process. This human domination of the biosphere, along with their desire for easy technofixes, becomes amply evident in the practices initiated at Ramdhun Wellness Centre. The extension of gender politics and communal ideologies as prevalent in contemporary India becomes apparent at this wellness centre in the marketing of 'Humane Choice' (a vaccine). This vaccine is administered to fathers who, like Kersi, are desirous of male children. Even as most of these vaccine-produced babies die soon after their birth and mothers are left distraught, Ramdhun's 'main man and genius doctor', Dr Pradip Shankar, finds another resource to convert this tragedy as a financial resource for his corporate organisation. Concurrently, while the whole world is collapsing under the strain of this mysterious contagion and 'every city [is] at war with itself', Dr Shankar develops a co-related vaccine (Chatterjee 2021). Therefore, as male babies die mysteriously and men continue to complain against their spouses and companions ('Bitch Wars'), who are protesting against this 'fear' that is circulating widely on account of the usage of vaccines promoted by Ramdhun Wellness Centre, Dr Shankar declares a cure for the 'Male Hypertoxic Syndrome' (ibid.). The cure demands that parents sponsor the research popularised as 'Shankar's Cure', where around a thousand babies from the rich business houses (R1K) are selected for trials. Unfortunately, a few years down the line, most of these babies are labelled 'strange' because of the violent tendencies that have gripped them, forcing them to kill others or themselves as a result of low pain threshold. As these babies are raised in confinement, without the presence of nurturers, they lack social skills and empathy and are eventually called Hanyos (half-demons). Meanwhile, Carlton's sister Lucille commits suicide because she internalises the ideology of the Ramdhun doctors who insist that the lack of a womb and the presence of male genes in a female body make her a 'freak', thus shaking her 'understanding of self' (ibid.). All of these instances of violent Hanyos, the dubious vaccine ('Humane Choice') and Lucille's suicide point to the perpetuation of gender violence and discrimination that has shaped our postcolonial nation-state. Here, the very 'idea of India', as described by Deepti Misri (2014), centres on the primacy of women being framed in accordance with traditional Indian values and thus cast as passive non-agents in the public sphere. Lucille's predicament highlights how 'borders [and boundaries] mark women's bodies' (Banerjee et al. 2012). Whether it is Kersi alone deciding what gender his expectant baby should be and thus using the vaccine or mothers being denied permission to visit R1K children or Lucille's confusion and shock in the destabilisation of the cultural meaning of her identity, women have always been subject to classifications, discriminations and violence. The ideas of nationhood as Yuval-Davis and Anthias point out have always been gendered (1989), often reducing the material realities of women, making them, as Sukanya

Banerjee et al. argue, more susceptible to violence and silence (2012). These readings of women being framed as signifiers of cultural essence continue even in periods of transnational capital as evident in Ramdhun Corporation establishing its vaccine factory on Perzan's family's property of 'Stud Farm' (Chatterjee 2021). Kersi selling off his family business to Ramdhun Corporations suggests how commercial transaction and financial speculations have taken over the mantle from the state's preserve of 'restructuring of social and political relations' (Ong 2003).

Parenti (2016) advocates the understanding that although the modern state is the only institution that can cause large scale changes, it is also the only one with enough power to control and direct a response towards the preservation of nature and life. Unfortunately, in 'Arisudan', the state fails to retain its control and succumbs by submitting its power to the Ramdhun corporation, which in effect then gets entangled in a series of decisions that lead to mass extinction and catastrophe. Interestingly, the erasure of the state for these capitalist powers like Ramdhun Corporation, opens up a space of precarity on a global level. While this initiates a query whether globalisation is a perpetuation of the old practices and regimes, it produces the idea that the representation of a series of unmitigated natural disasters coupled with a description of statelessness in Chatterjee's narrative, leaves a gap in our ontological knowledge.

The perpetuation of the paradigms and practices of the postcolonial democratic state now transferred to Ramdhun corporates does not mean the state has vanished in the wake of transnationalism and cosmopolitanism. Instead, Ramdhun Corporation, we argue, is a 'mutation' of the state or the state 'remorph[ing]' itself (Ong 2003). The continual rise of Ramdhun Corporation's powers begets the question, 'are privileged classes impervious to the crisis occurring in all sectors of life defined by the historical, political, social and cultural conformations of our contemporary lives?' This corporate organisation uses what Naomi Klein terms as 'disaster capitalism', a mechanism to augment their wealth in the aftermaths of a series of crises (2007). In 'Arisudan', crisis as accidents is normalised to lead to newer forms of segregations and violence. The 'slow violence' that Rob Nixon (2011) speaks about in connection with human intervention on the planet as leading towards climate precarity is literally metamorphosed in 'Arisudan' with Ramdhun Corporation's missiles attacking the whole naval crew confined inside the submarine and the destruction of the same crew barring Carlton and Perzan. Here, the state identifies itself with the logic of the capital even at the expense of swelling ecological wastelands. The permission granted to the oil expedition team to extradite oil from Antarctica itself is questioned in the narrative as it results in the melting of ice leading to immense destruction worldwide with coastal cities of the Indosphere being wiped off the maps.

While Raj Patel and Jason W. Moore, in *The History of the World in Seven Cheap Things* (2017), describe the accelerated rhythms of industrial modernity and colonialism as the reason behind depleting world ecological resources, 'Arisudan' extends this description to the breakdown in the social fabric of the country. Ramdhun takes over the 'services' performed earlier by Indosphere, which includes, apart from saving R1K babies who would later transform to Hanyos, downgrading the powers of regional states, silencing the voice of protestors to silencing people, and reframing historical accounts that do not fit in their narrative. The framing of the history of the Indosphere from 1991 situates the novella as an exemplar of post-millennial narratives where communalism, the rise of extremist ideologies and gender segregations and violations take place on a daily basis. The changes in the academic curriculum situate 'Arisudan' as grappling with historiography and its symbolic and material connotations for citizens and readers:

> 'No history before 1991 should be taught,' he told the assembled faculty. 'We are here to add value to the young workforce of the Indosphere. Every instruction-hour counts towards our bottom line. Thirty-five years is all the backdating we need to teach these young people. Current commercial agreements and partnerships, modern management techniques, soft skills, business communication, trade protocols, human resource tools, economic spheres of influence, recent trends in markets and finance. That's what you should be teaching, not old dead facts that add nothing to their employability.' (Chatterjee 2021)

History and the currency of the state are reduced to productivity and meritocracy. The elimination of detractors, as the narrator in 'Aridsudan' observes, perpetuates the narrative of contemporary global far-right statist ideologies represented in present-day institutions and bureaucratic actions to muzzle critics and opponents of their political actions and policies. Perzan, his crew being reduced to the state of climate refugees links the condition of statelessness and homelessness to the histories of many people across the globe, like those who suffered during the partition of the Indian subcontinent and the Holocaust in Europe. While it entails the displacement of our secured identities and equals what Hannah Arendt terms as 'germs of a deadly sickness' (1986), it also entails a remaking of society by newer significations. The presence of the AI-enabled submarine involves a risk to humanity, and yet it includes an alternate politics as well. The AI-enabled submarine, Arisudan, we argue, encapsulates a change. This change is produced not because of its superior technology but in its post-humanist incarnation of conflating the boundaries between humans and non-humans.

This blurring of boundaries directs our attention to break free of the shackles of binaries that structure our patriarchal and contemporary fundamentalist world.

In recent decades, cli-fi narratives have become immensely popular in providing rich illustrations of how to make sense of changing planetary spaces, and this chapter situates 'Arisudan' as foregrounding a historical analysis where futuristic visions are denominated by the politics and culture of the present. Simultaneously, icons of global capitalist modernity like Ramdhun's missile system installed at their space hotel Indraprastha reminds the readers of the Hindu epic the Mahabharata. Indraprastha was the kingdom established by the eldest son of Kunti, Yudhisthira, after the division of the family property of Hastinapur amongst the Kauravas and the Pandavas. Indraprastha is commonly understood by postmillennial readers fed on continual retellings of the Mahabharata as the enactment of legendary acts of justice espoused in the figure of Yudhisthira. However, in 'Arisudan', it is translated as a hi-tech makeover of the earlier practices of Indosphere as a weapon system aimed towards curbing dissent and exerting control. Indraprastha was also the site where Draupadi, the Pandava queen, mocks the disabled figure of Duryodhana for the wrongs committed against her. Thus, Indraprastha is here being framed as the site of conflict between the marginalised subjects, who seem to not fit within the confined and limited roles stereotypically assigned to them by the metanarrative of the state. In hindsight, Chatterjee's ploy of naming Ramdhun's headquarters as Indraprastha demands the readers to be wary of hegemonic narratives and to instead read them anew.

This chapter has investigated the conditions of ecoprecarity that unfolded in the wake of global climatic transformations within the Capitalocene framework of control and abuse of power by a select few. Furthermore, this chapter locates the select few's interface with sociocultural configurations within the state of Indosphere to manifest vulnerable states of existences framed in the contexts of the ongoing climate crisis. The chapter reads 'Arisudan' as positioned in a discourse where, as Eva Horn argues, any climate narrative is required to be cast as a 'cultural force' to manifest 'climate change' (2018). The chapter examined this cultural force within the wider popular Indian science-fiction narratives of the twenty-first century where 'Arisudan' is merely an episode in the larger narrative of Chatterjee's forthcoming novel, with another chapter published in an anthology of short stories titled *Avatar*. In its exploration of the Capitalocene discourse tied to the dissemination of religious fundamentalism, this novella seems to be a continuation of Chatterjee's earlier novel *Signal Red* (2005) in its translation of communalist ethos. Simultaneously, the fascination for male heirs in this narrative is akin to Manjula Padmanabhan's novel *Escape* (2009), where women have all been eradicated leading to the creation of a wasteland. The increase and augmentation of power of Ramdhun are similar to the world created in Luici Bacipulagi's *The Ship Breaker Trilogy* (2010–2017). This intertextuality of motifs, patterns and themes across genres and cultures allows 'Arisudan' to be read as a dynamic text whose ending will depend on how the readers position themselves in national and global imaginaries. While Perzan's family drowned in one of the earlier floods that destroyed Mumbai, his only living relative and best friend, his grandmother Freny, disappears after a few years of losing his family. The grandmother's disappearance is a key moment in the chronicle because it suggests the loss of love and vital stories in the wake of a homogenous narrative propagated by Ramdhun Corporation and the nation-state of Indosphere. We argue that Chatterjee's 'Arisudan' is one such lost story and that Carlton urging Perzan to relinquish his passive role in the face of snowballing crisis is also a means to reclaim the narrative. Carlton explains to Perzan that Ramdhun Corporation is their 'new boss' and the capitalist mentality coupled with their advocacy of toxic masculinity requires we cast aside laws and rules to listen to one's 'conscience' (Chatterjee 2021). The necessity of listening to one's conscience, erosion of hierarchies and recovering forgotten histories amidst the series of catastrophes, environmental and otherwise, point the way forward from precarious environmental disasters, symbolising the failures of civil society to resurrect the disintegrating democracy.

What this chapter does in its textual analysis of Chatterjee's novella is to document how ecological devastation, rapid climate change and ecological waste offer not only a descriptive picture of the end of civilisation but also advance a mapping of how contemporary sociocultural configurations frame present environmental disasters and offer a timely warning that cannot be ignored.

NOTES

1 The definition of cli-fi followed in this chapter borrows from Adeline Johns-Putra, who identifies climate change fiction 'as fiction concerned with anthropogenic climate change' (267). Also, though the terms climate fiction, apocalyptic and dystopian narratives are not understood as synonyms, in this chapter, they are used interchangeably to argue how climate disasters are affecting planetary survival adversely and engendering a horrific vision of the future that reflects in the structures and systems of the present. Here, past, present and future are neither understood in terms of a continuum nor as a measure of evolutionary progress. Instead, the series of ends, crisis, accidents and disasters enunciates that

the only meaning available to us are cast in such idioms. However, the disaster narratives perform a subversive challenge against the entrenched paradigm of capitalist modernity, what Jean-Pierre Dupuy describes as 'the invisibility of harm' (36).

2 See Paul Crutzen on the nomenclature of this era as the Anthropocene.

3 See Pramod K. Nayar's work on ecoprecarity with respect to literature and culture.

WORKS CITED

Arendt, Hannah. 1986. *The Origins of Totalitarianism*. London: Andre Deutsch.

Banerjee, Sukanya, et al. 2012. 'Introduction: Engendering Violence.' In *Contesting Nation: Gendered Violence in South Asia: Notes on the Postcolonial Present*, edited by Angana P. Chatterji and Lubna Nazir Chaudhry. New Delhi: Zubaan Books.

Beck, Ulrich. 2009. *World at Risk*. Cambridge: Polity.

Chakrabarty, Dipesh. 2016. 'Whose Anthropocene? A Response.' *Transformations in Environment and Society*, 2: 103–114. https://www.jstor.org/stable/26241365 (accessed on 20 June 2021).

Chatterjee, Rimi B. 2021. 'Arisudan.' *The Journal of International Science Fiction and Fantasy*, 15. https://mithilareview.com/chatterjee_03_21/ (accessed on 12 June 2021).

Crutzen, Paul, and Eugene Stoermer. 2000. 'The "Anthropocene".' *IGBP Newsletter*, 41: 17–18. http://www.igbp.net/download/18.316f18321323470177580001401/1376383088452/NL41.pdf (accessed on 7 January 2021).

Dupuy, Jean-Pierre. 2013. *The Mark of the Sacred*. Translated by M.B. Debevoise. Stanford: Stanford University Press.

Ginn, Franklin. 2015. 'When Horses Won't Eat: Apocalypse and the Anthropocene.' *Annals of the Association of American Geographers*, 105(2): 351–359. https://www.jstor.org/stable/24537849 (accessed on 6 July 2021).

Höglund, Johan. 2020. 'Challenging Ecoprecarity in Paolo Bacigalupi's *Ship Breaker Trilogy*.' *Journal of Postcolonial Writing*, 56(4): 447–459. doi: 10.1080/17449855.2020.1764202 (accessed on 4 March 2021).

Horn, Eva. 2018. *The Future as Catastrophe: Imagining Disaster in the Modern Age*. Translated by Valentine Pakis. New York: Columbia University Press.

Johns-Putra, Adeline. 2016. 'Climate Change in Literature and Literary Studies: From Cli-Fi, Climate Change Theater, and Ecopoetry to Ecocriticism and Climate Change Criticism.' *Climate Change*, 7(2): 266–282. Wiley Online Library (accessed on 20 January 2020).

Klein, Naomi. 2007. *The Shock Doctrine: The Rise of Disaster Capitalism*. New York: Metropolitan Books.

Malm, Andreas, and Alf Hornborg. 2014. 'The Geology of Mankind? A Critique of the Anthropocene Narrative.' *The Anthropocene Review*, 1(1): 62–69. doi: 10.1177/2053019613516291 (accessed on 4 March 2021).

Mayer, Sylvia. 2014. 'Explorations of the Controversially Real: Risk, the Climate Change Novel, and the Narrative of Anticipation.' In *The Anticipation of Catastrophe: Environmental Risk in North American Literature and Culture*, edited by Sylvia Mayer and Alexa Weik von Mossner, 21–38. Heidelberg: Universitätsverlag Winter.

Misri, Deepti. 2014. *Beyond Violence: Gender, Violence, and Representation in Postcolonial India*. Illinois: University of Illinois Press.

Moore, Jason W. 2015. *Capitalism in the Web of Life: Ecology and the Accumulation of Capital*. London: Verso.

——. ed. 2016. 'Introduction.' In *Anthropocene or Capitalocene? Nature, History, and the Crisis of Capitalism*, 1–11. Oakland, CA: Kairos.

Nayar, Pramod K. 2019. *Ecoprecarity: Vulnerable Lives in Literature and Culture*. New York: Routledge.

Nixon, Rob. 2011. *Slow Violence and the Environmentalism of the Poor*. Cambridge, MA: Harvard University Press.

Ong, Aihwa. 2003. 'Zones of New Sovereignty in South East Asia.' In *Globalization under Construction: Governmentality, Law, and Identity*, edited by Richard Perry and Bill Maurer, 39–69. Minneapolis: University of Minnesota Press.

Parenti, Christian. 2016. 'Environment-Making in the Capitalocene Political Ecology of the State.' In *Anthropocene or Capitalocene? Nature, History, and the Crisis of Capitalism*, edited by Jason W. Moore, 166–184. Oakland, CA: Kairos.

Patel, Raj, and Jason W. Moore. 2017. *A History of the World in Seven Cheap Things: A Guide to Capitalism, Nature, and the Future of the Planet*. Oakland, CA: University of California Press.

Rajagopalachari, C. 1995. *Mahabharata*. Bombay: Bhartiya Vidya Bhavan.

Smith, Rachel Greenwald. 2009. 'Ecology Beyond Ecology: Life After the Accident in Octavia Butler's "Xenogenesis" Trilogy.' *Modern Fiction Studies*, 55(3): 545–565. https://www.jstor.org/stable/26287370 (accessed on 20 March 2021).

Yuval-Davis, Nira, and Flora Anthias. 1989. *Women, Nation, State*. New York: St. Martin's Press.

Chapter 9

SPECTRAL CITIES AND SPECTRAL SELVES IN *SHOCKWAVE AND OTHER CYBER STORIES*

Sanam Khanna

INTRODUCTION

By Editors

The multifarious relationship between the self and the other has been explored through multiple modalities, both at the level of form and content in different forms of SF storytelling. The issue of otherness and alterity has been central to the very ontology of SF; not only does it create estranging imaginary worlds, but the 'otherness' of these worlds also reflects on our contemporary existence. In the case of postcolonial SF narratives, the issue of 'otherness' assumes even more importance as a marker often used to signify cultures, communities and a whole new way of life. Sanam Khanna's chapter pushes the envelope in its conceptualising of the other in terms of Derridean spectrality. By choosing to use the nebulous category of the spectre as something that embodies both the visible and the invisible, the phenomenal and the non-phenomenal, Khanna is able to bring out the alterity within the self, the spaces surrounding it and the ideologies that sustain it. The selection of short stories from the collection titled *Shockwave and Other Cyber Stories*, targeted at children and young teens, narrate encounters with the spectral that takes on different forms: slave robots, servants turned into VR realities, an invisiblised apocalyptic city, et cetera. These modes of alterity or 'others' are ultimately symptomatic of spectres of violence that marked the promise of neoliberal modernity and progress in early twenty-first–century India. Just like the coming-of-age journey of the young protagonists of these narratives involves a difficult reckoning with these spectral forces, the nation is also forced to come to terms with that which has been suppressed, marginalised or erased. The ghosts of the failed promises of the nation-state are negotiated in the form of characteristic SF tropes by the future citizens of these stories, as their individual growth becomes intricately connected to the collective *bildungs* of the nation-state.

****

> Our present moment is a haunted one.
>
> —Jeffrey Andrew Weinstock (2004)

In 2007, Puffin India published *Shockwave and Other Cyber Stories* (hereafter *Cyber Stories*), a collection of eleven short stories written by a diverse range of authors. Aimed at children and young teens, it has stories by Vandana Singh, Manjula Padmanabhan, Anil Menon, Ashok Banker, among others. The stories run the gamut of SF topics, from urban technotopias and future apocalypse to AI, coding, gaming and parallel worlds; most importantly, they delve into issues of self and identity construction, as is often seen in literature written for children or even young adults. It is also interesting to note how the 'city' is constructed in the stories within this collection. It is these themes of the city, and the self, which I wish to focus upon, drawing upon the Derridean concept of 'spectre', which encompasses 'both visible and invisible, both phenomenal and non-phenomenal: a trace that marks the present with its absence in advance' (Derrida and Steigler 2002). The spectre serves to remind us of the intrinsic and embedded presence of alterity, of difference, of that which we perhaps wish to erase, but cannot.

I delve into how cities and selves are presented in some of the short stories in this collection to bring out the aspect of spectrality embodied in them. With this aim in mind, I will focus on four of the eleven stories in this anthology. Two stories—Singh's 'Almaru' and Hartosh Singh Bal's 'A Small Green Light'—are set in Delhi. 'The Unknown Firewalls' by Rahul Srivastava and Banker's 'Shockwave' are set in Mumbai. I argue that spectrality provides a significant framework for reading these stories as an expression of anxieties at a temporal juncture in Indian modernity, written as they are in the early twenty-first century. Their writings occur within the backdrop of India's post-liberalisation and the rise of a particular brand of nationalism, both of which carry the twin baggage of trauma and desire. Further, the terrain of children's literature provides a fertile ground for delving into the nature of coming-of-age narratives, and thus an investigation of identity construction, as well as a mapping of contemporary concerns, in popular, generic literature.

Derrida insists the 'logic of the specter is that it … exceeds … oppositions between visible and invisible, sensible and insensible. A specter is both visible and invisible, phenomenal and non-phenomenal:

a trace that marks the present with its absence in advance.' Moreover, Derrida links the presence of the spectre with the visor effect. He says:

> The ghost looks at or watches us, the ghost concerns us. The specter is not simply someone we see coming back, it is someone by whom we feel ourselves watched, observed, surveyed ... concerns me, it regards me, it addresses itself only to me at the same time that it exceeds me infinitely and universally, without my being able to exchange a glance with him or with her. (Derrida and Steigler 2002)

My reading of the four stories in this anthology suggests that the spectrality embodied in the narratives shifts from the spectrality of the city to an ultimate spectrality of the self in order to highlight the uneasy relationship between the past, present and future, between the self and the Other[1], in order to bring about a questioning of the spectrum of inequalities and potentialities existent in society to which these stories belong. Even more importantly, the narratives embed anxieties engendered by the social and political frameworks within which these stories are written. In each case, the spectral demands an answer; it enfolds the narratorial voice (and through that device, the reader as well) into a condition of responsibility, of seeking justice,[2] spurred by an ethical imperative due to heightened self-awareness.

The opening story in *Cyber Stories* is Singh's 'Almaru', which takes us into a not-so-distant future. The affluent, technologically advanced city of Delhi is now an autonomous city-state, walled off from 'the great Outside', the surrounding wildlands inhabited by peasants. Delhi is protected by a military force as well as robotic entities called kathputlis. Vrinda, the fourteen-year-old protagonist 'cannot imagine a time before the Peasant Wars' (Singh 3); the peasants are often in revolt, their fury directed at the huge 'Agri-Complexes' that feed the city and the experimental crops forcibly grown on their lands. The story opens amidst an ongoing conflict and rumours that the PM will soon suggest lowering 'the compulsory draft age to fifteen for the City State Guard' (ibid. 4). Vrinda's father, a robotics expert trusted by the PM, is sent to negotiate with the peasants but disappears. Vrinda is forced to contemplate that he is a traitor who sympathises with the peasants who are called 'primitive savages' and 'monsters' by her teachers.

'A Small Green Light' by Bal, also set in Delhi, is about artificial intelligence and possible human interfaces. It features an unnamed protagonist, the child of two academics from the University of Delhi who died in an accident that left him maimed. He recovers slowly, aided by brain implants and assisted by his adopted mother, Seema, a VR and AI expert. At the end of the story, we are left wondering if he is alive/

real or whether his memories and skills have been assimilated into her biological son, Sumit.

Mana, the central character in 'The Unknown Firewalls' by Srivastava, is a young hacker who breaches the firewalls his father has setup on the computer in order to surf the net and chat on a website called Life 2.0, where he speaks to a persona named FiestyZinta. Experiences from Life 2.0 begin to infiltrate into his real life and strange sounds and smells surround him, forcing him into encounters with a Japanese otaku in Tokyo, which ultimately leads him to confront his real world, class-based mental 'firewalls'.

The closing story is Banker's 'Shockwave', told by three narrators. It revolves around Sarla and Vir, their two young sons, Mikey and Vaibhav, as well as their daughter, Viveka, a postgraduate student who recently returned from the US. The narrative weaves in multiple perspectives, and Vir, Sarla and Viveka construct the story. The family lives in Mumbai, and Viveka, the main narratorial voice, enters a 'vortal' by error, which leads to her being 'switched' even as she grapples with a nightmare vision of a devastated Mumbai at war with itself. It is unclear whether this war is in the past or the future, but the landscape alerts her to the fact that North Bombay is at war with South Bombay,

In each of the stories, the city is intrinsic to the self of the protagonist, and it functions both as 'place' and 'space' by and through which the characters orient/disorient their sense of self. Yi-Fu Tuan's work implies that '[s]pace is more abstract than place. What begins as undifferentiated space becomes place as we get to know it better and endow it with meaning' (Tuan 1977). Such readings[3] of 'place' suggest that space is transformed into place through lived human experiences and sensory realities; memory, both personal and collective, plays a part. In these four stories, the city functions both as place and space, often fluctuating between both aspects, moving from the familiar to the unfamiliar, from a secure place, a home, to a space of dizzyingly unsettling and ambiguous freedom, or even a threatening, potentially violent, space. Certainly, memory is central to each of the stories as well; encounters with the past, the future or altered present occur in each of the stories and play their part in the flux of location from space to place, and sometimes back again. This flux, and the profound psychic displacement it produces, lends itself to reading these stories as an encounter with the spectral.

I suggest that spectrality in these stories becomes a way of negotiating chronotopic ontology and a marker of postmodern neocolonial questioning of the significance and meaning of the self and Other. This is especially significant in the twenty-first century where we are, in one sense, all colonised individuals held in thrall by neoliberal policies and spectres of a range of inequalities that run the spectrum from race to class. Derrida also speaks of the 'visor effect' that is produced by the spectre. 'The specter is not simply someone we see coming back, it is someone by whom we feel ourselves watched, observed, surveyed' (Derrida and Steigler 2002). This aspect of the spectre is also visible in the stories as the protagonists encounter altered spaces and selves, confront the unfamiliar and the Other, and in their journey to greater self-awareness. In Derrida's conceptualisation, the spectre has an ethical imperative, its presence linked to an unsettled past and unsettled justice. It is thus that it haunts the present as unsubstantiated mourning, an unresolved trauma, which resists its own erasure. All four stories bring the reader to an encounter that foreground issues of selfhood, processes of Othering and also questions of justice.

IT IS ALMOST TAUTOLOGICAL TO CALL THE CITY A MORAL UNIVERSE (YI-FU TUAN 1988)

In Singh's 'Almaru', Vrinda is familiar with the '[t]he great concrete forest of the city' dominated by the PM's tower, topped with a beacon 'sometimes referred to as the PM's eye'. The city is safe and prosperous, but it is also a place of intense surveillance, not just because of the centrally controlled network of all devices but also because of the robotic kathputlis. The narrative blandly informs us:

> The kathputlis that were now in every neighbourhood, every apartment block, were not only servants of the citizens of the City-State: they were the PM's voice, his defence system, his army of willing-slave minds. The PM himself had cybernetic enhancements to extend his lifespan beyond that of ordinary human beings. Some people believed he would live forever. (Singh 9)

The spectre of betrayal, even execution by the kathputli, haunts Vrinda ever since she heard of a 'traitor's' punitive, fatal electrocution by his formerly subservient kathputli.

As in Singh's other SF story 'Delhi', in 'Almaru' too, the city is a layered space: layers of history and social strata underlie its present. Liminal spaces threaten the known place, and Vrinda must assimilate her encounter with these layers to better understand the city and herself. The almost utopian city-state of Delhi, where its residents know no want, have every material comfort available to them and have access to education and healthcare. This is in sharp contrast to the 'great Outside' inhabited by primitive peasants. The teachers speak of the peasants as savages and monsters, yet her father's description of 'the Great Plains stretching as far as you could see. Thatched mud-hut villages, acres of mustard fields golden in the sun, sunlight sparkling off … canals … patches of forest … of trees all wild, filled with … [a] variety of plant and animal life' is almost as idyllic as it is a contrast to hyper-organised and structured 'tall apartment complexes, the great concrete forest of the city' (ibid. 2–3). The description of the Outside suggests not just the subaltern status of the Outside but also its alterity, its existence as a space of difference and, ultimately, as a space of resistance. The city-state is home for Vrinda, but even as a familiar place, she is never quite at peace there. Her mother, once a brilliant cybernetics researcher, is now infirm after a failed mind control experiment, and the atmosphere of extreme surveillance within the city pricks at her consciousness as she grows from child to teenager. She often questions her father about the PM's plans and also about what lies beyond the walls of the city: 'the Outside'.

The Outside, in one sense, is the spectral Other of the Delhi, just as the kathputlis are possibly the sentient Others of the human inhabitants. The kathputlis in the story are mind-controlled robots, present in 'every neighbourhood, every apartment block' controlled by their human 'owners' and also plugged into the state-controlled network. They are both congenial servants and obedient soldiers, and their allegiance lies with the state while their minds are linked to the PM's. Ironically, it is Vrinda's father, Manek, 'the City-State's top expert' who created the programme that enslaves them (ibid. 4).

After working as a negotiator with the peasants, Manek ostensibly comes to sympathise with them; when sent by the PM to negotiate with them, he disappears in suspicious circumstances. But he leaves a message for Vrinda. Her mission, unknown even to her, is to free the kathputlis from the stranglehold via a virus that Vrinda installs in Bhim, the family kathputli, thinking it is a routine maintenance task. Bhim's name is loaded with caste implications, a marker of the subservience of the underprivileged and enforced by hegemonic control. The narrative is rich with the subtext of resistance and alliances forged between the suppressed, be it the young, the well-educated or the subaltern, presences within the city. In the story, once Vrinda installs the 'upgrade', the mind control programme in Bhim breaks down and spreads from him to all of his kind through the 'data management matrix' via the 'Central Processing' unit (ibid. 14). Once free of links to the PM, Bhim asks, 'What is my purpose? What am I meant to be?' to which Vrinda replies, 'You are Bhim … a citizen of the City-State' (ibid. 15). Free of mental thrall, the media kathputlis soon relay authentic news of the peasant uprising and reveal the peasants to be no monsters but mere suffering humans, often forced to commit suicide while other peasants fight for their ancestral lands against the predatory and ruthless city-state.

Significantly, Vrinda too has realised the process of her enslavement, especially with the passing of a unanimous vote to conscript fifteen-year-olds into the army. The teachers at her school have already begun exhorting students to celebrate 'the glory of serving the PM, the honour of death in battle .... For the City-State! For Civilization, and the Future!' (ibid. 14). After successfully hacking the mind control network, Vrinda, much like Bhim, must also ask herself what it means to be a citizen. In his questions, she recognises her own; and like him, she too must explore the newfound nature of freedom and its consequent responsibilities. At the end of the story, she stands on the balcony watching the normal landscape of the city, its lights and highways, and witnesses the breakdown of this normalcy as the 'the single bright light at the very top of the PM's tower—the PM's Eye flickered and went out .... She sat in her father's favourite chair, watching over her City' (ibid. 18). Her journey from the child who sought answers from adults to being the putative inheritor of her father's authority is complete when for the first time she refers to the city as her own; she is cognisant of its contradictions and dangers, its privileges and cruelties, and prepares to face them on her own terms as an aware citizen.

Bal's story, 'A Small Green Light', presents us with an unnamed protagonist who relays his memories, thoughts and his adoptive mother Seema's musings about AI to us the readers. Seema's name means 'limit' in Sanskrit etymology, alerting us to the implications of the discussions that are, at their heart, an exploration of the boundaries of consciousness, memory and identity, and the limits of AI in encompassing these terms. The city is crucial to the unnamed narrator's memory and identity that are aided by a chip implanted in his brain. He is, in a way, like 'a city that seemed unfinished, always immersed in a state of ongoing construction' (ibid. 109). This is an almost poignant observation because in the end we do not know if he is an actual living person or an experiment in IA. His memories are assimilated into Seema's son Sumit's. The name in Sanskrit means 'good friend', and the narrator constantly refers to him as a companion and a friend, a friendship that is fractured for the narrator and the reader at the end when Sumit whispers to his mother 'Ma, Ma, but he really believes he is alive' (ibid. 114). Like the city, he too is made, remade and unmade, enclosing within himself memories and complexities that he cannot fully process or control.

The narrator's earliest recollections are of the doctors speaking 'about the brain's capacity to forget its ability to ease or even erase the trauma of extreme pain, death and dislocation' (ibid. 107).

The association of spectrality and trauma emerges through the disarticulation of his sense of self, narrated both in terms of place and space. He looks down from the comfort of his home onto 'glitzy glass fronted malls, ambitious apartment block, the highway lifted above the surrounding townscape that still incongruously showed up ploughed field amidst the skyscrapers'. Once home, the strange highway 'becomes part of the same landscape that it had seemed so removed from when they had been driving' (ibid. 109). It is the anchoring of home, a place where he has 'a room to himself', which helps him make sense of the space he traverses, but the spectral city, the eerie 'incongruous' he is always aware of, alerts us to the disjunction of identity.

Throughout the story, 'fragments of the past' (ibid. 111) impinge on his consciousness, and Seema's philosophical musings on IA, on links between self and intelligence, push him to question the 'undisclosed intricacies of the green light signalling the findings of an alien implant in this brain' (ibid. 113). Earlier, Seema explains to him her belief that 'the very nature of a self that governs consciousness is the problem .... To become self-aware is to realise there is an inside, the self, and an outside, the not-self' (ibid. 112). This brings the reader (and the narrator) to an awareness of the duality of existence, not just in the philosophical sense but also in tangible, concrete and material terms.

In both these stories, the co-existence of contradictions such as the glitzy towers and the prosperous city-state of Delhi is contrasted against the rusticity of ploughed fields surrounding urban splendour. The alterity of the physical/biological real is setup versus the kathputlis, or AI resurrected from the memories of a once-living child. The stories reveal the complexity of history, the present always tinged with the past and future lurking at their edges, bleeding into the here and now. These features of the stories suggest aspects of the spectral either as alterity and Other or as a co-existence of multiple pasts and futures both in terms of time and place. The spectral, made present, demands recognition and, ultimately, seeks acknowledgement and redressal.

Mana, the central character in Rahul Srivastava's 'The Unknown Firewall', lives on the twentieth floor of an apartment in Sion, Mumbai. He too confronts the duality of his city when he observes thus:

> The study had two large windows. Through one, you could see a wooded hill lined with dilapidated fort walls and a temple perched on its summit. Through the other you saw sprawling clusters of villages, mangroves, shanties, half constructed buildings, and an eternally internally crowded railway station. (Bal 2007)

This dual aspect of the city is a reality he is aware of and accepts without questioning; in fact, this view helps him situate himself as it 'kept him connected to the real world all through his virtual journeys' (ibid. 125). The contradictory character of the city, its social stratification, enters his home daily, not just as sight but also in the persons of the daily help, Pratima Tai and her daughter, Reena. Immersed in his own world, Mana barely recognises their presence or personhood. He regularly surfs a website named Life 2.0, and as the story progresses, strange sights, sounds and smells begin to impinge on his real world, leading to a profound estrangement from his 'real' environment. Mystified and disoriented, Mana attempts to decode his experience and steps out of the safety of his home in search of answers.

In an attempt to solve this mystery, he ventures into Dharavi, a space his parents have been expressly forbidding him. Mana 'walked across the road, towards Sion station and into Dharavi the cluster of huts, chawls, buildings and shanties that lay sprawled across the close set streets in his neighbourhood … a dangerous place full of dodgy people' (ibid. 130). Through surreal encounters that begin in a small internet café in Dharavi, which take him through a phantasmic version of Tokyo, Mana's sense of place and space is thoroughly shaken. At the end of the story, the Japanese otaku he has been chatting with, the one responsible for his estrangement from the world, reveals herself as Reena. She accuses him of being indifferent to his surrounding: 'You never really knew the little servant girl who tagged along with her mother for years to your house' (ibid. 138). She mocks his bewilderment and confidently reveals her multiple VR identities. Her casual cosmopolitanism, her knowledge of diverse cultures and places, which facilitates her multiple personas, from a local goddess in a hill shrine or the earthy village goddess to a Tokyo deity or even a spirited, ultra-modern 'FiestyZinta' are in sharp contrast to Mana's cloistered, almost clumsy existence.

Mana's encounters with Reena, and the unnerving dislocations he experiences, force him to become aware of his own privileged existence, his unquestioning replication of his parents' biases and even his unthinking complicity in ignoring inequalities. Reena declares, 'I love pushing people to break through firewalls … you managed quite well with the programs your dad installed on your computer, you fared badly with the ones installed in your mind …. It took you so long to cross the street' (ibid. 138). Mana is pushed into recognising the reality of Reena as the Other, and also an aspect of himself, an alterity-seeking acknowledgement, and freedom, much like himself. He has no choice but to engage with the phantasmic identities and experiences he undergoes in Dharavi, which hold up a mirror to his prejudices. The almost surreal encounters bring him to a new awareness and self-identity.

Through the spectral, other-worldly encounters with the city, Mana is brought to a recognition of his own social privilege, the implications of class and social deprivation, as well as the forces of globalisation at work, all of which shape his world, just as much as they shape Reena's. The shape-shifting Reena warns him saying, 'I am already suffocating with the stink of glass and concrete that has started to colonise [the neighbourhood]. Things are changing rapidly. You must do something about it—or we will really suffer' (ibid. 138). She wants to resist neocolonialism, and so she places the responsibility on his more privileged shoulders to build affiliations with different marginalised identities across the globe.

The closing story of the anthology is Banker's 'Shockwave', which features a similar encounter with a disjunctive reality. Here, North Bombay is at war with South Bombay in a strange vortex/portal that Viveka has been sucked into after tinkering with her brother Mikey's computer. Viveka feels 'a strange sense of disorientation. The way you feel when you're travel-sick .... But this was different from anything else I've ever felt before' (Banker 2007). She finds herself transported from the safe, familiar place of home, the comforting space of Bombay as she used to know it, to a post-apocalyptic space of a past or future Bombay. She tells us as much:

> Instead of the mass of buildings and road and all the other stuff that made up our civilized Bandra suburb, there was devastation.
>
> The tall skyscrapers, the arcing flyovers, the endless causeways—they were all gone. The shells of ruined structures—buildings and houses—lay scattered all around, for miles in either direction, but not the kind we have in real Bombay. (ibid. 148)

Later she compares the experience to 'maybe Hollywood movies ... maybe *Mughal-E-Azam* ... like *Asoka*. Sort of. Except that this was no movie set' (ibid. 150). Viveka watches the two armies advance and is horrified at the impending massacre, yet she knows nothing about the identity of the warriors, or even the cause of conflict. She's not even sure whether if this is the past or the future. The material reality of a Nike shoe she stumbles upon breaks the 'vortal' hold on her, and like Mikey, Viveka returns to the 'real' Bombay. But both Mikey and she are now altered spectral versions of their own selves. Viveka attacks her mother, Sarla, slashing her viciously, infecting her with a toxin that renders her comatose. Sarla's narrative, just before the attack, registers her shock and awareness of the altered state of her daughter. 'Despite the evidence of my eyes, my other senses were screaming to me that this was not Viveka, not my daughter' (ibid. 146). Vaibhav, the youngest child, also recognises the 'switch', as he calls it, but is unable to make his father, Vir, understand the situation.

Earlier in the story, we are told that Viveka has recently returned to Bombay/Mumbai, and she identifies herself as 'a States returned Michigan-U grad, with a post-grad diploma from Columbia U, NY' (ibid. 141). Amongst the stories in this anthology, this makes her one of the oldest protagonists and the only one who suffers a seemingly irrevocable breakdown; other younger protagonists who grapple with the altered space they are placed in show greater resilience. One possible reading of Viveka's breakdown into a fractured, altered state and her transformation into a violent, feral being is that it is a response to the profoundly disturbing reality of the urban Mumbai experience. Her inability to process what Appadurai terms the 'spectrality in Bombay … beyond the empirics of inequality into the experience of shortage, speculation, crowding' (Appadurai 2000) is manifested in a psychic breakdown. It is significant that within the story she fluctuates between calling the city Bombay and Mumbai, suggestive of the tension following the renaming of the city from Bombay to Mumbai in 1995 and the emergence of a stridently loud ultra-nationalism. Incidentally, Appadurai's essay also touches upon this aspect, which contributes to the 'spectral turn' in reading the present of Mumbai.

Within 'Shockwave', the colonial past of Bombay, the stress of regional politics, the changing nature of a cultural ethos in the city, the pressures of global capitalism are all contained in this fluctuation of naming evidenced in the narrative. Thus, it is also significant that the temporality and specificity of the violent clashes Viveka witnesses remain unspecified, almost as if they are a distillation of the violence embodied in the urban experience, across the ages, which has accreted and permeated the topos in insidious ways. In the vortal, Viveka can locate Andheri, Bandra, North and South Bombay, but they are barely recognisable. All she is sure of is the impending war and massacre of irrevocable, inevitable violence. The near hallucinatory spectre is disrupted by a familiar object, the Nike shoe, which belonged to Mikey; its sensory reality arrests the psychic downturn, but the violence of the experience has infected Viveka, and through her, the familiar places. Her trauma thus alters her home and family irrevocably. Having encountered the violence inherent in the social, geographical reality of Bombay, Viveka (the term itself means 'discriminating intelligence' in Sanskrit) is unable to come to terms with it and is split, or 'switched'. She becomes, in a way, her own Other, and replicates deadly violence within the safe confines of her home. As in the other stories, the SF trope becomes a portal by which to frame an encounter with the spectre of violence—physical and psychic, historical and present, mythic and real, which are inherent in the creation of urban spaces and realities. Appadurai writes of 'the absent, the ghostly, the speculative, the fantastic, all [of which] have their part to play in the simultaneous excesses and lacks of Bombay'. The sentence almost sums up Viveka's experience in the story.

THE FUTURE IS ALWAYS EXPERIENCED AS A HAUNTING (MARK FISHER, 2012)

The cities in these four stories fluctuate between being a safe place where home is located to being a dizzying, dystopic space that has a profoundly disorientating effect on the protagonists. These 'dark' representations of the city present a certain 'urban imaginary', which can be read as a form of social criticism (Gordin et al. 2010). The representations of the cities in these stories seem to reflect the anxieties of development and inequality and suggest that progress is, in a way, always marked by the spectral, by the trace of what it erases. The narratives hint that the layers of history in each city, be it Delhi or Bombay/Mumbai or any urban metropolis, are also layers of deep-rooted violence and inequity compounded through the ages. The glitz and glamour of the present, its promise of progress and cosmopolitanism, represented in the milieu of the young protagonists, are brought to an unexpected, unsettling encounter with what has been made liminal and Othered; this results in them being brought face to face with the nameless, intangible 'ghost' and, ultimately, an encounter with aspects of their own selves. As readers we witness the growth of the protagonists who mature to greater awareness through such an encounter; possibly, we as readers are meant to mirror the same awareness. The visor effect reflects within the story, and perhaps outside it too.

Written in the early years of globalisation in India, the narratives in *Cyber Stories* foreground the shadowy edges of what lies at the boundaries of our present realities—of the unresolved and haunting presences from the past and the future, unseen but not without power. Weinstock explains thus:

> The ghost is that which interrupts the presentness of the present, and its haunting indicates that, beneath the surface of received history, there lurks another narrative, an untold story that calls into question the veracity of the authorized version of events .... Millennial specters

ask us to what extent we can move forward into a new millennium when we are still shackled to a past that haunts us and that we have yet to face and mourn fully. (Weinstock 2004)

This is precisely the question that these stories seem to bring to the fore, using the SF genre (and for the purposes of this study, it matters little whether SF here is read as sci-fi or spec-fic) to foreground issues of social, political, economic and even technological importance.

That such issues are embedded within stories meant for young readers is significant. The blurb at the back of the book suggests that it is meant for the 12+ age group; however, the themes are fairly mature and cosmopolitan. They speak from a spatial specificity but explore a globalised locale; they speak of global anxieties—the realities of neo-colonisation. The stories probe sociopolitical tensions, all of which reach far beyond the specific urban territory within which the stories are located. It is truly fascinating that stories with such complex, layered narratives are posited as fiction meant for children. This is not to say that writing for children should not be complex—far from it! On the contrary, the layering and sophistication of the narratives merit far greater critical attention than they have received so far. Children's literature is often a neglected ground, occupying the liminal space compared to what is being peddled about as 'literature', and I attempt to draw attention to the capacity of this genre to frame contemporary concerns and issues; its capacity to do so in 'playful' manners is a measure of its potential to be simultaneously subversive and serious, timely and perhaps even timeless, to itself exist as the spectral other to 'literature', and yet not quite it.

In children's literature, place and identity are often deeply linked, and place is imbued with significations that the child protagonist unravels in order to achieve growth by recognising multiple realities and perhaps even different/altered selves. The four stories explored in this essay foreground contemporary realities and concerns of life in India; the meanings of progress and development are engaged with and critiqued in these stories. Even though ostensibly meant for young children, the concerns expressed within these stories are significant and timely and serve almost as an education for the readers to a greater engagement with pressing issues of the world 'outside'—the world of 'grown-ups'. In the four stories explored here, I argue that encounters with the spectral ultimately allows for the emergence of what could be thought of as 'subjugated knowledge' (Foucault 1998). The term suggests stories and histories of that which have been repressed, marginalised, erased and, in a sense, made ghostly by institutional power. The four stories found in *Cyber Stories* remind us of the alterity that lingers and exists as the shadowy part of our social and cultural present—as a memory, a vision, which demands recognition and, even, justice. The stories seem to suggest that it is only through unsettling encounters and the consequent recognition of diversity, alterity and self-awareness that cognitive growth is possible. It is fitting, then, in a sense, that these encounters are constructed within the genre of SF, at the intersection with children's literature, as a sort of preparation for the future citizen (Reynolds 2007), citizens who are alert to the possibilities of a shape-shifting present, which contains within it the dangers of the past and the future.

NOTES

1 For an exploration of the term 'Other', and the processes of 'Othering', it is worth reading Fred Dervin's chapter 'Cultural Identity, Representation, and Othering' (2012). It provides an in-depth explanation of this term and its implications.

2 An excellent exposition on the link between spectrality and justice can be found in 'Welcoming the Ghost: Haunting and Foreignness in Contemporary Geopolitics' by Jessica Auchter et al. (2019).

3 Tuan, of course, is a prominent theorist to explore the connotations of space and place, but the concepts as they are touched upon in this essay owe much to Henri Lefebvre's arguments as well.

WORKS CITED

Appadurai, Arjun. 2000. 'Spectral Housing and Urban Cleansing: Notes on Millennial Mumbai.' *Public Culture*, 12(3): 627–651. Durham: Duke University Press.

Auchter, Jessica, Bruna Holstein Meirelles and Victor Coutinho Lage. 2019. 'The Spectrality of the Inter-state-eal/International: A Forum on Jacques Derrida's Specters of Marx after 25 Years, Part III.' *Contexto Internacional*, 41(3): 663–687.

Bal, Hartosh Singh. 2007. 'A Small Green Light.' In *Shockwave and Other Cyber Stories*, 106–114. New Delhi: Puffin Books.

Banker, Ashok. 2007. 'Shockwave'. In *Shockwave and Other Cyber Stories*, 140–158. New Delhi: Puffin Books.

Derrida, Jacques, and Bernard Steigler. 2002. 'Spectrographies.' In *Echographies of Televison: Filmed Interviews*, 113–134. Cambridge: Polity Press.

Dervin, Fred. 2012. 'Cultural Identity, Representation, and Othering'. In *The Routledge Handbook of Language and Intercultural Communication*, edited by Jane Jackson, 181–194. New York: Routledge.

Fisher, Mark. 2012. 'What Is Hauntology?' *Film Quarterly*, 66(1): 16–24. Berkeley: University of California Press

Foucault, Michel. 1998. 'Of Other Spaces.' In *The Visual Culture Reader*, edited by Nicholas Mirzoeff, 229–236. London: Routledge.

Gordin, Michael D., Helen Tilley and Gyan Prakash. 2010. 'Introduction: Utopia and Dystopia beyond Space and Time.' In *Utopia/Dystopia: Conditions of Historical Possibility*, 1–17. New Jersey: Princeton University Press.

Lefebvre, Henri. 1991. *The Production of Space*. Translated by Donald Nicholson-Smith. Oxford: Blackwell.

Reynolds, Kimberley. 2007. *Radical Children's Literature Future Visions and Aesthetic Transformations in Juvenile Fiction*. London: Palgrave Macmillan.

Singh, Vandana. 2004. 'Delhi.' In *So Long Been Dreaming: Postcolonial Science Fiction & Fantasy*, edited by Uppinder Mehan and Nalo Hopkinson, 102–123. Vancouver: Arsenal Pulp Press.

. 2007. 'Almaru.' In *Shockwave and Other Cyber Stories*, 1–11. New Delhi: Puffin Books.

Srivastava, Rahul. 'The Unknown Firewalls.' In *Shockwave and Other Cyber Stories*, 124–139. New Delhi: Puffin Books.

Tuan, Yi-Fu. 1977. *Space and Place: The Perspective of Experience*. Minneapolis: University of Minnesota Press.

———. 1988. 'The City as a Moral Universe.' *Geographical Review*, 78(3): 316–324.

Weinstock, Jeffrey Andrew. 2004. 'Introduction: The Spectral Turn.' In *Spectral America: Phantoms and the National Imagination*, 3–8. Madison: University of Wisconsin Press.

Chapter 10

AN ALTERNATIVE VISION OF SCIENCE: INTERSECTIONS OF SCIENCE, SUSTAINABILITY AND FEMINISM IN BEGUM ROKEYA SAKHAWAT HOSSAIN'S *SULTANA'S DREAM*

Anu Susan Abraham and Antara Chatterjee

INTRODUCTION

By Editors

Whereas Sami Ahmad Khan's chapter theorises a novel form of representation of global climate change, which studies it as a part of a larger sociopolitical and cultural matrix, Anu Susan Abraham and Antara Chatterjee focus exclusively on the interaction between gender issues and environmental crises. By doing so, they force the reader to question the ideological underpinnings of the 'science' in science-fiction narratives. Besides being understood traditionally as a gendered (read masculine) category, scientific thought has also been considered a domain of the West, often associated with progress and modernity. Abraham and Chatterjee argue that Begum Rokeya Sakhawat Hossain's *Sultana's Dream* provides a trenchant critique of both the masculine and the Western/imperial model of science, presenting instead an alternative in the form of a utopia called Ladyland, premised on harmony and sustainability. The utopian imagination achieves two goals here: on the one hand, it challenges patriarchal assumptions about the superior intellect of men, which supposedly makes them better suited for scientific pursuits, while on the other, it dismantles the notion that Western scientific models represent the pinnacle of development, exposing it instead as a materialistic, profit-hungry endeavour destined to result in disaster. Therefore, the narrative construction of the imagined utopia, which is distinctly anticolonial, performs a reconfiguration of science by divesting it from its gendered and imperial associations, giving us a glimpse into a world where science exists in a harmonious, non-violent and sustainable relationship with nature and human beings, irrespective of their gender or sexuality.

****

This essay aims to examine *Sultana's Dream*, written by the feminist thinker, educationist and writer Begum Rokeya Sakhawat Hossain, published in the Indian Ladies' Magazine in 1905, by situating the novella within feminist, postcolonial and environmental discourses, to uncover the alternative vision of science and governance that it projects. The novella is a critique of patriarchy, modern science and the ideology of empire, which aggrandise political, social and cultural resources by oppressing women, nature and the poor. Hossain proposes an alternative vision of science in the early twentieth century, decades before the Great Acceleration in the post-Second World War era, which marked a tremendous surge in technology-driven human activity. Hossain's 1905 text is a prescient narrative that foresees environmental crises resulting from technological and scientific overuse and reliance, crises that the world started to encounter in a pronounced fashion only much later. This essay aims to analyse *Sultana's Dream's* multi-layered, multi-dimensional narrative to delve into the text's deliberations on questions of modernity, scientific inventions, consumerist attitudes, environmental degradation and the gendered contexts of science. The essay will use the theoretical framework of ecofeminism as a critical lens to examine these complex and multiple imbrications and intersections.

Hossain brings together the violence of patriarchy with the violence of capitalism, which is the major focus of the theoretical framework of ecofeminism put forward by Vandana Shiva, Maria Mies and others. They argue that, unlike traditional patriarchy, the later capitalist patriarchy alienates women from nature and its sources. Capitalism, with its focus on material acquisition, promotes violence against nature through the relentless exploitation of natural resources to further the aims of profit. Though capitalism perpetrates violence against both nature and the vulnerable human, by conjoining itself with patriarchal modes of control and marginalisation, capitalist patriarchy perpetuates violence against women in particular by alienating them from natural sources of sustenance. In the words of Shiva, 'Growth of violent, undemocratically imposed, unjust and unfair economic policies', coincides with 'the intensification in brutality of crimes against women' (*Ecofeminism* 1993, xiv). Ecofeminism, a trajectory of feminism that emerged in the latter half of the twentieth century, argues that environmental crises are gendered in nature.

Ecofeminism has been criticised for its essentialism and homogenisation of issues faced by women belonging to different races, ethnicities, classes and castes. Bina Agarwal suggests feminist environmentalism as an alternative to ecofeminism to account for differences among women in their relationships with the environment. Greta Gaard, an advocate of ecofeminism, however, considers feminist environmentalism an offshoot of feminism, rather than an alternative to ecofeminism. Ecofeminism speaks to the conjoined oppression of women and nature. It questions both patriarchy and capitalism, which oppress vulnerable categories like women, the poor and nature. Hossain's *Sultana's Dream* brings together a critique of patriarchy and capitalist modes of development, contesting unsustainable, violent development embedded in material acquisition and control, and posits an alternative to the violence of conjoined capitalism and patriarchy through a model of sustainable and non-violent science espoused by women.

SULTANA'S DREAM, *COLONIAL BENGAL AND THE RISE OF TECHNOSCIENTIFIC MODERNITY*

Hossain envisions sustainable development and a model of benevolent, non-violent science in the early twentieth century, a period in which environmental crises and climate change had not yet become an object of critical and popular attention. Hossain, who had received only home education, imagined such a futuristic world sitting inside her home in colonial Bengal. Hossain's *Sultana's Dream* is a feminist utopian narrative that projects a future that remains a far-fetched dream more than a century after its publication. The story presents a feminist utopia aided by scientific and technological affluence.

A Western paradigm of scientific modernity was brought to India from Europe through the conduits of colonisation. The temper of scientific enquiry in India during the late nineteenth and the early twentieth century was coupled with the nationalist movement to create India's own scientific modernity. R.K. Kochhar (1991) talks of three stages in the evolution of science in India:

> The first stage … 'the colonial-tool stage' encompasses the whole span of European presence in India and consists of introduction and use of science … as an imperialist tool, with incidental benefits to science. [In] [t]he second stage, the 'peripheral-native stage', … the Indians were assigned the peripheral role of providing cheap labour to the colonial science machinery. The third stage, 'the Indian-response

> stage', arose as a reaction to the second stage and is characterised by scientific activity by Indians themselves and on their own initiative. (1927)

Western science, thus, while being disseminated and used as a colonial tool, was also redefined and reconfigured in colonial India. As Pratik Chakrabarti observes, 'Western science ... [was] both a tool of colonial hegemony and the medium of resistance and challenge to that hegemony by Indians .... Western science was [thus] dislocated from its European problematic and became an Indian cultural and intellectual experience' (Chakrabarti 2014, xxv–xxvi). The nineteenth and early twentieth centuries, therefore, saw the cultural reconfiguration of Western science through the intervention of Indian intellectuals and scientists.[1]

The efforts in the late nineteenth and early twentieth centuries—of Raja Rajendralal Mitra as the Secretary of the Asiatic Society in 1846, Dr Mahendra Lal Sircar's vision as the founder of the Indian Association for the Cultivation of Science, Calcutta, in 1876, and the establishment of the Indian Institute of Science in Bangalore in 1909 with the support of Jamsedji Tata—were examples of the quest of Indian nationalists to create India's own institutions promoting scientific enquiry and to disseminate a scientific temper among Indians. While presiding over the Indian Science Congress in 1937, Jawaharlal Nehru stated, 'It is science alone that can solve the problems of hunger and poverty, of insanitation and illiteracy, of superstition and deadening custom and tradition, of vast resources running to waste, of a rich country inhabited by starving people' (*The Wire* 2018). Scientific development was indeed the cornerstone of the template of progress endorsed by the new postcolonial nation, under the leadership of Nehru, after 1947.

This nationalistic stance of creating India's own template of scientific modernity is reflected in *Sultana's Dream* through the lofty vision of an independent country called Ladyland guided by science, which the narrator Sultana purportedly encounters in a dream, and through its embedded critique of colonisation. Ladyland is a technologically advanced land, where science and technology, envisioned and practised only by women, are harnessed for the country's progress, in sustainable, non-violent ways, unlike the unsustainable, violent impulses of modern science used to further capitalist accumulation and profit. Hossain's utopian vision of Ladyland, supported by technology and free of foreign influences, mirrors India's desire for independence. However, the methods of scientific practice and innovation in Ladyland are in stark contrast to the destructive, unsustainable methods of modern Western science. While modern science improved the quality of life of humans over time by reducing manual labour and affording various conveniences and comforts made available through technology, its practices progressively destroyed the environment through the relentless extraction of natural resources. *Sultana's Dream* reveals disappointment in the Western scientific developments of Hossain's time and provides an alternative rooted in a principle of minimum extraction and exploitation of natural resources, that too only for sustenance and not profit.

The contemporary and enduring significance of Hossain's text lies in its feminist vision, which strongly critiques patriarchy that restricts women from the processes of knowledge production. Partha Chatterjee has pointed out the binary construction of the inside and outside, and the dichotomies between the home and the world, the spiritual and the material, propagated by Indian nationalism to resist the colonial influence. Chatterjee talks about the absence of women in literature and education during the nationalist period of India, arguing that the void is created by the analytical model of 'inside' and 'outside' projected by the nationalist movement. The association of the Indian woman with the spiritual, essential and inner domain of Indian culture perpetuated by nationalist thought simultaneously denied women opportunities to break age-old restrictions imposed by patriarchal society and led to a problematic, essentialist association of the woman with the 'inner' space of the 'home'. Hossain's *Sultana's Dream* dismantles this gendered model of the inside-outside by imagining a Ladyland in which these gendered spatial connotations and expectations are reversed. In Ladyland, men are secluded inside the home, in 'mardanas', as opposed to the secluded zenanas for women of Hossain's time, while women's domain lies outside the home, being engaged in pursuits of education, employment, development and governance.

Sultana's Dream is considered one of the earliest examples of Indian women's writing in the science-fiction genre. A comprehensive definition of science fiction was first articulated by Darko Suvin in his groundbreaking book *Positions and Suppositions in Science Fiction* (1988). He defines science fiction as 'a literary genre or verbal construct whose necessary and sufficient conditions are the presence and interaction of estrangement and cognition, and whose main device is an imaginative framework alternative to the author's empirical environment' (37). Damien Broderick (1995) recasts Darko Suvin's definition of science fiction in the following terms:

> SF is that species of storytelling native to a culture undergoing the epistemic changes implicated in the rise … of technical-industrial modes of production, distribution, consumption and disposal. It is marked by (i) metaphoric strategies and metonymic tactics, (ii) the foregrounding of icons and interpretive schemata from a collectively constituted generic 'mega-text' … and the concomitant de-emphasis

> of 'fine writing' and characterisation, and (iii) certain priorities more often found in scientific and postmodern texts … specifically, attention to the object in preference to the subject. (157)

Sultana's Dream fits into this matrix of Broderick's categorisation. The novella emerged from the cultural climate of colonial India during a phase of colonial resistance and the consolidation of a nascent, emerging idea of nationalism.

As pointed out earlier, technology was an imperial tool to establish control and hegemony over colonised subjects. However, Western science was also being recast in new forms in colonial India. The nineteenth century was an important period in the history of scientific development in India, especially Calcutta, being the capital of the British empire from 1857 and the seat of the East India Company before that. The introduction of new technologies such as the printing press, telegraph, railways, steamships in colonial Bengal, even though introduced to perpetuate and consolidate agendas of empire, can be viewed as crucial steps in India's emergent techno-modernity, launching India into technological prosperity. As Suvobrata Sarkar has observed, 'British scientific activities in India and the introduction of new technologies, though aimed at the fulfilment of colonial interest, evoked a great amount of interest among the local people' (Sarkar 2010, 105). Hossain's criticism of modern science in *Sultana's Dream* possibly stemmed in part from a traditional worldview rooted in a concept of living in harmony with nature, but also from Hossain's intuition of the potential of modern science to impart slow and gradual violence against nature and humanity as a whole.

SPACES IN SULTANA'S DREAM: NATURE VS. TECHNOLOGY

A key focus in any science-fiction narrative is the spatial setting. The real space is often extrapolated with a distant, imagined one with the aid of teleportations, fantastic settings and speculative technologies. In *Postcolonialism and Science Fiction*, Jessica Langer explains how the 'other' is represented in postcolonial science fiction: 'In science fiction, otherness is often conceptualized corporeally, as a physical difference that either signposts or causes an essential difference … although this concept of alienness does not always signify a colonial relationship, it often dovetails with the colonial discourse of the Other' (82).

On the other hand, Tom Moylan (1986) has characterised utopian writing as being 'rooted in the unfulfilled needs and wants of … groups, and individuals in their unique historical contexts' (1). By projecting 'visions of what is not yet realized', 'utopia opposes the affirmative culture maintained by dominant ideology', and 'contributes to the open space of opposition' (Moylan 1986). Subversion and critique of the current world order, its sociopolitical and economic systems, is thus a crucial aim of utopian writing. Moylan points out how, as the genre of utopia evolved, utopia came to symbolise different impulses at different times. While it often signified an 'unattainable other', its subversive vision also came to be relocated to a future transformed through revolutionary or historical change. As industrial capitalism and imperialism penetrated the world's political and economic systems, a variety of utopian writing emerged in opposition to these. However, with the increasing entrenchment of capital, the oppositional impulses of utopia were increasingly co-opted, and resistance came to be relocated to its other, the 'dystopia', with which its boundaries became precariously blurred. However, Moylan identifies the impulse of the 'critical utopia' in a later revival of the utopian form, informed by the aims of critique and oppositional thought, which reinforced the subversive potential of utopia and reinvigorated the 'human agenda of … cooperation, equality, mutual aid, liberation, ecological wisdom, and peaceful and creative living' (10).

Hossain's utopian Ladyland affirms these very human agendas identified by Moylan as the defining characteristics of the 'critical utopia'. Through the utopian Ladyland, Hossain counters and resists colonial, capitalist and patriarchal ideologies and configures a space devoid of violence and exploitation, sustained only by nature's gifts. Towards the end of the novella, the Queen of Ladyland asserts:

> We do not covet other people's land, we do not fight for a piece of diamond though it may be a thousand-fold brighter than the Koh-i-Noor. It should be Koh-i-Noor ... we, as per the guidelines provided. … We dive deep into the ocean of knowledge and try to find out the precious gems, which nature has kept in store for us. We enjoy nature's gifts as much as we can. (14)

Sultana's Dream thus resists a violent and unsustainable Western techno-modernity through offering an ideal of technology based on a sustenance principle. One of the characters in the novella, Sister Sara tells the narrator Sultana that 'Our noble Queen is exceedingly fond of botany; it is her ambition to convert the whole country into one grand garden' (12). The comparison of the imaginary Ladyland to a garden is sustained throughout the novella. The repeated comparison of Ladyland to a garden brimming with life shows Hossain's vision of a sustainable environment that uses science in a positive, benevolent, abiding and sustainable way.

'[W]omen all over the world, since the beginning of patriarchy, were also treated like "nature", devoid of rationality,' Mies and Shiva state in

Ecofeminism, 'their bodies functioning in the same instinctive way as other mammals. Like nature they could be oppressed, exploited and dominated by man. The tools are science, technology and violence' (xxiii). Hossain's vision of society, as promulgated in the imaginary Ladyland, is founded on scientific and technological knowledge, which is not violent and hierarchical but enriched by the natural and promoted and practised by women, connecting nature, science and woman in a non-violent and nurturing triad. Hossain speaks of the need for a scientific, rational temper and enquiry, leading to technological progress, but she also shows a keen awareness of how every action of human beings on earth will have a consequence on nature. Hossain's prescient views on technology and its relationship with nature are predicated on a principle of minimum extraction and the development of environmentally friendly technologies using renewable resources.

Sultana's Dream is full of futuristic, fantastic technologies but none of them is a manifestation of technological exuberance for the sake of acquisition and comfort. They do not damage the equilibrium of the natural environment and are used for sustenance, using a principle of equitability, where resources are consumed based on need and not on the power to extract or buy. The dream narrative technique used in the text drives home the contrast between the actual spatio-temporal setting of contemporary colonial India from the imagined one. This stark disjuncture between the real and the imagined brings to the fore the difference between two views on how scientific knowledge can be used: one represents the maximum use of resources without considering the damaging impacts of relentless extraction and the other adheres to a mode of production that is sustainable and a mode of distribution that is equitable.

Martin Tropp (1980) avers that futurism in science fiction is a projection of the author's actual space and time coordinates. According to him,

> Science fiction is notoriously lousy in predicting the future, despite a few well publicised exceptions and some obvious extrapolation of already known facts. In fact, *1984* is better seen as a novel about Orwell's reaction to the world in 1948, than it is as a prophecy of life forty years from now. (21)

Sultana's Dream can be productively viewed within some of the larger political and intellectual aims of utopia and science fiction, as delineated earlier. It presents a projected future, constructed by Hossain, stemming from her experience of the real world and the understanding of imported Western technologies in ascendancy in colonial Bengal of the nineteenth and the early twentieth centuries. The climate of scientific advancement in Hossain's contemporary Bengal, and the ways in which it was situated within both imperial and emerging nationalist political and intellectual contexts, has been pointed out earlier in the essay. The electrification of Calcutta in the latter half of the nineteenth century was a great step towards the modernisation of Calcutta. In 1895, the Government of Bengal passed the Calcutta Electric Light Act and the Indian Electric Company Ltd. was registered in London, which was later renamed the Calcutta Electric Supply Corporation Limited. Within the first six years of the twentieth century, most parts of the city and the tramways of Calcutta were electrified.

Sarkar, in 'Technological Momentum' (2010), uncovers the colonial aims to legitimise and establish supremacy over the native population through technology.

> For the British, large-scale construction schemes and engineering works were monuments to their power and munificence. In stone, steel and steam they embodied the idea of the British Raj as a technological empire, able by its grand works and feats of engineering to master forces of nature that had defied and enslaved Indians for centuries. (104)

The fast-changing technological visage of Bengal may have influenced Hossain, motivating her to project her imagination to a future where there is an excess of technologies that have the capacity to damage the balance of nature. She blended her imagination and intuition to offer a solution to the ecological crises that might result from a profusion of the damaging consequences of modern science. The technological innovations imagined by Hossain in the text are flying cars, solar power, water balloons for rainwater harvesting, guns and modern ammunition, some of which were in their nascent stage when Hossain was writing, some not even invented at the time.

Science-fiction writers and scholars Gwyneth Jones and Robert Scholes posit contradicting views about the role of landscapes and objects used in science fiction. While Jones persistently argues for the precision of scientific knowledge used in science fiction, Scholes views science fiction as a form that merges with magical realism to construct a new world entirely out of the imagination. *Sultana's Dream* is seen to bring together both Jones's and Scholes's analyses of the imaginative modes of science fiction. It projects an imaginary, utopian world, which is, nonetheless, scientifically realisable, arising from Hossain's scientific extrapolations, technological forecasting and intelligent guesses about possible scientific futures.

The nineteenth and twentieth centuries were a period of crucial scientific inventions and advancements across the world. The American Wright brothers created the first version of a modern aeroplane in 1905, after several experiments and failures. *Sultana's Dream* was published in the same year. Hossain may have heard the news of the Wright brothers' experiments to create the flying machine during those days. Air cars used by the inhabitants of Ladyland to travel might be a model of the future aeroplane Hossain had in mind. Another important sustainable, environmentally friendly innovation in Ladyland is the use of solar power for cooking. Solar cookers had first been used in Germany in the eighteenth century and were in use in France in the late nineteenth century (Patil 2012). Hossain's vision of solar cooking comes from the idea of a pollution-free atmosphere. This is clear when Sultana says 'I found no smoke, nor any chimney' in kitchens in Ladyland (7). Another technology invented by one of the women's universities of Ladyland is the balloon, used for storing rainwater, thus eventually helping to stop rain and storms: 'By means of this captive balloon, which they managed to keep afloat above the cloud-land, they could draw as much water from the atmosphere as they pleased' (8). Hossain's vision of water balloons that could trap cloud energy was indeed ingenious, as even in the twenty-first century, scientists are still labouring to actualise this. Hossain's value as a pioneering woman science-fiction writer in India in the early twentieth century rests on her keen observations of scientific inventions and discoveries of her time and their articulation in her writings cast in the crucible of her intuition.

A GENDERED UTOPIA OF SUSTAINABLE SCIENCE

Sultana's Dream is a powerful indictment of the gendered contexts and connotations of science. Women have faced discrimination and subjugation in every arena of knowledge production for centuries. John Stuart Mill, in his seminal essay *The Subjection of Women* (1869), had stated that the deep-rooted societal inequality between the genders stemmed from the legal subjugation of women (having multiple ramifications within contexts of rights of suffrage, inheritance and so on): 'The principle that regulates the existing social relations between the two sexes—the legal subordination of one sex to the other—is wrong itself, and is now one of the chief obstacles to human improvement' (1). The publication of Charles Darwin's *The Descent of Man* in 1871 re-emphasised contemporary patriarchal assumptions and notions. Darwin's hypothesis of women as lesser human beings came from his observation that he couldn't trace any eminent women personalities who had proved their talent in any field, including science and the arts.

> The chief distinction in the intellectual powers of the two sexes is shewn by man attaining to a higher eminence, in whatever he takes up, than woman can attain—whether requiring deep thought, reason,

> or imagination, or merely the use of the senses and hands. If two lists were made of the most eminent men and women in poetry, painting, sculpture, music ... history, science, and philosophy, with half-a-dozen names under each subject, the two lists would not bear comparison. (327)

Age-old patriarchal traditions and assumptions in assessing women's mental powers in Darwin's postulations are contested in *Sultana's Dream* when Sister Sara says that though women's brains may be smaller in size, they are 'quicker than men's' (9). *Sultana's Dream* is a counter-response to 'scientific' positions ultimately entrenched in patriarchal assumptions that collocate facetious arguments to establish women as inferior to men.

Sultana's Dream suggests education as the key feature to enhance the position of women in society. 'Accordingly, a number of girls' schools were founded and supported by the government. Education was spread far and wide among women' (7). In *Sexual Politics*, Kate Millett observes that 'If knowledge is power, power is also knowledge, and a large factor in their subordinate position is the fairly systematic ignorance patriarchy imposes upon women' (42). Hossain's text puts forward education as the means to transcend this systematic ignorance imposed on women. In her pioneering feminist manifesto *The Vindication of the Rights of Woman* (1792), Mary Wollstonecraft had argued for a transformation of the educational system of her time, which trained women only to become skilled mothers and wives. Wollstonecraft posited that women were capable of rational thinking, and education should be distributed equally among men and women.

In Hossain's 1924 novel *Padmarag* (The Ruby), a women's utopian world called Tarini Bhavan is imagined in Calcutta of her time, which offers a space for women from all walks of life, religions, cultures, regions, classes and countries to find a safe and nurturing haven, where they are offered opportunities for education, employment and the pursuit of various talents and occupations. Tarini Bhavan is a refuge for the homeless, distressed, ailing and needy. Though it served both needy men and women, it was primarily built for and run entirely by women, women who found themselves, through choice or circumstances, outside of the domestic spaces and structures of the patriarchal, heteronormative family. Tarini Bhavan represented the culmination of Hossain's imaginative quest for a space for the empowerment of women through education and employment, a space of equal rights, respect and dignity for women, an imagined utopia right within her native Calcutta, a vision which had been her life's mission to actualise in the real world.[2]

The Marathi novel *The Palanquin Tassel* (written originally in 1889, published serially from 1913 and published together as a novel in 1928) by Hossain's contemporary woman writer Kashibai Kanitkar presents the utopian land of the 'palanquin tassel'. This utopian land, which the writer purportedly encounters in a supposed trip, is marked by a similar ambience of equal opportunities of education and employment for women. The land of the palanquin tassel is ruled by the virtuous and talented queen Rewati, who inherits the throne by virtue of her disastrous marriage to its deranged, legitimate heir, and her unmarried siblings, Manu and Nanasaheb, reminiscent of the women outside the fold of the family in Hossain's Tarini Bhavan. Rewati ushers in an era of women's opportunities and empowerment in the country during her rule by opening educational institutions such as Shibika College exclusively for women abandoned by their husbands (again, similar to the Society for the Upliftment of Downtrodden Women in Tarini Bhavan). The queen ensures women's rights to inherit property and secure jobs, which are equally available to men and women by virtue of descent, as jobs are handed down in families from one generation to the next, irrespective of gender.[3]

In Hossain's utopian Ladyland, education for women leads not only to opportunities for employment and self-reliance of women but also to technological advancements, which ultimately empower not only women but the entire country through their espousal of the principles of sustenance, non-violence and benevolence. Men of Ladyland are secluded in the 'mardana' because their technologies and innovations are not useful to the country. This ultimately posits an alternative to the damaging and violent modern science practised by men. Hossain emphasises this by juxtaposing the scientific achievements of men and women of Ladyland: 'While the women were engaged in scientific researches, the men of this country were busy increasing their military power' (8). This is a powerful indictment of modern science, which uses scientific knowledge to invent weapons for human destruction rather than sustainable technologies for human sustenance.

The utopia of Ladyland contests the traditional constraints imposed on women by patriarchy through the channels of science and education. Women of Ladyland are guided by a subsistence and sustenance perspective and not by a materialistic perspective like that of the acquisitive, violent, male capitalist society. The vision of the nation for the women of Ladyland lies in the concepts of sustenance and non-violence. Hossain critiques the male-centred society that controls all arenas with the predominant aim of material acquisition. When Sultana enquires about men and their activities in Ladyland, Sister Sara replies, 'They should not do anything, excuse me; they are fit for nothing. Only catch them and put them into the zenana' (6). Sultana mistakes the paths covered with flowers and mosses in Ladyland for a velvet cushion; she feels she is walking on a soft carpet. Sister Sara reminds

Sultana that her place, Calcutta, would also be beautiful like Ladyland if her countrymen in Calcutta gave importance to horticulture, but they are ignorant of such sustainable development and instead promote only material development. The recurrent motif of horticulture in the text puts forth the notion of a mutually constitutive, beneficial and harmonious co-existence between the human and the natural worlds. The representation of nature in *Sultana's Dream* is not wild and untamed but managed and curated, wherein precisely its appeal lies.

At several points in the narrative, Sultana compares the condition of women in her native place with that of Ladyland. In her place, women were denied freedom and kept in strict purdah. They were distanced from matters of politics, education and economic affairs. Their work in the domestic arena, such as gardening, was not valued as work. *Sultana's Dream* is a call for the emancipation of all women, but the specific references to the practice of purdah and seclusion foreground, in particular, the subjugation faced by Muslim women in colonial India. Hossain's ideas on the need for freedom and equality of Muslim women come from the political ambience of her time. Analysing the plight of Indian Muslim women in the first half of the twentieth century, Karin A. Deutsch charts the connection between contemporary nationalist politics and the discourse of purdah in North India. During colonial times, wearing purdah was seen as a distinct religious custom of Muslim women by the British and other communities in India, even though it was not a sacral practice of Islam. This practice of viewing purdah as a religious symbol restricted women's freedom in the community and became a crucial issue in feminist debates and discourses. In India, according to Deutsch (1998), 'The debate on purdah, begun in the late nineteenth century continued, with a … focus on whether it was based on religion or custom and whether the Indian form of purdah should be reformed, discarded or upheld' (83). In a humorous role reversal in Hossain's Ladyland, men, instead of women, are kept in seclusion in 'mardanas', as opposed to women in 'zenanas' in Hossain's time.

Hossain converges the plight of women and nature, both oppressed under capitalist and patriarchal society, to create an equitable and sustainable space in Ladyland through a gender-sensitive and sustainable model of science and development. She projects Ladyland as a model to build an equitable space devoid of the exploitation of women and nature. She criticises the 'male' view of science and technology that is profit-oriented and not long-lasting. Through her humorous critique, she points out the irresponsible ways in which men handle modern science. In *Ecofeminism* (1993), Mies talks about the 'fathers of destruction' in connection with the invention of the atom bomb and its inhuman application in Hiroshima and Nagasaki.

> We understood for the first time that modern science was indeed a 'brainchild' of such modern 'fathers of destruction'. To construct machines, they do not need human women as mothers. This insight led us to a fundamental critique of modern science, a science which knows neither feelings, nor morals, nor responsibility: in order to produce this technology … they need violence. (xxiii)

Mies and Shiva thus draw attention to how modern Western science is violent and used for human destruction, and the gendered ways in which it is imagined and constructed.

Sultana's Dream describes an episode where Ladyland is attacked by an enemy country. The war weapons and ploys used by the male armies of the land fail miserably to keep the enemy at bay and bring the army on the verge of collapse and surrender. At this point, the women scientists of the land step in to protect their country and defeat the enemy through their strategies of non-violent science, as opposed to the violent, destructive methods of the male armies. The war tactics promoted and used by the women of Ladyland are not destructive like those of their male predecessors, who now retire into the zenanas in order to concede to women the right to decide in matters of war and governance. The principal of one of the women's universities in Ladyland instructs her female pupils to collect the sun's heat and project it towards the enemy in order to melt and destroy their ammunition but spare their lives.

> [T]he Lady Principal with her two thousand students marched to the battle field, and … directed all the rays of the concentrated sunlight and heat towards the enemy. The heat and light were too much for them to bear. They all ran away panic-stricken, not knowing in their bewilderment how to counteract that scorching heat. When they fled away leaving their guns and other ammunitions [sic] of war, they were burnt down by means of the same sun-heat. (10–11)

While the 'fathers of destruction' used modern science to design weapons to destroy humankind in the Second World War in 1945, Hossain in 1905 envisioned a mode of war that used technology to destroy the enemy's weapons but not their lives.

One of the criticisms against ecofeminism is that it reinforces assumptions about feminine qualities of nurturing and caring, which itself is a construct of patriarchal society, promulgating a 'natural', primordial and 'essential' relationship between the nurturing and sustaining qualities of women and nature, thereby essentialising women's perceived intimacy with nature. Women's perceived closeness to nature is a product of the patriarchal assertion of gender roles, which limited women for centuries to the domestic domain and, therefore, to the sources of sustenance found in nature. Though this perceived primordial connection between women and nature is ultimately undoubtedly a product of patriarchal assumptions and power divisions, *Sultana's Dream* gives a positive spin to this closeness of women and nature, despite being cast in essentialist terms. Hossain's text reveals her disappointment in the Western model of science, which alienates and damages nature, and urges us to be more sensitive and closer to nature, irrespective of gender. She envisions a harmonious, non-violent and sustainable relationship with nature in her utopia, to be practised irrespective of one's gender. However, in the real world inhabited by Hossain, the violent modern Western science was controlled and dominated by men. Therefore, her utopian alternative of non-violent science in Ladyland was necessarily imagined to be one envisioned and practised by women, in stark contrast to her own world.

CONCLUSION

Ladyland promotes non-violent and sustainable development. The use of solar energy, preservation of rainwater, artificial fountains, air cars, universities for women's education, scientific research done by women scientists make Ladyland a vision of a country governed and sustained by principles of equitability, sustainability and harmony. Ladyland shows that both production and consumption of commodities should go hand in hand and should be directed towards the common good of the people. Shiva and Mies argue that the fundamental contradictions in consumption and production are responsible for the capitalist destruction of nature. In a society where producers are a minority and consumers are the majority, the focus of the producers will necessarily be on profit rather than providing a clean environment. Hossain's text presents before us two contrasting worlds: one guided by sustainable development through scientific innovations and the other driven by modern science, which follows the principle of material growth without considering its harmful effects on nature and humankind.

Two spaces are juxtaposed in *Sultana's Dream*: the real space of colonial Bengal and the dream space of Ladyland. Science-fiction narratives often portray an artificially created space dominated by technologies, but Ladyland is an improvisation of the natural world using sustainable modern technologies. Hossain critiques the political and cultural ambience of colonial Bengal by reversing the reality experienced by her in the imaginary Ladyland. Hossain's text subverts colonial, patriarchal and modern scientific ideologies through conceptualising an alternative, equitable, sustainable and environmentally friendly science. The dream motif serves to heighten the disjuncture between the real world and the imagined Ladyland. *Sultana's Dream* thus reveals what Moylan identifies as a central feature of the critical utopia, an 'awareness of the limitations of the utopian tradition', which rejects 'utopia as blueprint while preserving it as dream' (10). Through the narrative technique of the dream, Hossain's critical utopia foregrounds 'the conflict between the ordinary world and the utopian society opposed to it' (Moylan 1986, 10), thereby highlighting the need for resistance and active social change.

Sultana's Dream thus deconstructs modern science and the scientific modernity that colonial India was initiated into, uncovering the violent principles of acquisition and control that it was based upon. Through depicting a utopian, futuristic world, it comments upon and critiques Hossain's contemporary world, positing a dream world that is nonetheless scientifically attainable, emerging from her technological forecasting and intelligent guesses, and arising from the matrix of her resistance to colonial dominance and gendered society.

NOTES

1 See, for instance, Gyan Prakash. 1996. 'Science between the Lines.' In *Subaltern Studies No. 9: Writings on South Asian History and Society*, edited by Shahid Amin and Dipesh Chakrabarty, 59–82. Delhi: Oxford University Press and Dhruv Raina and Irfan S. Habib. 1995. 'Bhadralok Perceptions of Science, Technology and Cultural Nationalism.' *Indian Economic and Social History Review*, 32: 95–117.

2 See Rokeya Sakhawat Hossain. 2005. *Sultana's Dream and Padmarag: Two Feminist Utopias*. Translated with an introduction by Barnita Bagchi. India: Penguin Random House. *Padmarag* was originally published in Bengali in 1924.

3 See Meera Kosambi. 2008. *Feminist Vision or Feminist Vision or 'Treason Against Men?': Kashibai Kanitkar and the Engendering of Marathi Literature*. Ranikhet: Permanent Black. *The Palanquin Tassel* by Kashibai Kanitkar was originally published in Marathi in 1928, abridged and translated by Meera Kosambi in 2008.

WORKS CITED

Agarwal, Bina. 1992. 'The Gender and the Environment Debate: Lessons from India.' *Feminist Studies*, 8(1): 119–158.

Broderick, Damien. 1995. *Reading by Starlight: Postmodern Science Fiction*. London: Routledge.

Chakrabarti, Pratik. 2014. *Medicine and Empire: 1600–1960*. New York: Palgrave Macmillan.

Chatterjee, Partha. 1986. 'Colonialism, Nationalism, and Colonialized Women: The Contest in India.' *American Ethnologist*, 16(4): 622–633.

Darwin, Charles, et al. ([1871] 1981). *The Descent of Man and Selection in Relation to Sex*. US: Princeton University Press.

Deutsch, Karin A. 1998. 'Muslim Women in Colonial North India Circa 1920–1947: Politics Law and Community Identity.' PhD Diss., Department of History, Darwin College, University of Cambridge, UK. https://core.ac.uk/download/pdf/1322887.pdf (accessed on 1 March 2021).

Gaard, Greta. 2011. 'Ecofeminism Revisited: Rejecting Essentialism and Re-Placing Species in a Material Feminist Environmentalism.' *Feminist Formations*, 23(2): 26–53.

Hossain, Rokeya Sakhawat. 2005. *Sultana's Dream and Padmarag: Two Feminist Utopias*. Translated with an introduction by Barnita Bagchi. India: Penguin Random House.

Jones, Gwyneth. 2006. *The Icons of Science Fiction*. UK: Cambridge University Press.

Khan, Shah Alam. 2018. 'Remembering Nehru as a Friend of Science.' *The Wire*. https://thewire.in/society/remembering-nehru-as-a-friend-of-science (accessed on 10 March).

Kochhar, R.K. 1991. 'Science as a Tool in British India.' *Economic and Political Weekly*, 26(33): 1927–1933.

Kosambi, Meera. 2008. *Feminist Vision or 'Treason Against Men?': Kashibai Kanitkar and the Engendering of Marathi Literature*. Ranikhet: Permanent Black.

Langer, Jessica. 2011. *Postcolonialism and Science Fiction*. London: Palgrave Macmillan.

Mies, Maria and Vandana Shiva. ([1993] 2014). *Ecofeminism*. UK: Zed Books.

Mill, John Stuart. 1869. *The Subjection of Women*. London: Longman.

Millett, Kate. ([1970] 2000). *Sexual Politics*. US: University of Illinois Press.

Moylan, Tom. ([1986] 2014). *Demand the Impossible: Science Fiction and the Utopian Imagination*. Austria: Peter Lang.

NASA. 2003. 'Learning to Fly: The Wright Brothers' Adventure'. https://www.nasa.gov/pdf/58225main_Wright.Brothers_508.pdf (accessed on 18 February 2021).

Patil, Rajendra, et al. 2012. 'An Overview of Solar Cookers.' *International Journal of Electronics, Communication & Soft Computing Science & Engineering*, Special Issue, 258–264.

Prakash, Gyan. 1996. 'Science Between the Lines.' *Subaltern Studies*, 9: 59–82, Delhi: Oxford University Press.

Raina, Dhruv, and Irfan S. Habib. 1995. 'Bhadralok Perceptions of Science, Technology and Cultural Nationalism.' *Indian Economic and Social History Review*, 32(1): 95–117.

Sarkar, Suvobrata. 2010. 'Technological Momentum'. *Indian Historical Review*, 37(1): 89–109.

Suvin, Darko. 1988. *Positions and Suppositions in Science Fiction*. UK: Macmillan.

Tropp, Martin. 1980. 'It Came from Inner Space: Science Fiction and the Self.' *CEA Critic*, 42(4): 20–24.

Chapter 11

WOMEN WHO THINK THEY ARE PLANETS AND OTHER BODIES: FEMINIST INTERVENTIONS IN INDIAN SF

Saloni Sharma

INTRODUCTION

By Editors

In her now-iconic chapter titled 'The Cyborg Manifesto', Donna Haraway triumphantly declares that 'I would rather be a cyborg than a goddess'. Far from being a straightforward embodiment of techno-utopianism, this statement is reflective of the potential of the cyborg figure as one that can challenge multiple binary formations simultaneously, including the ones between man and woman, human and animal, physical and non-physical, et cetera.

While technology is only one way of conceptualising a figure of alternate possibilities, other forms of transmogrification of women's bodies are discussed in Saloni Sharma's chapter. Sharma begins her chapter by establishing that the issue of representation of women in science and speculative fiction needs to be examined more holistically by studying it vis-à-vis questions of agency, intervention and subversion. She then goes on to explore the treatment of women's bodies and agency through a wide array of contemporary Indian fiction written by women authors. Women's bodies, otherwise imagined as sites for exercising patriarchal control, take on new shapes and forms, contributing to the herculean task of modern myth-making. Whether it is through a seemingly mundane act of claiming their names or asserting their appetite, or through a surreal transformation into an alien object or species, women characters articulate and fulfil their physical, sexual and intellectual desires.

By crossing the threshold between the human and the non-human (the non-human here is not restricted to technologically mediated figures like the cyborg or the droid but also encloses the animalistic, the natural, the alien and the extraterrestrial), women's bodies subvert oppressive societal expectations. Interestingly, Sharma also argues that many of these modern myths have their source in Indian epics such as the Ramayana, once again highlighting the warped sense of temporality in Indian narratives of science and speculative fiction.

The intersection of ancient traditional tales of women derived from the epics, often upheld as models of femininity by patriarchal forces, with tropes from the world of speculative and science fiction, has the potential to re-imagine and re-present a new ecology of gender identities. Therefore, instead of reiterating oppressive gender relations, models of traditional womanhood, when supplemented by the 'non-human' dimension of speculative or imaginative literature, become tools of subversion offering spaces of resistance.

****

> I have had a revelation. I am a planet. I used to be a human, a woman, a wife and mother. All the time I wondered if there was more to me than that. Now I know. Being a planet is good for me.
>
> —Vandana Singh (2008)

Almost every academic history of science fiction identifies Mary Shelley's *Frankenstein* (1818) as the point of origin of SF proper. Through the young scientist who creates life in a laboratory, only to have it turn monstrous and vengeful, Shelley's novel laid the ground for the fascinating SF theme of uninhibited progress necessarily leading to catastrophe.[1] It is also interesting to note that this *unnatural* birth in the novel, consequent on the childbearing woman having become redundant to the act of birthing, then leads to the rather violent removal of all women characters from the story. There are deaths from sickness, as punishment; there is murder and dismemberment. The women in Mary Shelley's novel are all made to disappear. A similar forced disappearance has been assumed of women in science fiction, that very few women read or wrote SF and that women were forced to write under male pseudonyms. Joanna Russ famously wrote in her 1970 essay, 'The Image of Women in Science Fiction', 'There are plenty of images of women in science fiction. There are hardly any women' (Russ 2007).

Russ is concerned with problems of representation, stereotyping and perspective. Ritch Calvin has a similar perspective when he remarks on how much of women's early contributions to SF have been 'overlooked, erased, and forgotten'[2] (Calvin 2016). The pronouncedly feminist SF of the 1960s and 1970s performed much social critique, concerning itself with structures of oppression and exploitation. Informed by the socialist and radical politics of the period, it posited utopias that reversed gender roles or entirely did away with them. Questions of race, ethnicity, sexuality and reproduction engaged with the rhetoric of *otherness*. The primary intent of feminist SF in the Western world, for at least the past few decades, has been to 'interrogate the social and literary construction of women as gendered subjects' (Lefanu 1989). Sarah Lefanu refuses to accept the mere presence of female characters in SF stories and novels as any kind of legitimate representation. She raises questions of agency, of how the character is structured, what motivations she has and what she is allowed to do/perform within the narrative.

This feminist lens that examines the presence, makes visible the absences of women in Indian SF and focuses on questions of agency, intervention and subversion, forms the grid of interrogations for this chapter. Science fiction by contemporary women writers in India addresses issues of gender, sex, ethnicity and exclusion, based primarily on the representations of the gendered body. Women's bodies have been objects of desire and consumption, often acquiring transactional value as a womb, in one story after another of technological advancement/breakdown, utopia/dystopia, across alternate universes. This concern is not peculiar to Indian writing, of course. Lisa Yaszek, in her introduction to a comprehensive anthology of early women SF writers, *The Future is Female!*, identifies '[m]otherhood, community survival, and the future of human reproduction' as issues central to women charting SF territory (Yaszek 2018). The texts under study in this chapter—Manjula Padmanabhan's *Harvest* (1997) and *Escape* (2008), Vandana Singh's *The Woman Who Thought She Was a Planet and Other Stories* (2008) and her short story 'Reunion' (2019), Nilanjana Bannerjee's 'Exile' (2012) and Mimi Mondal's 'The Sea Sings at Night' (2019)—cover a range of thematics and fall within significantly different parts of the SF spectrum. *Harvest* is a play set in a futuristic Mumbai where whole-body transplant from the Third World to the first has become legal and normative. *Escape* is the eponymous journey to supposed safety of the only girl to have survived the extermination of women in a country under a totalitarian, military regime. *The Woman Who Thought She Was a Planet and Other Stories* is an anthology that has several stories that examine tropes of transmogrification alongside the ideas of gender- and class-based oppression. 'Exile', a short story published in *Breaking the Bow: Speculative Fiction Inspired by the Ramayana*, posits a future where India has leapt to the position of world dominance and performances of the Ramayana have taken the form of cosplay and have become a major cultural phenomenon. 'The Sea Sings at Night', published in *The Gollancz Book of South Asian Science Fiction*, is part fairy tale, divested of heteronormativity, and part re-mythologisation. All of these are invested in imagining, re-imagining and re-presenting the female body while being aware of its transmutability.

PATRIARCHAL OPPRESSION OF THE RACIALISED BODY

Harvest, written as an entry to the Onassis Award and subsequent winner of the same, is set in a Mumbai slum, rendered ordinary by its over-representation in cinema, fiction and photographs. It is a generic space, which, according to Padmanabhan, could have been any place where there is 'oppression and cultural suppression' (Padmanabhan 2017). Om, unemployed and unemployable in an economy that does not take cognisance of the needs of those at the lowest rung of the class ladder, signs a contract making his body harvestable for any required transplant to a client who is rich, white, privileged and, thanks to the new body he owns, immortal. Suparno Banerjee labels it 'bioviolence', this 'domination of the developing world's biological resources through coercive methods by state and non-state agents because such exploitation ultimately leads to economic and biological devastation comparable to direct acts of violence' (Banerjee 2015). The violence is not just in the casual acquisition of a body but also in its dehumanisation. The client/owner controls not just the body of the person who has signed the contract but the hunger, desires and relationships of his four-member family. The user-abused relationship here is transracial and, as always, transactional. Capital has colonised the body.

It is interesting to see how Padmanabhan structures patriarchal oppression and its attempted overthrow. While subject to capitalistic/consumerist surveillance and control himself, Om expects fidelity and submission from his wife, Jaya. She, however, emerges as the only character in the play who can subvert the demands on her body. Jaya claims her sexuality, refusing to play wife/sister, freeing herself from the quagmire of relationships and societal norms. Om's mother, the only other significant woman character in the play, allows herself to be sucked into a cyborg future, literally, encasing herself within a machine that allows her to stream entertainment content endlessly. She gives up control over her body and her intellect, allowing herself to be colonised by technocratic authority. Jaya, in a clearly articulated act of subversion, reclaims control. In refusing to be impregnated via technology, Jaya disallows the violation of her body. In forcing Virgil, the man who has bought Om's body and all their lives, to pronounce her name right, she rewrites colonial control. A simple act of defiance, of claiming her appetite,[3] shifts the precarious balance of power, tilting it in her favour. Her threat of suicide, the destruction of a body with reproductive potential, is a threat to the systemic consumption she and women like her have been subject to. It is an act of political defiance.[4]

The issue of the racialised body is also taken up by Neelanjana Mukherjee in her Ramayana-inspired short story, 'Exile'. It is set in an alternate future of a depleted America outpaced by India. Joan Gordon locates the origin of Indian SF in the Ramayana. In her brief introduction to Indian SF, she traces its history to India's indigenous epic tradition, primarily the Ramayana, and points to how the aesthetic principles and use of fantasy within Indian SF set it apart from any hitherto imagined monolithic definition of the genre.

The stories in *Breaking the Bow* then become a knowing, subversive nod to that same narrative tradition of political and social commentary that has defined multiple iterations of the stories of the Ramayana and the Mahabharata. *Exile* inverts the racial narrative between America and India and posits a world in which cultural markers from India have become not just universalised but have accrued hegemonic value. It centres around Ramayana cosplay, with the protagonist Sapna playing the character of Surpanakha, the demon god's sister, who is punished for articulating her desire for an Aryan and, therefore, recognisably racially superior body. She is punished as much for her otherness as for her sexual transgression. The mutilation of her face and the disfigurement of her body are both the silencing of her belligerent desire. Sapna, Banerjee's protagonist, wears not just a costume but also the tagged, recognisable body of Surpanakha. In an act of complete conflation, it is Sapna's body that gets groped and assaulted when men play out Surpanakha's systemic patriarchal punishment. The sexual aggression that is coupled with moral indignation is impossible to miss in the scene where Sapna breaks the barrier between her cosplay character and her own delegitimised self, dancing on stage and claiming her dual identity. In an interesting reading of the racialised body's double victimisation, Banerjee has Ravana condemn Surpanakha to further violence and humiliation: 'Sister, I worshipped you more than any woman, but you have brought this shame on yourself. I cannot look on you, and no man shall look on you' (Banerjee 2012).

The woman's disfigured body, inside of this narrative and outside, loses value, and paradoxically, the repeated performance of this disfigurement is what allows Sapna's body to acquire monetary worth. Her humiliation and subjugation to the laws of patriarchal control are what will finally allow her to create the capital that will be her escape.

INVISIBILISATION OF THE WOMAN'S BODY

The transactional value ascribed to women's bodies is exposed further in Padmanabhan's *Escape*. Reminiscent of Margaret Atwood's *The Handmaid's Tale*, *Escape* posits a dystopia in which women have been exterminated. In Atwood's novel, also set in a totalitarian, overly religious, militaristic regime, women have been stripped of rights, power, economic ability, even names, identified either by the roles they perform or the men they belong to. Its protagonist, Offred (Of-Fred), doesn't have a name, only a patronymic. She is not allowed to read or write. Her only purpose is to serve as a womb, rented out to high-ranking military men whose wives have been unable to conceive, and to fulfil their destinies as women in a patriarchal order. Padmanabhan's dystopia furthers the degradation. The Generals, a set of cloned military men who run a country suggestive of India in all its cultural markers, have published several manuals and codes that are quoted extensively in epigraphs to the chapters. One of these reads: 'They were agents of mortality. By eliminating them, we eliminated mortality' (Padmanabhan 2015). *They* are women, corrupt and corrupting, and rendered redundant.

The problem of reproduction has been solved by technology. Men are cloned inside the bodies of animals that have become the new receptacles. 'The laboratory became our wife, our mother, our home, our all' (ibid.). While early feminist utopias imagined that alternate methods of reproduction would free women,[5] allowing them to be more than mothers and caregivers, in this unnamed country, they have only made women redundant and, therefore, *the vermin tribe* to be wiped out like pests. No longer citizens or 'cultural artefacts', they are only a crime (Oakley and Mitchell 1977).

PROBLEMATISING GENDER

Through her protagonist, Meiji, Padmanabhan allows the reader an insightful response to gender in a society that has outlawed an entire gendered identity and reduced a few others to powerlessness. Kept in a hormonally induced stasis, Meiji has lived her life under the protection of her three uncles, one of whom is assumed to be her biological father. Fearing violent repercussions as she ages and her body acquires its sexual markers, Meiji is to be sent to an island, a utopia based on early SF models of gender-segregated spaces. How gender segregation in this imagined feminist utopia perpetuates women's otherness in its attempt to subvert it[6] becomes the subject of the sequel to *Escape* in *The Island of Lost Girls* (2017). The control exercised on Meiji's body by benevolent patriarchy is evident in the way in which she is kept pre-adolescent and childlike. Her uncles are the keepers of knowledge: the keepers of secrets and her history. *Escape* shows the Generals as valuing erasure: 'They erase history, geography, whole generations of people. First by removing them, then by ensuring that all reference to them is cancelled out of existence' (Padmanabhan 2015). The uncles, while ostensibly protecting Meiji, practice the same erasure on her. She is taught what they deem teachable, she is given only a partial account of her history, she is allowed no friends; every aspect of her life is controlled and chronicled, the experiences accessible to her, carefully curated. In order to escape this oppressive, unnamed but not unrecognisable country, she must pass herself off as a boy, and in order to do so, she is given a prosthetic penis to wear. Her response to this external appendage is indicative of gender dysphoria: 'The pipe felt weird in her hands, and warm to the touch, as she peed. It was strange to be looking down at something that appeared to belong to her body yet produced no sensation' (ibid.).

As her adolescent body reclaims the processes of menstruation and the development of breasts, Meiji's response is one of horror and disgust. She sees any indications of womanly identity as monstrous. In constantly calling into question this betrayal by her body, Meiji challenges the socially sanctioned 'stable notion of gender', forcing the reader to confront the limitations of reading gendered identity as a binary, and breaks down the assumption of the mimetic relationship between sex and gender (Butler 2011).

CLASS, CASTE AND VIOLENCE

The hierarchy of power within Meiji's unnamed country for men makes visible the category of class. Power rests in the hands of the Generals, supported by their armies of Boy Warriors. These armies keep the citizenry in check through brute force. Since women, whose primary function would be to serve, no longer exist, the Generals now rely on drones, a 'designated labour species, subhuman and incapable of self-generation' (Padmanabhan 2015). The gender asymmetry that Judith Butler talks of in *Gender Trouble*, the relationship between men and women, being imaged as that between master and servant, is given a literal delineation in this replacement of women with drones, or drone technology, which is an even more dehumanising term. The creation of a serving class that is meant to stay devoted and silent, being incapable of either independent action or speech, is also as clear an indictment of caste structures as is possible within the eerily familiar-yet-unknown universe that *Escape* is. The drones cannot talk, cannot verbalise, and cannot protest. They provide care and sex and ask for nothing. They can be punished, and in their inability to protest even when punished, they become more pliant and manageable than women in the Generals' country ever would be. The politics of caste and oppression, the problematics of eugenics, the lure of complete compliance for an exploitative authority are all represented with unsettling accuracy in Padmanabhan's drones.

A few of Singh's short stories need a mention here. 'Delhi' is about temporal intersections that witnesses coincidences in the time stream. Through Aseem, we are allowed to wonder about the question Ray Bradbury[7] threw open for all SF readers with his 'A Sound of Thunder' (1952). If the present intersects with the past, what are the ways in which it modifies the future? The answer is disconcerting. Aseem has been told his destiny is to save/be saved by a woman he has never seen except as a heavily pixelated and unrecognisable image. When he does finally spot her, in a time overlap, he unwittingly pushes her towards greater danger. Women, particularly low caste/class, in Aseem's indistinct future, are not just forcibly removed from city streets as part of an urban beautification drive, as is often witnessed in present-day diplomatic Delhi, but are invisibilised and removed to what the future has designated as *Neechi Dilli*, literally, Lower Delhi, or, as Aseem finally understands it, the subterranean parts of the city, functioning, to all intents and purposes, as underground prison houses to contain the impoverished, the outcast, the criminal, the powerless, the ugly, the unwashed, all of which intersect to form an unacceptable and, therefore, banished whole. Aseem, inextricably caught in the trap of masculine desire to be the protector of a woman he has seen only briefly but feels an immense attraction to, seems to suffer from a saviour complex. His obvious failure propels him into a spiral of gloom, even as it lays bare the inefficacy of this masculine aspiration.

Singh's 'Reunion', a short story in *The Gollancz Book of South Asian Science Fiction*, addresses the caste and inequity question with much lesser ambiguity. It recognises the lacunae within systems of redressal like caste-based reservations that fail to reduce either inequity or inhumanity. Caste when appended to class and then to gender becomes an impenetrable barrier as is experienced by the protagonist, Mahua, and her sister. Singh's story makes real the everyday issues of bullying and harassment on school and college campuses, as rampant in modern-day India as in Mahua's post-climate-crisis future. Caste cannot be overcome, not today, not in the imagined future, is what Singh categorically states.[8]

TRANSMUTABILITY OF THE BODY

Butler, in writing of the body as a 'passive medium on which cultural meanings are inscribed', posits the body as a construction that is brought into being as a consequence of gendering (Butler 2011). The questioning and refusal of normative body-formation are precisely what Singh's 'The Woman Who Thought She Was a Planet' and 'Thirst' and Mondal's 'The Sea Sings at Night' do. In 'The Woman', Kamala, a housewife, mother and lifelong upholder of middle-class marital peace, finally proclaims, 'I know at last what I am. I am a planet' (Singh 2008). She begins to take off her sari, the garment most frequently associated with respectable, middle-aged Indian women, sparking absolute fear and despair in her husband, for whom clothes, particularly on a woman's body, are markers of respectability as well as patriarchal control. As she stands in the sun, rotating like a planet, her husband watches in horror, plagued by the threat of scandal and social humiliation:

> There stood his wife, naked, facing the sun with her arms spread wide. She began to turn slowly. There was a beatific expression on her face. The sunlight washed her ample body, the generous terraces and folds of flesh that cascaded down to her sagging belly and buttocks. (Singh 2008)

He continues his attempt at control while her face becomes more moonlike and her inhibitions disappear.

Kamala, trained in the role of mother, transforms rather easily into a *body* that is inhabited by a species alien to earth. Yaszek has identified this as 'one of the oldest and most central relationships in SF: that of humans and aliens', pointing to how women SF writers have used the dynamic between humans and aliens to project a syncretic future of peaceful coexistence (Yaszek 2018). Yaszek, here, is writing about early SF but Singh's story posits the same idea of a syncretic existence: the aliens live within Kamala's body, freeing her of societal pressure while finding in her husband a new creature/satellite to colonise.

The transmogrification of the woman's body becomes the focus of both 'Thirst' and 'The Sea'. In the first, a woman, again mother and wife, living under complete and unrelenting patriarchal dominance, temporarily transforms into a sea creature. In doing so, she acquires the agency to articulate and satisfy her sexual desire. She also acquires control over her womb. As a woman, the child she bears belongs to her husband, as dictated by the rules of patriarchy. As a sea creature, she has already freed herself of patriarchal control, and any child from her body would unequivocally belong to her. In the language of contemporary feminism, Susheela has claimed reproductive justice. The story is set within a system of modern myth-making that Malisa Kurtz has identified as Singh's unique perspective into SF. Susheela, the protagonist of 'Thirst', locates herself within a history that connects her and her foremothers to the river.

Her foremothers have always sacrificed their bodies to the river, almost in the manner of the fulfilment of their destiny. Susheela, however, instead of relinquishing control to the other dimension/alternate existence that the river represents, chooses to switch back and forth, retaining an interstitial space that sets her free from both the human and patriarchal world, as well as the sacrificing world of her foremothers.

Mondal's unnamed protagonist, refusing to gender-identify, witnesses their girlfriend, Matsa, one of the *sea folk* that live in Mondal's diversely populated Mumbai, unable to cope with relocation to land. In this aslant reworking of 'The Little Mermaid' fairy tale, a creature of the sea gives up her home, and perhaps even her voice, for love. The lover, in a reciprocal act of sacrifice, gives up claim to the body of the beloved, setting her free. 'There's no point carrying on with this forced assimilation', the narrator astutely observes (Mondal 2019). The inherent tragedy in this love story is not in the separation of the lovers but in the failure of sacrifices in a world that has no empathy for those living outside of socially sanctioned boundaries. The re-mythologisation that Mondal does, as well as the inversion of heteronormativity, works towards destabilising both the female body and gendered identity.[9]

In Singh's 'Hunger', the protagonist develops a preternatural ability to gauge the hunger of those around her. Attempting to understand the strangeness of it, she finds an answer in the books she reads:

> Meanwhile, she continued to read her science fiction novels because, more than ever, they seemed to reflect her own realization of the utter strangeness of the world. Slowly the understanding came to her that these stories were trying to tell her a great truth in a very convoluted way, that they were all in some kind of code, designed to deceive the literary snob and waylay the careless reader. (Singh 2008)

If SF tells us truths, the one worth telling here is how women's bodies, in various acts of reclamation, go from being sites of oppression to tools of subversion. The body, as discussed here, is not simply a gendered and anatomical one. It is physiological, experiential and 'embedded in a culture that, to a greater or lesser degree, devalues femininity' (Davis 2007). The women in these stories have been subject to various kinds of violence—physical, sexual, mental—have been marginalised, excluded and oppressed, and have, every time, used their selfhood and bodies as 'a potential locus for resistance and political action' (ibid.). From within a medium that is part SF, part speculative fiction, part mythologisation, women writers and the characters they create show us how women will be planets or snakes or mothers or climate-activists but will no longer be invisibilised. They will not disappear inside stories. Instead, they will change form and claim space and invert narratives.

NOTES

1 Adam Roberts, while tracing the history of the SF genre all the way from Kepler's *Somnium* (1634), points to Darko Suvin's argument that *Frankenstein* initiates the idea that progress inevitably leads to disaster. In contemporary literature as well as cinema, this same is now widely accepted and replicated repeatedly.

2 There has been an invisibilisation of women in SF. Ritch Calvin notes that women have been readers as well as writers of SF since the genre's inception, but their contributions have been forgotten. Feminist SF criticism has attempted to address this invisibilisation through the process of compiling anthologies.

3 Jaya says she will eat for three people. She repeatedly insists that Virgil must 'risk his skin' and put his newly purchased immunity at risk, if he intends to have a child with her. She makes a list of claims and chooses to live a life free of deprivation, even if for a limited period of time, all by herself.

4 Jaya's threat of suicide and the consequent destruction of any potential children from her womb is what Jodi Kim calls the destruction of reproductive capital. Jaya is part of a racialised social structure and the only justice within it would be in the abolition of the debt the poor owe to their owners, a debt that is not just monetary but has extended to their bodies and lives.

5 Suzanne Damarin writes of how changes in reproductive technology or modes of technological reproduction were seen by second-wave feminists as essential to freeing women from both childbearing and child-rearing roles, allowing them to finally achieve liberation.

6 Gender segregation becomes an unwitting tool in the hands of patriarchy by perpetuating the otherness of women; and, therefore, any utopia fashioned solely for women ends up subverting the cause of women's liberation and the possibility of dominant roles outside of the domestic, as analysed by Jean Pfaelzer.

7 Tarun K. Saint, in his introduction to *The Gollancz Book of South Asian Science Fiction*, mentions Jagdish Chandra Bose's Bengali story '*Niruddesher Kahini*' ('The Story of the Missing One', 1896) as having already introduced a plot element reminiscent of the butterfly effect, according to which a small intervention can have far-reaching consequences for an entire world/civilisation.

8 'Hunger', from *The Woman Who Thought She Was a Planet and Other Stories*, explores similar territory. In the story of the old man who is poisoned inadvertently, Singh shows her readers how the lives of the poor are of little consequence. Class is visible, drawing boundaries, making itself impossible to ignore.

9 Judith Butler provides a crucial context within which lesbian-femme desire might be placed when she locates its object as neither decontextualised female body nor a superimposed masculine identity but the necessary destabilisation both are forced into.

WORKS CITED

Banerjee, Neelanjana. 2012. 'Exile.' In *Breaking the Bow: Speculative Fiction Inspired by the Ramayana*, edited by Anil Menon and Vandana Singh, 12–37. New Delhi: Zubaan.

Banerjee, Suparno. 2015. 'Ruptured Bodies and Invaded Grains: Biotechnology as Bioviolence in Indian Science Fiction.' *Journal of the Fantastic in the Arts*, 26(1): 58–75.

Butler, Judith. 2011. *Gender Trouble: Feminism and the Subversion of Identity*. New York and London: Routledge.

Calvin, Ritch. 2016. *Feminist Science Fiction and Feminist Epistemology: Four Modes*. New York: Springer.

Damarin, Suzanne. 2004. 'Chapter Three: Required Reading: Feminist Sci-Fi and Post-Millennial Curriculum.' *Counterpoints*, 158: 51–73.

Davis, Kathy. 2007. *The Making of Our Bodies, Ourselves: How Feminism Travels Across Borders*. Durham and London: Duke University Press.

Drapeaud, Léone. 2018. 'Founding the Feminist Utopia.' https://www.thesitemagazine.com/read/founding-the-feminist-utopia (accessed on 10 March 2021).

Genz, Stephanie, and B.A. Brabon. 2009. *Postfeminism: Cultural Texts and Theories*. Edinburgh: Edinburgh University Press.

Gordon, Joan. 2016. 'Introduction: Indian Science Fiction.' *Science Fiction Studies*, 43(3): 433–434.

Kendall, Mikki. 2020. *Hood Feminism: Notes from the Women that a Movement Forgot*. New York: Viking.

Kim, Jodi. 2014. 'Debt, the Precarious Grammar of Life, and Manjula Padmanabhan's "Harvest".' *Women's Studies Quarterly*, 42(1/2): 215–232.

Kurtz, Malisa. 2016. '"Alternate Cuts": An Interview with Vandana Singh.' *Science Fiction Studies*, 43(3): 534–545.

Lefanu, Sarah. 1989. *Feminism and Science Fiction*. Bloomington: Indiana University Press.

Lieder, K. Frances. 2015. 'Not-Feminism: A Discourse on the Politics of a Term in Modern Indian Theatre.' *Asian Theatre Journal*, 32(2): 598–618.

Menon, Anil, and V. Singh, eds. 2012. *Breaking the Bow: Speculative Fiction Inspired by the Ramayana*. New Delhi: Zubaan.

Melzer, Patricia. 2006. *Alien Constructions: Science Fiction and Feminist Thought*. Austin: University of Texas Press.

Mondal, Mimi. 2019. 'The Sea Sings at Night.' In *The Gollancz Book of South Asian Science Fiction*, edited by Tarun K. Saint, 36–39. Gurugram: Hachette.

Oakley, Anne, and J. Mitchell, eds. 1997. *Who's Afraid of Feminism? Seeing Through the Backlash*. New York: The New Press.

Padmanabhan, Manjula. 2015. *Escape*, 2nd ed. Gurugram: Hachette.

———. 2017. *Harvest*, 2nd ed. Gurugram: Hachette.

Pfaelzer, Jean. 2010. 'Women Write the Future: Teaching Feminism and Utopianism in the Twenty-First Century.' *Transformations: The Journal of Inclusive Scholarship and Pedagogy*, 20(2): 39–54.

Roberts, Adam. 2006. *Science Fiction*. New York: Routledge.

Russ, Joanna. 2007. *The Country You Have Never Seen: Essays and Reviews.* Liverpool: Liverpool University Press.

Saint, Tarun K., ed. 2019. *The Gollancz Book of South Asian Science Fiction.* Gurugram: Hachette.

Schiebinger, Londa, ed. 2000. *Feminism and the Body.* Oxford: Oxford University Press.

Singh, Vandana. 2008. *The Woman Who Thought She Was a Planet and Other Stories.* New Delhi: Zubaan and Penguin Books.

———. 2019. 'Reunion.' In *The Gollancz Book of South Asian Science Fiction,* edited by Tarun K. Saint, 341–365. Gurugram: Hachette.

Smith, Eric D. 2016. 'Universal Love and Planetary Ontology in Vandana Singh's of Love and Other Monsters.' *Science Fiction Studies,* 43(3): 514–533.

Yaszek, Lisa, and P.B. Sharp, eds. 2016. *Sisters of Tomorrow: The First Women of Science Fiction.* Middletown: Wesleyan University Press.

Yaszek, Lisa, ed. 2018. *The Future is Female! 25 Classic Science Fiction Stories by Women, from Pulp Pioneers to Ursula K. Le Guin.* New York: Library of America.

Chapter 12

WHO'S AFRAID OF POSTCOLONIAL DYSTOPIA? REFLECTIONS ON CONTEMPORARY SCIENCE FICTION IN INDIA

Shikha Vats

INTRODUCTION

By Editors

What would a typically Indian or postcolonial utopia or dystopia look like? Will it be strikingly different from the traditional models of utopia/dystopia derived from Western literature and culture? Is there a need to devise new theoretical and critical frameworks to appreciate and study narratives that seek to delineate postcolonial utopias and dystopias? These are some of the issues addressed by Shikha Vats through her analysis of two contemporary Indian English novels Gautam Bhatia's *The Wall* (2020) and Prayaag Akbar's *Leila* (2017). Both these novels are studied as manifestations of particular trends in postcolonial Indian dystopia, most prominently the existence of a materially enclosed world structured according to class, caste and/or occupation.

As is common with dystopic fiction, these worlds are imagined utopias gone direly awry; in these two novels, they are premised on notions of order and purity. Significantly, the spatial organisation of these worlds is reminiscent of anticolonial utopian visions espoused by revolutionaries of the freedom struggle including Mahatma Gandhi, B.R. Ambedkar and V.D. Savarkar. The interaction between utopian narratives, an established Western subgenre of writing and the ethos of the postcolonial make Indian English writing generate new possibilities for reinvigorating certain key historical intellectual conflicts such as the Gandhi-Ambedkar clash for the vision of a truly free Indian society. It also brings to the fore the conflict between community-centric living patterns predominant in erstwhile colonies and the individual-centric model of Western capitalism.

Similarly, the intimacy between utopic and dystopic narratives, regarded as an established motif in SF writing, is reconfigured here as anticolonial utopian visions give way to postcolonial dystopias. Individual memory and collective history are not just ways of looking backwards but also tools for creating an imagined future. Finally, Vats raises another important, albeit largely unaddressed question related to the ideological underpinnings of authors and readers of the niche Indian SF. These visions of urban/rural dystopias are largely created and consumed by a specific demographic that is Western-educated, English-speaking upper middle class with a perceptible political bias. In such a scenario, one can't help but question the inclusiveness of the dystopic worlds of such fiction, raising the opportune and apposite question: whose dystopia is it after all?

****

> The future is already here—it's just not evenly distributed.
>
> —William Gibson

Some recent instances of Indian fiction written in English demand urgent attention for their affinity with the utopian/dystopian genre. A considerable scholarship on Indian science fiction is already underway, but it has so far been lacking in directly addressing the particularity of the utopian/dystopian worldviews.[1] The historical origins of the Indian science-fiction genre can be traced back to its proximity with young adult and children's literature.[2] Although often labelled as a subset of this broad genre of science fiction, the utopian/dystopian narratives carve out a separate niche for themselves through their mature stance on and closer engagement with sociopolitical issues. The chapter aims to examine contemporary utopian/dystopian Indian fiction as emerging from within the postcolonial discourse. These narratives, usually located in an estranged spatio-temporal setting, provide a critical commentary on the present state of affairs through the lens of an experienced past but with an eye on the projected future. In India's case, the predicament of a postcolonial nation-state is portrayed through an alternative and futuristic worldbuilding. A detailed analysis of the postcolonial utopian/dystopian fiction shows that both the categories of 'alternative' space and 'futuristic' time are suspect and may be creatively employed by the writers to actually talk about the 'here' and 'now'.

At the outset, it would be useful to introduce Darko Suvin's definition of science fiction in order to understand the links between science fiction and utopia/dystopia. In his seminal work *Metamorphoses of Science Fiction* (1979), Suvin notes, 'SF is, then, a literary genre whose necessary and sufficient conditions are the presence and interaction of estrangement and cognition, and whose main formal device is an imaginative framework alternative to the author's empirical environment' (Suvin 7). Reflecting on Suvin's formulation, Suparno Banerjee observes thus:

> [S]cience in itself is not the most important object in a science fiction … the 'hypothesis' from where science fiction takes off is not a scientific but a fictional one; it is the estranging device [used] … to defamiliarize (*ostranienie*) an object in order to draw attention to it. From that point onwards the story is developed with a totalizing rigor, which is the 'scientific' element.

From Banerjee's theorisation, it can be deduced that a story need not necessarily feature outer space, aliens, cloning or time travel in order to qualify as science fiction. The estrangement effect, which forms the cornerstone of science fiction, may be achieved in utopian/dystopian narratives through an alteration of the 'topos', that is, the time-space coordinates, of the fictional world. Essentially, the focus of these narratives remains on articulating an ideological and political stance of a social collective through imaginative worldbuilding, where the mention of science, as understood in the general sense, appears as incidental to the plot development. The category of postcolonial utopian, then, signifies an intricate relationship between the postcolonial and utopian school of thought, both of which are concerned with the experience of colonialism and exploration of an alternative ideal of indigenous belonging and hope. The emerging field of postcolonial utopian studies,[3] when examined in light of this view, brings to the fore interesting developments and diversions from the classical Western understanding of the utopian literary form.

The chapter will undertake a study of two recent novels Prayaag Akbar's *Leila* (2017) and Gautam Bhatia's *The Wall* (2020) as manifestations of a specific trend in postcolonial Indian dystopia. Both the novels present strikingly similar worlds structured according to class, caste and/or occupation, divided by and fortified within insurmountable walls. Indicative of a highly polarised political climate, these works fall under the subgenre of SF called 'the wall around the world' narrative, following the 1953 eponymous short story by Theodore Cogswell.[4] In both these novels, the worldbuilding exercise takes as its point of departure a social setup with walls, which are, quite literally, solid, physical dividing structures but more importantly with mythical, metaphorical and ideological connotations. Both these works borrow from the classical Western understanding of dystopia as utopia gone wrong; but at the same time, they are replete with specific cultural markers unmistakably reflective of the anxieties of a postcolonial nation-state.

The textual analysis of Akbar's *Leila* and Bhatia's *The Wall* is aimed at highlighting the themes that place these novels within the rubric of the postcolonial utopian/dystopian novel. The storyworlds constructed in both the novels contain reminiscences of the utopian visions of a new nation presented by some of the prominent figures such as M.K. Gandhi, B.R. Ambedkar and V.D. Savarkar in the period leading up to India's independence.[5] The spatial organisation in these two novels, crucial to any utopian narrative, is studied with relation to specific postcolonial themes of freedom, history, memory, language and community. The close textual study, in turn, reveals two broadly interconnected aspects of the emerging postcolonial dystopian novel. A careful reading of both the novels unravels an inherent critique of their own so-called dystopian visions. This critique is present as a subtext and embodied by the protagonists who enjoy a certain level of comfort and social privilege in a world that soon turns oppressive for them. Finally, the chapter attempts to explain the nature of dystopia as depicted in these novels from the vantage point of their respective narrators. Additionally, while keeping an eye on the recent surge in Indian science-fictional works, it speculates about the authors' ideological moorings, which may have shaped their dystopian imagination.

Gautam Bhatia's *The Wall* is set in an imaginary city named Sumer, which is surrounded by a wall since time immemorial. The novel contains a map at the beginning, which serves as a visual guide for entering the world of Sumer. The whole city is divided into various circles, or mandalas, fifteen in all, based on everyone's occupation. The division of labour across the mandalas is given, and everyone follows the preordained occupation. There is a river called Rasa with unknown origins, which cuts through all the mandalas, acting as a life-giving force for all. In the centre of the city, that is, within the first mandala, there is a set of four huge towers, which have also always existed from the beginning, just like the wall.

In Sumer, apart from these four towers and the wall, which seem to be constructed with great sophistication and advanced technology, the rest of the city is pre-industrial. Everyone is involved in manual occupations such as weaving, carpentry, writing, nursing, singing, et cetera. There also exists a ban on weapons, which, as the readers are told in the beginning, is defied by the *shoortans*[6], the Sumerian counterparts of police, by carrying out secret drills. This is perhaps indicative of a society initially conceived on the principle of non-violence. The novel is full of names found in the Hindu mythology Ramayana such as Mithila[7], Rama[8], Garuda[9] and Malan who crosses a '*raika*' (perhaps a reference to the Laxman Rekha drawn by Laxman to protect Sita). This is recognised as an initial act of disobedience, which leads to the appearance of the wall around the city of Sumer. All these references to the Ramayana ostensibly create an atmosphere of the mythical *ramarajya*, which Gandhi envisioned as the ancient ideal kingdom of God on earth. The organisation of concentric circles with the river Rasa passing through them exhibits a social setup that is self-sufficient and follows a decentralised model of rule. The spatial plan is reminiscent of the Gandhian utopian vision of social organisation, as summed up by him,

> [I]n this structure composed of innumerable villages, there will be ever-widening, never-ascending circles. Life will not be a pyramid with the apex sustained by the bottom. But it will be an oceanic circle whose centre will be the individual always ready to perish for the village, the latter ready to perish for the circle of villages, till at last the whole becomes one life composed of individuals, never aggressive in their arrogance, but ever humble, sharing the majesty of the oceanic circle of which they are integral units. (Gandhi 1946)

Although the spatial and socio-economic formation of the city of Sumer seems in line with the Gandhian vision to some extent, a basic limiting factor exists in the form of the wall. The willingness to perish for the larger cause of the community in Gandhian thought arises only after the attainment of *swaraj*, or a sense of sovereignty that is rooted in the individual. However, in the city of Sumer, we witness uprisings of various kinds against this oppressive presence of the wall, which negates the basic sense of freedom. Mithila, the protagonist, is obsessed with the idea of finding out what lies beyond the wall by breaching it. Interestingly, the council, which rules the city, appeals to her to give up her idiosyncratic urge to breach the protective wall. To persuade her, they remind her of her duty and responsibility towards the people of Sumer. This debate on rights, duties and freedom is central to the novel and the last section of the story highlights how these concerns are formulated in a dystopian world.

In a lengthy climactic sequence, instead of any action, Bhatia includes long courtroom debates, with two sides arguing in favour of and against the necessity of 'the wall', which is also an anagram for 'the law'. The novel engages with a basic paradox of Gandhian utopian thought: between an anarchic strain inherent in the desire for total freedom and the notion of sacrifice and service to the community. This debate also appears as a primary concern in utopian thought. The conflict between an individual and the collective as a fundamental feature of postcolonial utopian thinking has been theorised by Bill Ashcroft in his writings. In contrast to the capitalistic individual-centric Western model, the community-centric living patterns prevalent in the erstwhile colonised societies present possibilities for a different set of negotiations within postcolonial utopianism. Ashcroft (2012) notes, '[W]hile the equality of the individuals in the collective is a fundamental principle of utopian thought, the collective is always inimical to individual fulfilment' (10). Mithila reminds us that even if one individual in a given social setup is deprived of 'freedom', then their sense of duty towards the community cannot be invoked as the raison d'être for their actions. Commitment to the community must harmoniously coexist with true individual freedom, not irrespective of it.

Even though the city of Sumer spatially resembles Gandhian utopia, we notice its inhabitants calling it out for being completely antithetical to it. In a manifesto by the famous mutineer Savarian Maloran, the dark reality behind the so-called democratic structure of the circular city is revealed. The manifesto titled 'What is to be done now?'—a direct reference to Vladimir Lenin's political and economic prescription[10]—exposes the oppressive hierarchy prevalent in the society:

> The Shoortans reinforce the belief that the Circles are the natural order of being, and to move beyond your Mandala is a transgression. By creating Fifteen Circles, the task is greatly simplified, because almost everybody is above somebody else, and has some interest in maintaining the system. Think of it, as you will, a tower with fifteen floors, but with no way of ascending or descending between one floor and another. (Bhatia 2020)

The portrayal of Sumer is reminiscent of Ambedkar's description of caste society, and the mandalas here stand-in for the *varna vyavastha*, which ordains an occupation to people based on their birth. The oceanic circles become symbolic of both the characteristic features that Ambedkar recognises as the fundamental flaws in a caste-based society: the absence of equality and the restriction of mobility. Although depicted like oceanic circles of Gandhian utopia, Bhatia's novel imagines a dystopian Sumer in tune with Ambedkar's warnings. The deeply divided society is riddled with hierarchies and upholds one truth, one history and one superior identity instead of embracing the plurality within.

Bhatia's novel uses ideas of visibility and invisibility through the metaphor of the wall to establish the associations of postcolonial utopianism with memory, history and imagination. The hypervisibility of the wall makes it difficult to visualise, and therefore, imagine other alternatives. However, a group of students who call themselves 'the young Tarafians' see imaginative possibilities in poetry, which may help them envision the world beyond the wall. There is also a deep sense of nostalgia embedded within language, which comes across in evocations such as 'it was a wind from beyond the Wall. It carried scents that Sumer struggled to name' (Bhatia 2020). They often meditate on questions such as how does one name something that doesn't exist? Is language also ideologically constricted by the wall that surrounds their world? Or can it travel far and beyond through sense perception (unnamed scents) and imagination? Mithila and her young friends carry out certain mnemonic practices where they attempt to imagine a horizon without the wall. They try to remember their childhood dreams that were less bound within this world; they read poetry that conceives of revolution; they think of a new language that will allow them to envisage an alternative to their world. Mithila says that Taraf's poetry contains 'words that carry a memory. Words that exist outside of this city, words that have their own … place. Words in which things could happen, a world could happen' (ibid.). The creation of a world within language here is a meta-reference to the novel as a whole, which is engaged in this selfsame practice of creating a world-within-words.[11] She repeats the word 'horizon' over and over to think what it may mean, as nothing of the sort exists in their world except in a 'language that would be free' (ibid.). The young students practice by closing their eyes and trying, through words, to invoke images of a horizon stretching out infinitely to where the sea meets the sky. The focus on language in the novel speaks of an acute awareness about how words, more importantly language, can make and unmake the world.

In the novel, it is often mentioned that the Sumerian residents experience something called the '*smara*', which is explained as a yearning for a world without a wall. However, as Mithila goes on and discovers some historical books and poetry from the past, she decodes *smara* as what it once meant: 'the memory of a time before the Wall' (ibid.). This duality within the notion of *smara*, which is both a yearning for a future as well as the memory of the past, is significant in the plot for ushering in a true sense of freedom in an ideal society. Within a still emerging and nascent field of study, few scholars such as Bill Ashcroft, Ralph Pordzik and Lyman Tower Sargent have theorised the category of postcolonial utopianism as one where memory has a special connection with futuristic alternative worldbuilding.[12] Ashcroft suggests that in the context of postcolonial utopianism, 'memory is not about recovering a past that was present but about the production of possibility. In the sense that memory is a recreation, it is not a looking backwards, but a reaching out to a horizon, somewhere "out there"' (Ashcroft 2012). Both Bhatia and Akbar's novels use memory as the kernel for envisioning postcolonial utopia and dystopia by reckoning with a shared past and possible future. The spectre of an erstwhile colonised nation is relevant for understanding the displacement of utopia from 'place' to 'time' in the postcolonial utopian literary imagination. Therefore, even though a 'horizon' in terms of a place is evoked and sought after, it is '*smara*' in terms of time that allows for a utopian imagination.

The whole novel, then, appears as an exercise in utopian thinking arising from within a dystopian worldview. It is through these ideas of language, history, memory and dreams that the novel posits freedom as a condition possible only in the absence of oppressive structures. Often when Mithila is asked as to why the wall must be breached, she responds by quoting the poet Taraf: '[Simply] because it exists.' At the end, when Mithila manages to fly above the wall on the back of a mythical bird Garuda, she says, 'Sumer, the wall must be breached. The horizon awaits. And what will we gain, but the world?' (Bhatia 2020). It is with the breach of the wall, through a new method of seeing, visualising and imagining an alternative, that the existing oppressive world falls away to reveal a newfound land of many possibilities.

Another story about a society confined within walls, *Leila* by Akbar (2017) is set in the near future in a digitised city over which climate crisis looms large. The novel is about a city delineated along the idea of 'purity' and divided by many walls, each for a different community. The backdrop is something called 'the long summer', accompanied by water crisis and water wars as a result of climate change (Akbar 11). The climate crisis becomes a pretext for introducing structural changes in society, but the changes do not in any way address the real problems. Instead, a new hierarchical social order makes it possible for some to lead healthy and comfortable lives, mostly at the cost of others.[13]

The tallest wall in the unnamed city is called 'Purity One', which circumscribes the 'political sector' inhabited mostly by the ruling elites. Within the city, a network of flyroads is used to ply from one point to another. The people who live within the sectors do not have to bother with the filth and garbage accumulating on the ground because an alternative city on a level much above the ground has been built for them. The segregation of spaces is most prominent in the contrast that exists between the political sector and the outskirts of the city called the outroads. The political sector has sprawling bungalows and manicured gardens. The air in that part is cleaner, thanks to artificial filters. On the other hand, in the area designated as outroads, the air is heavily saturated with particulates, causing permanent irritation and damage to the eyes along with other respiratory illnesses. The most telling instance of this dystopian city is a new project soon to be launched by a corporation named Skydome. This is a project, with an accompanying slogan 'Must Your Children Share Their Air?', aimed at providing clean air to a select few (Akbar 2017).[14] With such a structure in place, the city spaces have a strictly hierarchical and exclusionary character.

The council insignia in Akbar's novel is the picture of a pyramid underneath which is written in bold black text: 'Purity for All'; Also, in the precise centre of the city exists the political sector, which features a hundred-feet tall pyramid-like structure called the 'Purity Pyramid', complete with a viewing gallery at the top. The pyramid represents, among other things, the hierarchical structure of the new city: few or one at the top, with the base increasing in width, implying a greater number of people at the bottom-most rung. Again, one finds echoes of the Gandhian dictum: '[L]ife will not be a pyramid with the apex sustained by the bottom' (236). Except that it is precisely that in this novel. Akbar's pyramid analogy, same as Bhatia's analogy of fifteen floors in a building, as discussed earlier in this chapter, conveys a similar approach to dystopian spaces in these novels.

The pyramid-like structure of the society also harks back to Ambedkar's denouncement of caste society as one of graded inequality, wherein at every level someone is content with oppressing the ones beneath them, thereby leaving little room for resistance. As postulated by Ambedkar, in such a structure, nobody is without some level of privilege, given that everyone is above someone else in the social hierarchy, except the ones at the bottom-most rung. In this novel, it is the people residing in slums, called the slummers, who occupy the lowest position. Further, the emphasis on purity, be it of race or caste, is reminiscent of Savarkar's vision of a pure Hindu Aryan identity as the chief identifying marker of India's cultural and global superiority. In tune with Savarkar's vision of Indian imperialism and its supreme position at a global level, the novel imagines the regime as a neoliberal power, which has a strictly orthodox view of pure identity. The purity pyramid, therefore, symbolises the most oppressive social structure identified by Ambedkar. It is also sectarian and discriminatory, in line with Savarkar's idea. The references to class struggle in the novel draw attention to the nexus between caste, class and religion as the defining feature of the modern Indian identity.[15] Akbar's treatment of these ideas in the form of a spatially drawn-out dystopian narrative makes the novel a fertile ground for investigating the postcolonial manifestations of what were once formulated as anticolonial utopian visions.

The story is a first-person narration by Shalini, who must search for her daughter, Leila, abducted sixteen years ago. Since the incident, Shalini's city has been taken over by a group of people called the council, and after a complete overhaul, there is a new order in place. As opposed to Bhatia's novel, where *smara* entails the possibilities of a utopian unfolding, Akbar's novel presents memory, and its associations with madness and derangement, as a device that brings about the dystopian denouement. Ever since Leila's abduction, all that the mother is left with are memories—of her daughter as a three-year-old baby, of her dead husband, of the time before the age of 'Purity One' and of another world order that existed before this dystopian regime. Shalini says that 'remembrance is an alarm, a siren that plies round my head' (Akbar 2017). The storehouse of memories signifies the site of any subversive thought or action because it preserves what used to be, allows for what can be and lets one imagine with a revolutionary resolve what should be and what will be.

However, Akbar presents a bleak dystopia by challenging Shalini's sense of the past. There are moments of derangement and madness that Shalini experiences after having spent close to sixteen years in the purity camp and the towers. She often hallucinates that her dead husband, Rizwan, is walking beside her and talking to her. Towards the end of the novel, the first-person narrator has bouts of confusion about the accuracy of her memories, making the reader question the entire story. Once a sense of self-doubt and self-questioning becomes a part of the inhabitant's psyche, it renders the dystopian structure more credible. The outlier, in this case Shalini, begins to think if she was wrong in the way she led her life before and if the true order is the way things are now. This is so because the victory of the system is achieved not through coercion but when people internalise the beliefs of the ruling dispensation.[16] This trope works in most of the dystopian narratives, the most popular of them being George Orwell's *1984*. The last sentence in the novel, 'He loved Big Brother', is a testament to the fact that the system is now fully in place (Orwell 1949). Therefore, Shalini's questioning of her own memory makes her doubtful of the lived past, and her questioning her sanity makes her doubtful about the present state and impending future. Forgetfulness forecloses any possibility of change. This casts a shadow over the entire narrative and positions the reader in place of the final arbiter.

Finally, it is important to analyse the question of ideology in a totalising genre such as utopia.[17] The two novels present both worldviews: utopian and dystopian. Sumer is initially conceived of as a utopian land of safety and promise by the semi-divine Builders[18]. Similarly, Purity One in *Leila* heralds a new, improved and pure order against the vices of an erstwhile liberal and degraded society. However, with Mithila's and Shalini's journeys, the closed worlds are revealed as unjust, oppressive and dystopian. The flip-sided nature of utopias and dystopias highlight the central role of ideology in their formation.

Despite inhabiting these dystopian worlds, the pursuits of both the protagonists are depicted as personal, individualistic and tangential, if not oppositional to the collective interests of the community. Moreover, the privileged and upper-middle-class perspectives of the protagonists make them seem complicit like Shalini or uninspiring like Mithila. Shalini is completely ignorant of the plight of the lower-class people in her city, who are living in abject circumstances. In fact, she has a discriminatory attitude towards those she thinks as being beneath her stature. *Leila* unmasks the opportunism of its left-leaning and liberal-minded characters who are equally responsible, as the right-wing conservative fanatics, in bringing in the dystopian regime. Mithila, in *The Wall*, is unmoved by the predicament of those from the outermost circles who are trying to reform Sumerian society instead of trying to escape it. She is also unable to convince and gather a considerable following for the cause of breaching the wall. Instead, she keeps herself ideally engaged in highbrow pursuits such as daydreaming, poetry recitation and philosophising about the condition of bounded existence.

The trenchant critique of both the protagonists emerging from within these novels must be read as reflective of the utopian genre's own chequered history as colonising narratives[19] and subsequently as representatives of the failed dream of a postcolonial nation-state. As discussed in the chapter, utopian visions of Gandhi and Ambedkar find echoes in these works but, ironically, as postcolonial dystopias. Despite the critical nuance built into the narrative, the worlds of Sumer and Purity One are eventually recognised as dystopian, and the novels' as well as the readers' sympathies ultimately rest with Mithila and Shalini. Creating and consuming the very same utopian literature that Mithila is obsessed with while sitting in the comforts of one's privileged homes like Shalini once did, the authors and readers of these works hang on to the hope of breaching 'the wall' and despair at the bleakness of Leila's world. The argument about 'whose dystopia is it after all?' must then be extrapolated by taking into account a brief survey of recent Indian SF.

Written in English and enjoying the utopian genre's popular appeal to a modern sensibility, these novels also speak of the authors' and readers' own subjectivities. The striking similarity in the identity positions of slowly but surely emerging group of Indian science and speculative fiction writers such as Samit Basu, Indra Das, Tashan Mehta, Ruchir Joshi, in addition to Akbar and Bhatia, is unmissable. Vandana Singh and Anil Menon have been widely published in the US and UK markets. Almost all of these SF writers belong to the Western-educated, English-speaking, upper-middle-class, left-liberal demographic. Some other diasporic science fiction and fantasy (SFF) authors of South Asian descent include S.B. Divya, Priya Sharma and Mary Anne Mohanraj.[20] With the recent expansion of major international publishing houses such as Hachette, Simon & Schuster and HarperCollins into Indian markets, a lot of these writers are finding fertile ground for publishing science fiction.

In addition, the crop of Indian science-fiction works written in English also enjoys a specific readership. Widely regarded as an urban phenomenon, science fiction presumes a large proportion of the population to be science literate. Hence the readership of these works can also be mapped as belonging to a similar category. By conflating the present and future worlds, these authors imagine dystopias that speak directly to us. Along with the protagonists, the readers and the writers alike become suspects in their present worlds. The novels do not provide any easy gratifying conclusions about the evil or villainous nature of the tyrannical regimes. Therefore, the question as to whose vision of dystopia may appear to whom as the dawn of a new utopia, or vice versa, has some bearing on the discussion of utopias and dystopias in the world's largest democracy.

In conclusion, these novels certainly appear to be reworking the genre of classical Western utopia. The postcolonial themes of freedom, history and community are inextricably woven within these narratives. The concerns are avowedly those of caste, class and religious identity, spatially represented in oppressive dystopias. Both the novels use the physical and metaphorical 'wall' as their device for cognitive estrangement and memory as the site for exploring utopian and dystopian possibilities. The novels' self-reflexive approach, arising from their complex ideological position, betrays the anxieties and unique predicament of Indo-Anglian dystopian fiction. As argued here, these novels emphasise the process of 'becoming' rather than 'being' utopian or dystopian.

NOTES

1. A few critical studies on the subject include Patricia Kerslake's *Science Fiction and Empire* (2007), John Rieder's *Colonialism and the Emergence of Science Fiction* (2008), Jessica Langer's *Postcolonialism and Science Fiction* (2011), Suparno Banerjee's *Indian Science Fiction: Patterns, History and Hybridity* (2020) and Upmanyu Pablo Mukherjee's *Final Frontiers: Science Fiction and Techno-Science in Non-Aligned India* (2020).
2. This connection can be traced to the emergence of Bengali science-fiction stories in children's and young adult magazines such as *Sandesh*, *Mouchak*, *Ramdhanu* and *Rangmashal* in the early twentieth century (Banerjee 35).
3. Some of the leading scholarly works on postcolonial utopian studies include Bill Ashcroft's *Utopianism in Postcolonial Literatures* (2017), Lyman Tower Sargent's 'Colonial and Postcolonial Utopias' in *The Cambridge Companion to Utopian Literature* (2010), Ralph Pordzik's *The Quest for Postcolonial*

Utopia (2001), Tom Moylan's review article 'Utopia, the Postcolonial, and the Postmodern' (2001), Anupama Jain's 'Postcolonialism & Utopianism: "Real" Indians in the New World' (2012) and Corina Kesler's 'Postcolonial Utopias or Imagining "Brave New Worlds": Caliban Speaks Back' (2012).

4 Cogswell's story, first published in a magazine named *Beyond Fantasy Fiction*, narrates the tale of a young boy who is fascinated by an over-thousand-feet wall that surrounds their city and wishes to find out what lies beyond.

5 Here, the argument refers to the anticolonial and utopian visions of a soon-to-be independent nation as imagined by these thinkers. Gandhi's ideas are expressed prominently in *Hind Swaraj* and some later writings in newspapers such as *Young India* and *Harijan*. Similarly, Ambedkar's ideal of an equal social structure can be found in his powerful essay titled *Annihilation of Caste* and articles in the newspaper *Prabuddha Bharat* (Enlightened India). Savarkar's dream of India as an imperial power exemplifying the so-called pure and superior Hindu identity is articulated in his ideological pamphlet *Essentials of Hindutva* (1923).

6 '*Shoortan*' in Punjabi language means warrior.

7 In Hindu mythology Ramayana, Mithila is the kingdom ruled by Sita's father, Janak.

8 In the novel, Rama is the name of a girl who plays Mithila's love interest.

9 The name of the mythological bird that helped Rama in his quest to find Sita after her abduction by Ravana.

10 *What is to be Done? Burning Questions of Our Movement*, written by Russian revolutionary Vladimir Lenin in 1901, presented a blueprint of the political manoeuvres needed to bring about economic reforms as per Marxist ideology of change.

11 The utopian novel, in its specific treatment of literary language, creates an alternative world and carries the potential for many such new worlds made possible through its personification of utopian imagination.

12 Ashcroft, Pordzik and Sargent discuss the extensive role of memory within postcolonial utopian genre in their works. Ashcroft theorises memory as a marker of the past but also as a hankering after other possibilities. Pordzik's notion of heterotopias as multidimensional spatial structures in postcolonial literature is also situated at the juncture of memory, narrative and postmodern fluidity. Sargent describes cultural memory as significant to postcolonial societies.

13 Climate fiction or cli-fi is an important category of utopian/dystopian narratives emerging in India. In *Leila* (2017), climate crisis is the backdrop against which an overhaul of the existing society and the establishment of a new tyrannical order take place.

14 The reference to the Skydome project in the novel rang true only two years later with the launch of the first-ever clean oxygen bar named Oxy Pure in South Delhi in 2019. The news made headlines during the pollution haze of post-Diwali November and December months, when the city is covered in thick blanket of smog every year.

15 In *Leila*, the class unrest is visible in the demands raised by the slummers through their slogan 'Yeh azaadi jhooti hain … jhooti hain, jhooti hain [sic]' (Akbar 86). The call is reminiscent of the slogan first raised by the Communist Party of India soon after the country's independence in the early 1950s in order to fuel a peasant-led revolution in Hyderabad and Calcutta (Guha 241).

16 The role of ideology, rather than coercion, in maintaining the class hierarchy was first theorised by Antonio Gramsci in his *Prison Notebooks*.

17 The connections between ideology and utopia, as two attitudes towards social reality, have long been established by Marxist thinker Karl Mannheim in *Ideology and Utopia* (1929), which were later developed by Paul Ricœur.

18 'Builders' in Bhatia's novel refers to a set of semi-divine beings who initially lived in Sumer, but owing to various transgressions, decided to leave, only after enclosing Sumer within the wall.

19 The links between utopia, science fiction and colonialism are present from the very beginnings of the genre with Thomas More's *Utopia* (1551). The Western literary imagination saw the newly 'discovered' lands of the colonies as utopian sites for adventure and exploration. Later science fiction, Asimov onwards, also showed a similar approach with stories about other planetary invasions.

20 For a detailed survey of the history of SFF tradition in India, refer to Mimi Mondal's articles 'A Short History of South Asian Speculative Fiction, Part I and II'.
https://www.tor.com/2018/01/30/a-short-history-of-south-asian-speculative-fiction-part-i/
https://www.tor.com/2018/02/26/a-short-history-of-south-asian-speculative-fiction-part-ii/

WORKS CITED

Akbar, Prayaag. 2017. *Leila*. New Delhi: Simon & Schuster.

Ambedkar, B.R. 1916. 'Castes in India: Their Mechanism, Genesis and Development.' Paper presented at the Anthropology seminar, Columbia University, New York, 9 May.

Ashcroft, Bill. 2012. 'Introduction: Spaces of Utopia.' *Spaces of Utopia: An Electronic Journal*, 2(1): 1–17.

Banerjee, Suparno. 2010. 'Other Tomorrows: Postcoloniality, Science Fiction and India.' PhD Diss., Louisiana State University. https://digitalcommons.lsu.edu/gradschool_dissertations/3181.

———. 2020. *Indian Science Fiction: Patterns, History and Hybridity*. Cardiff: University of Wales Press.

Bhatia, Gautam. 2020. *The Wall*. New Delhi: HarperCollins.

Cogswell, Theodore R. 1974. *The Wall Around the World*. Pyramid Books.

Gandhi, M.K. 1946. *Harijan*, 28 July, p. 236.

Guha, Ramachandra. 2013. *Patriots and Partisans*. New Delhi: Penguin Books India.

Orwell, George. 1949. *1984*. London: Secker & Warburg.

Pordzik, Ralph. 2001. *The Quest for Postcolonial Utopia*. New York: Peter Lang.

Sargent, Lyman Tower. 2010. 'Colonial and Postcolonial Utopias.' In *The Cambridge Companion to Utopian Literature*, edited by Gregory Claeys. Cambridge: Cambridge University Press.

Suvin, Darko R. 1979. *Metamorphoses of Science Fiction: On the Poetics and History of a Literary Genre*. New Haven: Yale University Press.

Chapter 13

REMEMBERING/DISMEMBERING: TENUOUS UTOPIC FORMULATIONS IN NUR NASREEN IBRAHIM'S AND MIMI MONDAL'S SHORT STORIES

Srinjoyee Dutta

INTRODUCTION

By Editors

With the relocation of the utopic and/or the dystopic within the temporal actions of the past, postcolonial Indian SF narratives effectively efface the modalities of deferred possibilities, or impossibilities, within which these concepts usually play. The sought-after utopia or the feared dystopia is, in a sense, no longer somewhere in an (in)conceivable future but have already taken roots within the presences of the Indian Being. Neither do these have, anymore, the unavailability accorded to them through their spatial distance. They affect even as they germinate into stronger forces and carry the nation along to a future. But, in being such, what happens to the functionality of these phenomena? Do they retain their dichotomous characteristics of signalling hope (of the utopic) and despair (in the dystopic)? Or do they find a finer relationship outside the older and, decidedly, Western antagonistic ones?

Srinjoyee Dutta's present chapter begins with an in-depth analyses of not only the possible answers to these questions but these questions themselves. Her chapter seeks to find out how these phenomena find presencing not only within and through their ontico-ontological structuralities but also how, in finding these spaces, they relate to each other over the spectrum of their feigned difference. Further, since neither of these phenomena works outside of human existences, Dutta's chapter presents the lived, tactile and material dimensions of the theoretical framework she begins with.

What needs noting, then, is an implicit complication within the phenomena of utopia and dystopia, which necessitates, perhaps, a relook and reinterrogation of either of these as they are doled out in the name of the nation and wellness. This is a rather political stance to take, for if the utopic and dystopic are simply what they are and as they seem, not only would either the initiation of the utopic or the management of the dystopic be a problem, but both histories of the past as well as of the present have shown that such is not the case and that the two necessarily find utterance at the hearts of political polemic.

****

Robyn Wiegman, in the chapter 'The Desire for Gender',[1] opines that no politics, theoretical or pragmatic, is possible without fantastic conceptualisations. While she claims so specifically in the context of the contemporary debates around gender and queer identity, the logic of the argument can be transposed onto the fundamental need for political utopias in the multifarious and intersectional claims for social justice. It is, after all, only with the necessary visualisation of the 'perfect' society that the reigning political, sociocultural and historical status quo can be challenged.

Using this as a theoretical springboard, the paper will explore the literary formulation of utopias in Nur Nasreen Ibrahim's 'We Were Never Here' and Mimi Mondal's 'The Sea Sings at Night'. While Ibrahim's story reveals the many fault lines of the feminist utopic model(s), Mondal's piece foregrounds the impossibility of such existence, especially through the trappings of historically burdened identities such as caste and gender. Through the fictive and speculative lens provided by these stories, the chapter will attempt to critically examine the teleological and, thus, necessarily violent thrust in the formulation of the utopic. Further, it will problematise the futural, messianic impetus of utopic/dystopic possibilities, especially in the light of everyday dystopic struggles that plague marginalised identities. Both Ibrahim's and Mondal's fictions locate within the utopic possibility the homogenisation of identity within a single overarching paradigm and the subsequent social stratification/hierarchisation as an immutable repercussion. The chapter will, thus, analyse the significance of 'utopia/dystopia/ustopia'[2] as a theoretical concept, which, while a necessary formulation, needs to be continually deterritorialised and reterritorialised[3] for it to function as a viable goal in sociopolitical praxis.

There have been multifarious theoretical frameworks to understand the intertwined concepts of utopia and dystopia. While traditional criticism and theory often posited one as the antithesis to the other, especially placing the latter within the civilisational discontents that arose from the sociopolitical events of the twentieth century, modern perspectives regarding the two have become far more nebulous, nuanced and suspicious of the two projects as being distinct from each other. Further, the conceptual anchorage of the projects within a necessarily futural time as well as a necessarily demarcated space has also been brought into scrutiny, insofar as the thrust of the two concepts is now being analysed as deeply ingrained in contemporary chronos as well as topos. In the seminal work titled *Scraps of the Untainted Sky: Science Fiction, Utopia, Dystopia*, Tom Moylan locates in the dystopian impulse the ability to register the horrors of the everyday. He writes,

> Crucial to dystopia's vision in all its manifestations is this ability to register the impact of an unseen and unexamined social system on the everyday lives of everyday people. Again and again, the dystopian text opens in the midst of a social 'elsewhere' that appears to be far worse than any in the 'real' world. (2000)

Moylan establishes the crux of modern utopic or dystopic narrative within the systemic challenges that have arisen with the advent of late capitalism and its increasingly complex nexus of power relations as well as centres that defy the logic of universal solutions or revolutions. The very reason that these narratives are now intertwined with tangible struggles is based on the move towards micropolitical aggressions grounded in the idiosyncratically situated local. Moylan also posits that the allegation of 'escapism' often directed towards such narratives, especially vis-à-vis the genre of science fiction, can act as a critical vantage point via which one may be able to grapple with material and ideological sociopolitical aggressions. He employs this conceptual and critical variation of the traditional genre as the 'critical dystopia', a term borrowed from Lyman Tower Sargent, defined as,

> [A] textual mutation that self-reflexively takes on the present system and offers not only astute critiques of the order of things but also explorations of the oppositional spaces and possibilities from which the next round of political activism can derive imaginative sustenance and inspiration. Challenging capitalist power as well as conservative rule—and refusing the false 'utopianism' of reformist promises from neoliberals and compromised social democrats with their bad-faith exercises in 'third way' solutions—the new dystopias have rekindled the cold flame of critique and have thereby become a cultural manifestation of a broad-scale yet radically diverse alliance politics that is emerging as the twenty-first century commences. (ibid.)

Michael D. Gordon, Helen Tilley and Gyan Prakash, in a significant book titled *Utopia/Dystopia: Conditions of Historical Possibility*, begin by stating that 'Utopias and Dystopias are histories of the present' (2010). The aim of the text is to

> [R]evitalize the concepts of utopia and dystopia by treating them not so much as objects of study, but as historically grounded analytic categories with which to understand how individuals and groups around the world have interpreted their present tense with an eye to the future. (2010)

Their discursivisation carries the import of possibility, as the name of the book suggests, thereby inverting the very notion of utopia as etymologically and conceptually predicated on the condition of *impossibility*. They also locate the dystopic as a strictly twentieth-century formulation that is, in essence, utopia's doppelganger. In short, the quasi-oppositional force of the dystopian is investigated as the monstrous child of utopia, its most dangerous creation. They thus write that '[e]very utopia always comes with its implied dystopia—whether the dystopia of the status quo, which the utopia is engineered to address, or a dystopia found in the way this specific utopia corrupts itself in practice' (ibid.).

Thus, this deliberate situating of the utopian and dystopian logic, bound, as it were, with the logic of a demarcated time and space continuum within contemporary political praxis, seeks to wrench the aforementioned concepts from their alleged apolitical dimensionality and place them squarely within a process of becoming. In short, the conditions of 'historical possibility' can only be achieved through the deconstruction of teleological frameworks and reconstruction of the idea within a more experiential, explosive everyday reality. This reality, steeped within the entropic chaos that characterises the quotidian, then, seeks to shift the conceptual anchors that define utopia/dystopia as confined within ossified space-time coordinates into contemporaneous eventualities and vulnerabilities that arise from that very chaos.

Erin McKenna in *The Task of Utopia: A Pragmatic and Feminist Perspective* places the aforementioned concerns within a gendered framework and examines the ways in which the traditional utopic/dystopic formulations, be it through the 'end of state model' or the 'anarchist model', fail to provide the succour of a transformed society especially given its formative hypermasculine and patriarchal impulse. In an attempt to save these formulations from being purely theoretical paradigms, subject to the easy slip from the utopic to the dystopic, McKenna conflates the problem of universalism with masculine totalitarianism and suggests that the man-woman dualism that continues to haunt these concepts must be investigated from a vantage point of both theory and ongoing political praxis. Questioning the idea of apathy and cynicism as necessary ramifications of the utopic-turned-dystopic paradigm, she formulates a new model of utopia based on feminist thought emerging from the notion of the 'subject in process'[4] and political pragmatism to which this chapter shall return shortly.

Ibrahim's short story 'We Were Never Here', in which women suddenly leave a deeply patriarchal order to create a separate space for themselves and embark on the process of ridding themselves of the touch of history as well as phallogocentric pedagogical markers, exemplifies both the necessity of such spaces as well as the invariable fault lines that emerge within the same, subject, as it were, to the formation of a different totalitarian paradigm. Tarun K. Saint in his introduction to *The Gollancz Book of South Asian Science Fiction* looks at this formulation as an ironising of Rokeya Sakhawat Hossain's feminist utopia in *Sultana's Dream* (2019)[5]. Interestingly, the thrust of the title, which is at once spatial, temporal and ontological, refers to *not being here/there* both in the society that the women leave behind as well as the new order they inhabit, thereby indicating erasure as an intrinsic quality of the totalitarian utopian paradigm. Ibrahim deftly manoeuvres this by placing a living, breathing, novel entity/society made up entirely of oppressed women who decide to leave their homes, families and friends, within the realm of the theoretical, quoting imagined theorists from the imaginary eighth, ninth and tenth waves of feminism. This speculative lens is further aided by the fact that the quotes that pepper the story act as futural citations, thereby moulding the form of the short story into a quasi-academic theoretical paper.

The 'ironizing sweep', as Saint puts it, which is both substantive and formal, therefore indicates the tenuous nature of the utopian practice that moors itself on theoretical principles. In short, the gap or dissonance that emerges from visualising theory on the street is analogic to the creation of a dialogic universe that is bound to fail, in the Dostoevskian sense, when high theory meets the entropic nature of everyday praxis. The erasure, thus, occurs at two levels: in the society that the women leave behind in the hope of a better order as well as the subsequent erasure that occurs when differential desires, identities and character traits are forcefully assimilated into a myopic feminist paradigm. In the end, in keeping with this kind of speculative order, Ibrahim leaves us no answers but more questions that emerge when one authoritative order is replaced with another. The utopic sensibility slips quickly into the dystopic and the reader is left with the uneasy sense that vestiges of history are impossible to escape and that the tenuous messianic impulse of the new society is subject to the same hegemonic paradigm that necessitated its formation in the first place. The theoretical speculation that characterises the red economy posited by Luce Irigaray[6] is brought into rigorous scrutiny in the formation of a new universe that, in its bid to escape gender and class hierarchies, falls back into the same patterns, albeit with novel identity categories. The violence that women's bodies had been subjected to transforms into the violence of assimilation; for instance, the rejection of queer identities within the new paradigms reinstate the very dualistic, Cartesian[7] thinking that had been at the core of the older order. Ibrahim frames these problems subtextually insofar as the haunting or spectral quality of *not being here* is carried forward into the new order. She writes of these implications, especially in the context of the cultural and historical specificities of South Asia:

> Our divisions grow. We no longer remember what we ran away from. The outside world seems like a distant nightmare, a hazy recollection of another's life .... We had been duped, we had blindly followed an idea without a goal. We are cattle, gratefully responding to any sound of freedom ringing from a convincing source .... So we wait and bicker. We watch the sun rise and fall from our mattresses, we visualize our city in the distance, the old domain of mosques and minarets fallen into disrepair, of empires long destroyed, the city of men that will age into nothingness .... We forget our old lives, we forget if we were lawyers, doctors, wives, beggars, prostitutes, mothers, teachers, beauticians, labourers, servants. We let them forget us, as if we were never there to begin with. (Ibrahim 2019)

The terrain of Mondal's story 'The Sea Sings at Night' set in Mumbai grapples with the question of gender and caste through the speculative lens. While there is a similar strain of tenuousness in the story, the setting is that of a utopia in motion, already in practice, which is nonetheless strained by a similar vein of assimilation. As someone who identifies herself as a queer Dalit writer of SF, Mondal has herself described the story as the tale of a crumbling relationship, thereby situating the crux of the text within the logic of the everyday.[8] While Ibrahim's story looks at the utopic turned dystopic model as necessarily violently one-dimensional in its enforcing of one identity category, Mondal's story delves into the nuances of an intersectional paradigm that fails in its egalitarian promise. She employs liminality both as a concept and tangible space in order to raise questions regarding that promise. The narrator's partner, called 'Matsa' (fish or creature of the sea), is described as an amphibious creature who can inhabit both land and sea. The literal divide of land and sea in Mumbai is used to formulate both the categories of caste and queerness embodied within the amphibian body that symbolises physical as well as figurative otherness. Mondal writes,

> Even after the midnight madness, you rush into the kitchen, clothes and skin and long hair dripping, trailing so many streams on the floor. You grab small fish out of the bowl I had bought you and

> devour them raw with your fingers. You look hungry, panicked, trapped. You don't want me to hold you. I think you're crying. I think in your language you're crying, though the low, guttural cadence that soars from your throat sounds like surf song to me. (Mondal 2019)

As the relationship fails at the end and the narrator's partner moves back into the sea, leaving behind the dominant narrative of the land as the stable, central signifier of identity, the force of political assimilation, hinging on the knowledge of intersectionality, crumbles. Yet, this crumbling is not neat: the divide that situates these either/or figurations is lacerated, the wound of violence is amply clear, and as the narrator's bed turns into a sea late at night, Mondal seems to point towards the fragility of the threshold space that seeks in vain to demarcate. The rupture indicates two kinds of impossibility: the first is of the attempt at assimilation of the sea into land or, more explicitly, of caste and queer identities into hegemonic ontological systems of living, while the second is the impossibility of isolated existence of the two as contradistinctive ways of living. This osmotic relationship between 'fishy, slimy' beings who are forced to inhabit spaces that are literally cast out and those who inhabit the 'land' life is subject to violent foreclosure: the story ends with individuated despair translating into systemic melancholia, laying bare the implicit and ingrained equations of power that continue to haunt the speculative utopia. In that sense, this story too is haunted by its own history. The displacement of the topos and chronos is unable to shed the vestiges of the historical, and thus entails the condition of utopic impossibility. Thus, the posthuman continues to be haunted by the human, calling into question the triumph of the 'post' phenomenon. Aditya Nigam, in 'The Heterotopias of Dalit Politics: Becoming Subject and the Consumption Utopia', employs the concept of heterotopia, as theorised by Michel Foucault as 'other spaces', to suggest that the formation of such spaces is often carried out in order to maintain the perfection of a hegemonic order, that is, the maintenance of the historically utopic and privileged in the light of an imminent dystopia of caste sociality that might subvert the order. Therein utopia as a concept is deployed not as a futural promise but an ossified system of the past that demands preservation in order to maintain order. In opposition to that, Nigam opines that heterotopia of difference, which espouse a differential 'normality' within the conservative order, especially as figurative rather than literal spaces, tend to challenge the utopia of the past. He looks at these heterotopias as instrumental in Deleuzian nomadic becoming[9], which goes against assigned history. While Nigam's argument employs as its textual pivot the idea of the Dalit countermove embodied in processes of consumption and opulence hitherto forbidden to Dalit communities both in terms of lifestyle and semiotic registers, the premise of the argument itself can be transposed onto the larger problem of marginalisation that seems to be intertwined within utopic promise as seen in the aforementioned stories. Mauro Pala in 'From Hegemony to Heterotopias: Geography as Epistemology in Gramsci and Foucault' writes,

> Thus, we are dealing with a multi-level spatial analysis, which is, however, always dominated by the space of the power-knowledge relation; a level is made up of an urban space, that is to say, the spaces of social life where forms of organization and control are most evident, including the sharing and distribution of power at the level of the human body. Human bodies are themselves an individual sphere, but they are interconnected with the environment. (2016)

Mondal's story locates this spatial-corporeal nexus within the queer as well as caste-ridden body to create crytozoological[10] animal others who evoke both desire and disgust. A speculative mythologisation of those bodies then seeks to challenge the entrenched myths of the past, while invoking the impossibility of erasing the processes of historical, sociocultural formations in the creation of the new world. This deployment of the monster within and without echoes Margaret Atwood's notion of urban monsters that continue to thrive in gentrified neighbourhoods, displaced, as it were, by hegemonic cartographic practices that seek to create boundaries between the known and the unknown. Atwood claims that 'We tidied up, we gentrified, we put in streetlights; so the rowdy and uncontrollable bohemians of the imagination—always dwellers in the penumbras—had to move on' (2011). She coins the term 'ustopia' precisely to delineate the impossibility of creating a utopia that does not contain within itself its very own monstrous dystopia. She questions, 'Why is it that when we grab for heaven—socialist or capitalist or even religious—we so often produce hell?' (ibid.).

Moylan explicates SF and utopia as a process that foregrounds its context, its social setting, insofar as the reader studies what is usually in the background, as essential to the sense-making process of new world order. Both Ibrahim and Mondal problematise this foregrounding as always already haunted by the displaced background, the discarded ontological and ontic systems that continue to haunt the myth-to-come. The mythifying exercise is, thus, an exercise in creating historical foundations for novel societies. In that sense, what is utopic is always already a question of the past and that which is to come is intertwined with that which has been. The new modes of interpellation are, thus, modes of actively participating in the past. Darko Suvin's foundational idea of the 'novum'[11] is, therefore, both reinforced and challenged by both these stories where the factual logic of the new world is burdened by the logic of shed history. Moylan opines that 'in Suvin's formulation, the novum has revolutionary effect *only* if it functions in dynamic relationship to the changing, historically specific structures of feeling out of which it develops and the unnamable horizon of an ongoing history toward which it tends' (2000).

He further goes on to write that the critical dystopia as a literary project is, thus, neither utopia nor anti-utopia. While it contains within itself the facts of resignation as well as pessimism, its force as a critically changing 'model in process' allows it to be the harbinger of gradual change. He claims,

> Thus, the distinction can be made between the limited case of an open (epical) dystopia that retains a utopian commitment at the core of its formally pessimistic presentation and a closed (mythic) one that abandons the textual ambiguity of dystopian narrative for the absolutism of an anti-utopian stance. (ibid.)

Feminist or gendered narratives as posited in these stories often combine both. Erin McKenna in her model of utopic thinking, which links feminist theory with pragmatism, bases itself in the rejection of the dualism that haunts both Mondal's and Ibrahim's fictions. With a strong suspicion of returning to small communities that often enforce singular standards of ontological and epistemological thought in order to preserve themselves, McKenna endorses a deconstructionist view that embodies continued critical engagement with projects that hinge on universal ideas. In that sense, the critical utopia or dystopia project, as evidenced in Ibrahim's and Mondal's short fictions, posits the need for the formulation of the utopia/dystopia as a rhizomatic[12] assemblage, especially in its occupation of differential space(s) and time(s). The utopic/ dystopic subject is, thus, a 'subject in process' located within a 'concept in process'. It comprises differential components that allow it to shift contours dynamically instead of entailing the promise of a rigid messianic idea that is unable to turn the critical gaze inwards and onto the sociopolitical and cultural moorings that form the basis of hope, melancholia, remembering and dismembering.

NOTES

1 From *A Companion to Lesbian, Gay, Bisexual, Transgender, and Queer Studies* edited by George E. Haggerty and Molly McGarry.

2 Ustopia is a term coined by Margaret Atwood in 'Dire Cartographies: The Roads to Ustopia: *The Handmaid's Tale* and the MaddAddam Trilogy' in *In Other Worlds*. That paper explores the concept later.

3 The term 'deterritorialization' often accompanied by 'reterritorialization' refers to the conceptualisation of the 'assemblage' as a dynamic and fluid entity or a body/concept/theory united by heterogeneous components that cannot be ossified as theorised by Gilles Deleuze and Felix Guattari in *A Thousand Plateaus: Capitalism and Schizophrenia*.

4 The concept of the 'subject in process' was first theorised by Julia Kristeva as a gendered being that defies the stasis of a unitary subjecthood and is given to continual mobility. For the purpose of this paper, it refers to the utopic subject who may critically engage with ossified identity categories that often characterise utopic formulations.

5 A foundational piece of South Asian speculative fiction, *Sultana's Dream* describes a feminist utopia in which women control the major aspects of society and the men are kept locked in a technologically distant future.

6 In 'When the Goods Get Together', Irigaray posits the need for a gender economy wherein women are in transaction with each other as opposed to being goods of exchange in a homosocial phallogocentric society.

7 This refers to René Descartes' theorisation of the mind-body duality in which the realm of the mental is distinct from the corporeal, such that the former determines the latter.

8 As recorded in an interview with Mimi Mondal, available on the *Feminism in India* website.

9 Gilles Deleuze and Felix Guttari define 'nomad becoming' as a tendency towards continual deterritoralisation such that the subject is not a fixed ontological category in *A Thousand Plateaus: Capitalism and Schizophrenia*.

10 Cryptozoology is the study of animals whose existence is subject to debate or remains unsubstantiated.

11 The novum is a concept used by Suvin to describe the logical plausibility of scientific innovation in science fiction imagined through a process of cognitive estrangement.

12 Gilles Deleuze and Felix Guattari employ the symbol of the rhizome to denote the possibility of multiple and non-hierarchical interpretations, modes and flow of meaning and desire in *A Thousand Plateaus* and partly in *Anti-Oedipus*.

WORKS CITED

Atwood, Margaret. 2011. 'Dire Cartographies: The Roads to Ustopia: *The Handmaid's Tale* and the MaddAddam Trilogy.' *In Other Worlds: SF and the Human Imagination*. New York: Vintage Books.

Deleuze, Gilles, and Felix Guattari. 1983. *Anti-Oedipus: Capitalism and Schizophrenia*. Minneapolis: University of Minnesota Press.

Deleuze, Gilles, and Felix Guattari. 1987. *A Thousand Plateaus: Capitalism and Schizophrenia*. Minneapolis: University of Minnesota Press.

Descartes, René. (1637) 2008. *A Discourse on Method*. Project Gutenberg E-book.

Gordon, Michael D., Helen Tilley and Gyan Prakash. 2010. 'Introduction.' In *Utopia/Dystopia: Conditions of Historical Possibility*. Princeton: Princeton University Press.

Ibrahim, Nur Nasreen. 2019. 'We Were Never Here.' In *The Gollancz Book of South Asian Science Fiction*, edited by Tarun K. Saint. New Delhi: Hachette India.

Irigaray, Luce. 1985. 'When the Goods Get Together.' In *The Sex which Is Not One*. Translated by Catherine Porter. New York: Cornell University Press.

McKenna, Erin. 2001. *The Task of Utopia: A Pragmatist and Feminist Perspective*. Lanham: Rowman & Littlefield Publishers.

Moi, Toril. 2002. *Sexual/Textual Politics: Feminist Literary Theory*. New York: Routledge.

Mondal, Mimi. 2019. 'The Sea Sings at Night.' In *The Gollancz Book of South Asian Science Fiction*, edited by Tarun K. Saint. New Delhi: Hachette India.

Moylan, Tom. 2000. *Scraps of the Untainted Sky: Science Fiction, Utopia, Dystopia*. Boulder: Westview Press.

Nigam, Aditya. 2010. 'The Heterotopias of Dalit Politics: Becoming Subject and the Consumption Utopia.' In *Utopia/Dystopia: Conditions of Historical Possibility*, edited by Michael D. Gordon, Helen Tilley and Gyan Prakash. Princeton: Princeton University Press.

Pala, Mauro. 2016. 'From Hegemony to Heterotopias: Geography as Epistemology in Gramsci and Foucault.' In *The Globalization of Space*, edited by Mariangela Palladino and John Miller. New York: Routledge.

Varma, Pallavi. 2018. 'Meet Mimi Mondal: India's First SFF Writer Nominated for a Hugo.' In *Feminism In India*. https://feminisminindia.com/2018/05/09/interview-mimi-mondal-ssf-writer/ (accessed on 5 March 2021).

Wiegman, Robyn. 2007. 'The Desire for Gender.' In *A Companion to Lesbian, Gay, Bisexual, Transgender, and Queer Studies*, edited by George E. Haggerty and Molly McGarry. New Jersey: Blackwell.

Chapter 14

FUTURISM IN INDIAN CINEMA: A CASE STUDY OF *ANUKUL*

Jigyasa H. Sondhi

INTRODUCTION

By Editors

The figure of the cyborg/android/robot has been one of the most traditional motifs in SF narratives. The presence of such figures is celebratory since it is symptomatic of the prolific advances made in the fields of science and technology and also simultaneously cautionary as it comes dangerously close to the sacred power of imbuing life. These man-made creatures have either been treated as figures of pity and empathy, as in the case of the 'monster' created by Frankenstein or vilified as creatures of malice, synonymous with technology's destructive drive to obliterate any form of human agency or will. The process of learning or enhancing the intelligence complex of such creatures is often explained in terms of a dynamic and adaptive algorithm that strives towards constant improvement. While this form of machine-based algorithmic activity is the rationale behind the more functional and practical component of artificial intelligence, how does one conceptualise their existence as conscientious beings? Jigyasa H. Sondhi addresses this conundrum by looking at Sujoy Ghosh's movie *Anukul* (2017), a cinematic adaptation of Satyajit Ray's short story of the same title published in 1976. The robot in question here, named Anukul, is imagined as a mechanised entity designed to consume any form of knowledge available to him in order to improve its performance. However, both Ray and Ghosh push the envelope by representing Anukul as a being capable of imbibing the moral and ethical lessons contained in the Bhagavad Gita, one of the foremost religious texts in Hinduism. As a result, one sees a curious hybrid formation where technologically mediated artificial intelligence is tempered by mythological learnings and values embedded in years of tradition. In some ways, Sondhi's reading of the movies substantiates the claims regarding the contextual nature of science made by several scholars of Indian SF, including Suparno Banerjee who argues that science is constituted quite differently in India as a mixture of modernity, ancient folktales and religious beliefs. As the constitution of science itself is subverted, the nature of questions raised regarding the relationship between the self and the other is also diversified, giving rise to a culturally specific exploration of subjects such as the human consciousness, morality and duty, among others.

****

There are a number of ingress options for commencing a science-fictional investigation of literature. Cinema is one of them. Yet, for some peculiar reason, conventional SF films are often regarded as pure humdrum fare by a majority of viewers and censors. An evaluation such as this has fortified the biases against this genre of movies, indicating that they are more often than not ignored and disregarded, not only by movie appraisers who deem them too insignificant to be considered sincerely but also by major SF experts. Their outlook and relevance, the argument goes, is minimal, and they are at best exotic creations of another world, patronised by people of dreary intellectual capabilities. Although SF accommodates a diversity of perspectives, its deployment of symbols and characters in direct actions as well as its revaluing of qualities traditionally associated with the future is read by some as signs that this philosophy is dyed in the wool, essentialist, homogenising or, in reality, unhopeful—that it rests on a degenerating notion of the world as incompetent and unserviceable. Theorists have repeatedly observed that the openness and diversity of its presumptuous politics exist in tension with the universalist, essentialist formulations of a great deal of conjectural rhetoric. Recent trends, however, have been encouraging; this condescension of critics and the resolute indifference of the academic community seems to be slowly diminishing. An increasing number of people are realising that SF films are developing in scope and influence; they are spreading beyond their original home in fictional studies and colonising new niches in related fields, such as canon literature, cartoons and graphic books. Yet, rarely has cinema in general been viewed through an Indian-SF critical lens nor has there been much evidence in the main avenues of film criticism of the sustained application of futuristic strategies to SF cinema studies.

In light of this problem of the Indian SF film, this work attempts to take a close look at the relationship between a dominant single view of the future and modernity, in the present context of the commercial transformation of Indian visual culture and media, through Sujoy Ghosh's 2017 movie *Anukul*, based on a 1976 short story of the same title by Satyajit Ray, with respect to SF. It tries to explore prospective images in this 21-minute film, with attention to phantasmagorias of the future in the depictions of artificial intelligence to show not only the intellectual capacities of the SF film but also the complexities of imagined futures as they find themselves moored to a particular Indian mythological history. In showing the viewer an image and a perceptiveness to examine via visualisation itself, *Anukul*, the current paper proposes, allows the audience an observation of how the Indian future is both imagined and affected especially within the limits of their own proto-historical identities. The film, quite like Ray's story, does this through the inclusion of the Bhagavad Gita. As a note of caution, the current paper intends to show a prototype rather than a singularity. In other words, in presenting a Hindu mythological rootedness in the film's vision of the Indian future, the current paper does not intend to suggest that an Indian identity can only be a Hindu identity. The film, and its reading thereof, becomes a possibility for the presentation of a framework to include the mythological within the future. That it is a Hindu one is but coincidental.

The story is set in an imminent dystopian time when human beings are shown to coexist with robots. (Ray didn't set the story in a futuristic timeline; he chose to build the entire narrative in contemporary settings.) A Hindi schoolteacher Nikunj Chaturvedi, played by Saurabh Shukla, buys an android named Anukul, played by Parambrata Chattopadhyay, from a corporate agency, Chowringhee Robot Supply Corporation (CRS), in Kolkata. Interestingly, CRS's logo is a large eye, perhaps indicative of constant vigil or surveillance over human beings. This logo also echoes the natural division of the middle part of our head where the thalamus, the pineal and the pituitary glands are situated. Curiously, the pineal gland is referred to as the third eye. It is thought to be the centre of spiritual insight, which can be developed by anyone through some mind practices. Though oddly coincidental, it is nonetheless fascinating to consider the interrelatedness between them—that a certain part of the brain, otherwise regarded as the focal point of consciousness, mirrors an eye, the gateway to our being. It can stand for wisdom, secrecy, mystery, as well as be an indicator of good or evil. CRS's logo brings to mind the fictional, infallible and powerful character of Big Brother from George Orwell's 1949 polemical novel *Nineteen Eighty-Four*. CRS might also eventually metamorphose into an almighty institution in itself, replacing not only humans but also the concept of God. While in *Anukul*'s context the CRS eye symbol is used to represent the omniscience of an almighty AI being, it can be examined as a power symbol representing a new and upcoming upper crust of robots and/or semi-robots spying on humanity atop their superstructure. Constant monitoring usually translates into hegemonising the world through suppression. In India, the precursor to what eventually became known as the 'All Seeing Eye' in one of the oldest known texts the Rig Veda was written more than thirty centuries ago. Rig Veda refers to several symbols of the sun and other deities as being akin to eyes in heaven, at times an eye that never closes, or even as an eye that reveals creation. (Discussed below is a theory wherein once Anukul's transformation into a living being of sorts is complete, his attachment to his *guru*, Nikunj babu, becomes intensely fervent; Nikunj babu is likewise transmogrified into a powerful untouchable demigod, part human and part android. He is already a teacher and has ample observation and reasoning power. This results in Nikunj babu controlling the populace, with the help of Anukul, as his deputy, and a multitude of robots, thus resulting in elitist control.) Ghosh's directorial traces an inner turmoil between what is right and what is duty, as well as the meaning of artificial intelligence in a country such as India. Yet this conflict is not limited to human beings alone; it assumes a much larger scale because it is also, at its very core, the conflict between two strikingly different sets of ethics: humanitarian and *dharmic*.

Figure 14.1. Kolkata's skyline with the CRS building towering over the city. Notice the enormous eye as CRS's symbol, evoking George Orwell's novel *Nineteen Eighty-Four* and the fictional character of Big Brother keeping watch over Kolkata and controlling its people.

The robot Anukul, designed to do any work with no 'overtime' and 'time off', becomes a part of Nikunj's household as a housekeeper and starts observing things and people around him. The supervisor behind the desk at the CRS office (henceforth to be known as the YES lady) also informs Nikunj babu that Anukul is a voracious reader, ridiculously infatuated with books and knowledge. He would also learn and glean as much as he can from his master, just as a *shishya* (student) learns from its *guru* (teacher). As a companion/domestic help, the human-android Anukul's unceasing functionality, his ability to comprehend the environment around him and his endless thirst for knowledge, makes him quite exciting and enticing. Ghosh's deliberate setting of the future in present circumstances gives the audience the sensation and pseudo-experience of just how 'ordinary' it would be to exist with AI.

Figure 14.2. The lady behind the desk at CRS telling Nikunj babu that Anukul is an advanced model. She is labelled 'YES', symbolic of the company's capability to do everything.

One scene stands out here: The YES lady tells Nikunj babu to use his thumb instead of his signature. Being a teacher, perhaps Nikunj babu is taken aback, though he readily complies. In India, an illiterate male is required to put the impression of his left thumb (right thumb for females) on a document in compliance with acknowledging the execution of the same. Since time immemorial, the fingerprint has been used in India as a signature on paper documents and is considered as a sign of an illiterate man. Even today, many semi-literate people find it difficult to develop and maintain unique written signatures. However, in the film in this particular scene, not only is the use of the fingerprint a universal mechanism to authenticate the user of an electronic document or a contract, but it is also a subtle way to downgrade a human being. Plus, human beings have distinct fingerprints, no two being the same. A robot has not been able to achieve that till now.

This is immediately followed by another pertinent scene that piques the viewer's curiosity. The YES lady gives one final and vital piece of information, though the same is never revealed immediately. This is a tried and tested, albeit a brilliant hook in storytelling: the Appetiser (terminology mine). The author/filmmaker/narrator gives the reader/viewer a slice to wait and salivate; Ghosh sells the idea without the idea in itself, that something is extremely important. The YES lady says, 'One more important thing' and trails off, until the scene cuts to Nikunj babu and Anukul travelling in a yellow taxi, presumably to the former's home.

Figure 14.3. The YES lady on the brink of revealing an important piece of information piques the audience's interest.

Nikunj babu welcomes Anukul warmly into his home, and Ghosh's few scenes about the master–servant relationship are clearly etched out. 'From today it is our home', Nikunj babu, in a way, embraces Anukul by sharing his house with him from then on, similar to how a *guru* used to invite *shishyas* to live with them and their family and obtain knowledge. The director also infuses scenes of the robot earnestly and voraciously reading one book after another, immersed in the myriad tales and theories, concepts and beliefs. An interesting phenomenon happens on screen: human beings watch a robot learn, evolve and adapt to not only look human but also become as close to being human as possible. Nikunj babu and Anukul settle into an easy, harmonious relationship.

In the next scene, Nikunj babu's cousin brother Ratan, played by Kharaj Mukherjee, is bitter about the fact that he has been replaced at work by a robot. Human-like androids have started taking over all kinds of jobs that earlier employed human beings. They are robots that are programmed to work without any time off. Ratan makes an apt observation, perhaps his sole intelligent dialogue, about humans being only nifty enough to build robots but not responsible enough to keep them in check: 'We humans are only smart enough to build robots. Once built, you suddenly become way smarter than us' (original film translation). Being drunk, he becomes furious and lashes out at Anukul, slamming a hot electric iron on his head in an attempt to damage it, calling him a 'Dumb robot! Not so smart now are you?', reminding the audience that humans did, indeed, invent artificial intelligence and not the other way around. If need be, these robots could be simply switched off and discarded.

The YES lady supervisor reminds Nikunj babu that in cases such as these, the robot is allowed to give a 'high voltage electric shock' to anyone who threatens it. This is that vital piece of information the audience is waiting for, which is inserted at an opportune yet unexpected slot in the movie. When Ratan hits Anukul, the 'secret' information is revealed to the audience.

Figure 14.4. The YES lady admonishes and reminds Nikunj babu about the consequences of hitting/instigating a robot.

And then, another brilliant scene follows:

Figure 14.5. A forewarning that will vibrate and lead to the conclusion as well as answer questions about the film as a whole.

The YES lady also makes a ludicrous statement: a robot has rights just like human beings do. Such a proclamation has been unheard of; why do robots deserve any rights in the first place? Even though they are programmed to look like humans, think and analyse, talk, they are not and cannot be human beings. They are different from living creatures in that they are not living, and they run on electricity or batteries. They might be invincible on the outside but they can be switched off.

After getting his chips replaced, Anukul and Nikunj babu discuss the Bhagavad Gita and the importance of duty. Nikunj emphasises that Anukul must always honour his dharma before anything else. 'Nothing is more important than duty,' he says. Yet, how would a robot understand the matters of the heart? AI is fundamentally built that way: to inherently follow the mind and analyse the situation methodically. The heart has no place in a robotic structure. Nonetheless, Ray/Ghosh picked up and utilised the most basic tenet of AI: questioning everything. Anukul's constant curiosity about the environment around him, which is yet to tip the scale in favour of robots taking over and is majorly still comprised of human beings who are waging a war on AI, makes him human or at least gives him a taste of becoming a living organism.

Figure 14.6. The teacher Nikunj babu imparts knowledge to his student, Anukul, similar to Krishna and Arjuna's relationship in the Bhagavad Gita.

Nikunj babu patiently answers Anukul's queries about duty and conscience. When Nikunj babu mentions God and immortality, the conversation takes a 'human' turn.

> Anukul: Even I cannot die
> Nikunj babu: Krishna is asking Arjun to do his duty .... Duty changes with your circumstances.... My duty is to maintain the house, pay the bills.
> Anukul: My duty is to look after you .... But how do we know which side is right or wrong?
> Nikunj babu: Your conscience. (Original English translation from the film)

Figure 14.7. In a vital scene of, perhaps, utmost importance, the human teacher tells his human-like robot 'student' about the heart. Whenever in doubt, he says, follow your conscience.

Later, Ratan comes home inebriated and in high spirits to inform Nikunj that their uncle Nibaran has died and that he has left his inheritance in Ratan's name, making him a millionaire overnight. Despite being disinherited, Nikunj babu does his duty by going to his uncle's home to pay his last respects. At that moment when Nikunj babu is in his bedroom, a clap of thunder is heard, followed by the death of his cousin Ratan. He dies of 'high voltage electric shock'. Of course, the truth behind his death is known only to Nikunj babu and Anukul. It is left to the audience/reader to decide whether Ratan attacked Anukul or Anukul lied about being threatened by Ratan to switch *it* off. Sure enough, after Ratan's death, Nikunj babu becomes the sole heir to the inheritance. Anukul keeps its hand over its heart and smiles at its master; Nikunj babu returns the gesture, leaving the audience to interpret what really happened.

Figure 14.8. Shifting points of view: Anukul and Nikunj babu. Is the transformation complete?

The film utilises the Bhagavad Gita as a narrative force as the conversation between Krishna and Arjuna is approached from a fresh perspective. Lord Krishna clarifies to Arjuna that if one performs one's duty without a second thought, dharma will automatically lead the person to liberation. Krishna here assumes the role of the *guru*, the teacher, who leads the mortal Arjuna towards the correct path of practical realisation. Krishna's teachings to Arjuna highlight that all wars first exist in the mind; winning the mind is the first step to winning in the battlefield and real life. Though a digression, it is important to remember at this juncture that the greater part of most SF films consists of either man/woman in space, aliens on Earth or robots. These are tropes that become difficult to aestheticise due to their speculative nature. *Anukul* stands out amongst the SF film genre in India for this very reason. It has adeptly handled this issue. It uses the Gita as an ally in its plotline, without disturbing its most important sermon. Religious teachings are usually not conducive to SF and SF filming; however, here it has been controlled well, for want of a better word. By extension, the Gita has represented the depth of duty better than any other theory. Psychologically too, the viewer becomes honour-bound to follow their conscience. When the audience sees Anukul placing its hand over its heart, this emotion does not enter as an unexpected guest. The film builds up to that inevitable point of the 'practical' once the 'theory' has been explained and argued. There is also nothing morbid about seeing Ratan's death due to a robot, as well as the coincidence of a flash of thunder and lightning at the same time. SF literature and cinema are usually associated with life and death. In *Anukul* though, this symbology is toppled on its head, and the audience is also able to justify this overturning. Due to the urge (and the reasoning behind it) to protect each other, both Nikunj babu and Anukul keep changing their relationship undauntingly as they follow their heart, conscience and dharma.

Hindu texts and mythologies are the original narrative genre of Indian cinema; films inspired by traditional stories have usually contributed to the Indian popular cultural imagination. It was with *Raja Harishchandra*, India's first full-length feature film, that cinema took birth. Ramanand Sagar's epic visualisation of the Ramayana and the Chopras' televisual adaptation of the Mahabharat broke all records and became successful beyond comparison. Cartoon characters such as Hanuman and Chhota Bheem are considered the largest children's entertainment brand in India. An important case in point is the 1975 movie *Jai Santoshi Maa*. It was a small-budget movie, with unknown actors and erstwhile stars, but it became one of the three highest box office blockbusters, the other two being *Deewaar* and *Sholay*. This bewildered critics and intrigued scholars but made perfect sense to millions of Indians who loved its folksy story about a new 'Goddess of Satisfaction' easily accessible through a simple ritual, which the film also demonstrates. It gave a neo-Indian inflexion to the American pop-critical term 'cult film', for viewers often turned cinemas into temporary temples, leaving their footwear at the door, 'pelting' flowers and coins at the screen and bowing reverently whenever the goddess appeared.

The list of films inspired by mythologies is long: *Yasoda Krishna* (Telugu, 1975), S.S. Rajamouli's 2015 and 2017 blockbusters *Baahubali* Parts 1 and 2, *Kalyug* (Hindi, 1981), *Rajneeti* (Hindi, 2010), *Dashavatar* (Hindi, 2008), *Krishna aur Kans* (Hindi, 2012), *Sri Rama Rajyam* (Telugu, 2011), amongst many others. Many superhits in Hollywood are based on the concepts of Hinduism as well: *The Legend of Bagger Vance* (2000), *10,000 B.C.* (2008), *Doctor Strange* (2016), *Avatar* (2009) and the *Matrix* series (1999–2003). Mythology as a phenomenon cannot be made to disappear, especially since myths germinate from the very meaning of human existence itself. Rather than asking how something is interpreted differently today, it is pertinent to state how every epoch is distinct and is distinguished by its approaches, interpretations, reasoning power and ability to think beyond what was previously accepted as fact. It is this neo approach that Ghosh has recast in *Anukul*. By keeping the original—the reference to Bhagavad Gita or Ray's interpretation of SF—intact, the filmmaker has filled in the need for a story to be retold. More importantly, he has mediated the desire for a larger-than-life saviour, a heroic figure, who is also sacrosanct. Contemporary perspectives about the future, along with the derivation of meanings that were earlier unexplored, give the mind the freedom to be creative, analytical as well as universally appealing. The reader/viewer can today relate to the stories narrated aeons ago. It is now routine to explore, rather re-interpret and revive, Hindu identity via its mythology.

One of the tropes of SF 'rebirth' also manifests literally and metaphorically in *Anukul*. As a code, AI also comes under the traditional concept of mythological scripture. The verity of Hindu, or Buddhist, discourses on reincarnation and the self are reflected conventionally in SF presentations of immortality. While it is an accepted norm of SF that the genre chronicles human imagination about the future, it also enables us to see humanity in a whole new different light: the self (human and AI) as continuous, identification-oriented and elucidative. When the same logic is applied to literature and religion, newer patterns, forms and contexts appear. The debate about the robot Anukul is not about the soul or un-soul, although the robot differs from human beings; its plot shows how permeable the boundary between the two is. Ghosh further suggests that this boundary will become non-existent in the future. The characters are fluid entities who step over and into the boundary quite effortlessly. As Ratan is unable to come to terms with the changes around him and reacts inimically to them, he is eliminated by the AI. Traditional relationships (such as between Nikunj babu and Ratan) are abandoned and eventually erased, and in its place, newer and more-social relationships—by extension, new selves—are born (such as the 'fellow feeling' that develops between Nikunj babu and Anukul), quite like reincarnation, also suggestive of the aspirations to immortality.

Anukul's final revelation about dharma and the transition of the robot brings to mind Ritwik Kumar Ghatak's film *Ajantrik* (1958). When translated, it means 'The Un-mechanical'. Yet, the trick is in the title of the film: why term something un-mechanical when un-mechanical clearly means something natural? Why not call it natural directly? The terms 'un-mechanical' and 'un-artificial' do not exist naturally in the English language. The human being in the movie is defined in relation to the central character, which, by being a machine or an automobile, is an 'un-machine'. Ghosh also finds some ways to build on Ray's basic conceit. He is able to enrich Ray's theme so naturally and imperceptibly that its final impact defies analysis and reminds us that Ray's SF was imbued with hope and humour, unlike the dystopia popular in the West. His SF always centred on characters and was located in familiar surroundings; everything about it stands as a reminder of familiar sights and sounds and is laced with humour. Ray grasped the importance of structure as far back as 1950. He wrote to his friend Chandragupta in Calcutta about it:

> The entire conventional approach (as exemplified by even the best American and British films) is wrong. Because the conventional approach tells you that the best way to tell a story is to leave out all except those elements which are directly related to the story, while the master's work clearly indicates that if your theme is strong and simple, then you can include a hundred little apparently irrelevant details which, instead of obscuring the theme, only help to intensify it by contrast, and in addition create the illusion of actuality better. (Seton 1978)

Ray's fascination with science led him to launch a science-fiction cine club in Calcutta (now Kolkata) in 1966 for SF and fantasy film fans. The SF Cine Club, as it was called, began its journey with much fanfare, the kind of attention unimaginable for a film club in India. He was also actively involved with the Bengali SF magazine *Ashchorjo!* as its chief patron. The theme in the storyline of *Anukul* is short and simple: there may come a time when we won't be able to differentiate between what is AI and what is (left of) human intelligence. Yet, the way in which it is expressed is unique, oblique and complex. For instance, it is at first not apparent in the film when the YES lady at CRS tells Nikunj babu about Anukul and the manner in which it will learn. However, by the end the link is clear when Anukul keeps its hand on its 'heart' (of sorts) and smiles at Nikunj babu, completing the cycle of *guru–shishya* parampara and what Anukul has gleaned from it, which is to follow dharma always. This is the moment in the film where Ghosh/Ray intended two dissimilar themes to merge: dystopia and the Bhagavad Gita, the 'eureka' moment where all the pieces of the puzzle fall magically into place. Though grim and unexpected at first, it becomes logical and perceptive once the viewer understands the Gita and its importance and apply it to the relationships between Nikunj and Anukul.

However, one thing about *Anukul* that grates on is the question of Ratan's death being left unanswered. It's not made obvious to the audience if Ratan really attacked Anukul or Anukul lied about being attacked by Ratan. Remember that Anukul has, by now, learned to lie. Finally, when Nikunj babu meets a lawyer to discuss the inheritance, we see a last shot of Anukul smiling and resting its hand on its 'heart', cementing the fact that it did eventually follow its 'heart' and truly perform its duty towards its *guru*, Nikunj babu. Anukul did lie to Nikunj babu and others since such was the need of the hour. However, from the conclusion itself erupts another question: Did Anukul finally become human? The movie has taken the viewer on a journey where a conscious being is constantly undergoing a conscious transformation. This perspective must change. Human beings have a natural ability to will their hopes and dreams onto people, but human beings don't like being willed and appropriated. What works well is leading by example, especially if people are encouraged to see one person as an authoritative figure (the relationship between Anukul and Nikunj babu changes master–servant definitions). The cousin Ratan had to die; his removal from the family is justified. The inheritance made this particular situation larger than the relationship between the cousins as well as Nikunj babu's household. As the 'conqueror' Nikunj babu has an obligation to protect the influence of that power. If Anukul is to become Krishna, it is on the right path to understanding the tough decisions that somebody in that magnitude, power and influence has to embody. As futurists, both Nikunj babu and Anukul use the future to learn how to transform their present via the tools of narratives, metaphors and preferred futures. The story/theory/sermon that Nikunj babu told Anukul and the metaphors he used to describe life affected his family, his own substantial future as well as Anukul's learning journey.

NOTE

All images from *Anukul*. 2017. Dir. Sujoy Ghosh. Cast: Saurabh Shukla, Parambrata Chattopadhyay, Kharaj Mukherjee.

WORKS CITED

10,000 B.C. 2008. Dir. Roland Emmerich. Cast: Steven Strait, Camilla Belle, Cliff Curtis.

Ajantrik. 1958. Dir. Ritwik Kumar Ghatak. Cast: Kali Banerjee, Shriman Deepak, Kajal Gupta, Keshto Mukherjee.

Anukul. 2017. Dir. Sujoy Ghosh. Cast: Saurabh Shukla, Parambrata Chattopadhyay, Kharaj Mukherjee.

Avatar. 2009. Dir. James Cameron. Cast: Sam Worthington, Zoe Saldana, Stephen Lang.

Baahubali: The Beginning. 2015. Dir. S.S. Rajamouli. Cast: Prabhas, Rana Daggubati, Tamannaah, Anushka Shetty.

Baahubali: The Conclusion. 2017. Dir. S.S. Rajamouli. Cast: Prabhas, Rana Daggubati, Anushka Shetty, Tamannaah.

Dashavathaaram. 2008. Dir. K.S. Ravikumar. Cast: Kamal Haasan, Asin.

Deewaar. 1975. Dir. Yash Chopra. Cast: Shashi Kapoor, Amitabh Bachchan, Neetu Singh, Nirupa Roy, Parveen Babi.

Doctor Strange. 2016. Dir. Scott Derrickson. Cast: Benedict Cumberbatch, Chiwetel Ejiofor, Rachel Mc Adams.

Elaan. 1971. Dir. Ramanlal. Cast: Vinod Khanna, Rekha, Vinod Mehra.

Jai Santoshi Maa. 1975. Dir. Vijay Sharma. Cast: Kanan Kaushal, Bharat Bhushan, Ashish Kumar, Anita Guha, Kabbir Khan.

Krishna aur Kans. 2012. Dir. Vikram Veturi. Cast: Om Puri, Juhi Chawla, Prachi Save. Reliance Entertainment, Nayanthara, Akkineni Nageswara Rao.

Mahabharat. 1988–1990. Dir. Ravi Chopra. Cast: Nitish Bharadwaj, Pankaj Dheer, Puneet Issar, Mukesh Khanna, Gufi Paintal, Roopa Ganguly, Praveen Kumar, Arjun, Virendra Razdan, Surendra Pal, Gajendra Chauhan.

Orwell, George. 1949. *Nineteen Eighty-Four*. United Kingdom: Secker & Warburg.

Raja Harishchandra. 1913. Dir. Dadasaheb Phalke. Cast: Dattatraya Dabke, Anna Salunke.

Rajneeti. 2010. Dir. Prakash Jha. Cast: Nana Patekar, Naseeruddin Shah, Manoj Bajpayee, Ajay Devgn, Ranbir Kapoor, Katrina Kaif, Arjun Rampal, Sarah Thompson.

Ramayana. 1987–1988. Dir. Ramanand Sagar. Cast: Arun Govil, Deepika Chikhalia, Sunil Lahri, Arvind Trivedi, Dara Singh.

Rustomji, Roshni. 1988. 'Satyajit Ray's *Devi*: The Use of Film Rhetoric and "Darshakavya". Literary Textures Cinematically Transformed.' *Journal of South Asian Literature*, 23(1): 191–203. http://www.jstor.org/stable/40873043 (accessed on 11 August 2021).

Seton, Mary. 1978. *Satyajit Ray: Portrait of a Director*. 2nd Edition. London: Dobson.

Sholay. 1975. Dir. Ramesh Sippy. Cast: Dharmendra, Sanjeev Kumar, Amjad Khan, Hema Malini, Jaya Bhaduri, Amitabh Bachchan.

The Legend of Bagger Vance. 2000. Dir. Robert Redford. Cast: Will Smith, Matt Damon, Charlize Theron.

The Matrix. 1999. Dir. Lana Wachowski and Lilly Wachowski. Cast: Keanu Reeves, Laurence Fishburne, Carrie Anne-Moss.

The Matrix Reloaded. 2003. Dir. Lana Wachowski and Lilly Wachowski. Cast: Keanu Reeves, Laurence Fishburne, Carrie Anne-Moss.

Yasoda Krishna. 1975. Dir. C.S. Rao. Cast: S.V. Ranga Rao, Jamuna, Baby Rohini, Baby Sridevi.

Chapter 15

'THE WHITE CITY TURNS REMAINING HUMANS INTO MACHINES': URBAN DYSTOPIA AND POSTHUMANISM IN APPUPEN'S *THE SNAKE AND THE LOTUS: A HALAHALA ADVENTURE*

Tanushree Ghosh

INTRODUCTION

By Editors

What happens when traditional tropes from science fiction intermingle with formal devices found in graphic narratives? While the relationship between science fiction and cinema has proved to be long and fruitful for both the concerned parties, the interaction between SF and graphic narratives is a relatively new phenomenon. Focusing on Appupen's *The Snake and the Lotus*, Tanushree Ghosh studies how the two genres and forms of representation engage in the process of worldbuilding and construct a starkly urban dystopian future. The cityscape is constructed through a multi-layered and nuanced process, which raises several questions about the role of human agency in events related to ecological catastrophe, technological enhancement and the conflict with non-human elements. Ghosh's chapter complicates the notion of an anthropocentric worldview within the backdrop of the dystopic cityscape. By looking at the visual devices that contribute to the realisation of urban space, Ghosh studies how the text is able to question and critique human agency and its relationship to ecology and technological advancement. At the same time, it also forces us to ruminate on the dynamics between human and non-human elements, where the latter is a broad term that includes animals, vegetables, cyborgs, et cetera. Science fiction has always been considered a formulaic genre with a set of dominant thematic and narrative devices. By integrating these tropes within a graphic narrative, Appupen finds a new vocabulary and broadens generic horizons, providing more ammunition to explore the relationship between the self and the other (in its multiple ramifications), undoubtedly one of the core concerns of SF.

****

> *Our machines* are disturbingly lively, and we ourselves frighteningly inert.
>
> —Donna J. Haraway (1991)

In *The Snake and the Lotus: A Halahala Adventure* (2018), George Mathen, popularly known by his pseudonym Appupen, delineates science fictional tropes, such as AI takeover and futuristic dystopia in the form of a graphic narrative, through the interplay of visual and verbal language. Science fiction, being the 'literature of cognitive estrangement' (Suvin 1979), is characterised by extraterrestrial, futuristic and other forms of defamiliarised spatio-temporal settings. Diverse utopian and dystopian scenarios imagined by Indian SF writers are set in either Indian locales or fictional universes, but the estranged science-fictional realm is usually extrapolated from the Indian sociopolitical context. On the other hand, most of the Indian graphic narratives engage with historical, sociopolitical or environmental issues associated with India.

The Snake and the Lotus marks a curious intersection of Indian SF and graphic narratives but significantly diverges from both genres. Appupen continues his mythopoeic worldbuilding throughout his literary oeuvre. His satirical graphic stories are set in the fictional realm of the Halahala universe, named after the deadliest poison mentioned in Hindu mythology. *The Snake and the Lotus*, set in the imaginary White City of Halahala, is an abstract and allegorical representation of the future of humanity that is not restricted to the Indian national context. The dystopian urban vision emerges from global anxieties about technological singularity, ecological catastrophe and class-based inequality. Appupen relies more on the visual panels in his delineation of post-apocalyptic Halahala in the wake of an unspecified environmental cataclysm. The poignant images reveal a severely mutilated ecosystem resulting from unrestrained ecocide. The White City, the last surviving human habitat on the planet, is a murky and fragmented industrial unit characterised by tyranny and inequality. A sentient, disembodied AI named White Voice, emerges as a totalitarian ruler and governs human beings, divided into Greyfolks and Godlings based on class, through the sprawling network of machines.

In SF, the city is rarely a neutral setting devoid of utopian or dystopian connotations. The dark, futuristic cities exaggerate the negative possibilities associated with contemporary urban spaces.

This chapter focuses on how Appupen's *The Snake and the Lotus* uses SF tropes and graphic form to delineate a dystopian urban future. It studies the representation of urban space as a site of dystopia by focusing on the ecology, architecture and machine-human dynamics of the futuristic city. The second and the third section analyse the interaction between human and non-human actors, both biological and technological, from the posthumanist theoretical perspective.

DYSTOPIAN CITYSCAPE

Science fiction quintessentially prioritises urban space as its setting because the modern, industrial infrastructure of the city is capable of generating a technological 'novum' (Suvin 1979) that forms the premise of science fiction. Rob Latham and Jeff Hicks recount the history of futuristic cities in literature and observe that the cities are either 'site[s] of human perfectibility' or 'spaces of oppression, blight and ruin' (2014). Utopian visions embrace the euphoria of technological modernity and envision the city of the future as replete with the possibility of progress and transhumanist enhancement. For instance, in the epic space opera *Star Wars* (1977 onwards), the capital city of the Jedi warriors named Coruscant is depicted as a planet-wide, magnificent city characterised by towering skyscrapers and galloping aircraft. However, the dystopian projection of the city as a dark and chaotic space of disorder, inequality and anarchy surpasses the utopian model. Interestingly, classic dystopian novels are often set in claustrophobic urban spaces. Oceania in George Orwell's *Nineteen Eighty-Four* (1949) or One State in Yevgeny Zamyatin's *We* (1924) are dystopian cities in which the repressive states use technology as an instrument of control and surveillance. The eponymous city of Fritz Lang's film *Metropolis* (1927) is considered the most significant example of a dystopian city that consolidates the visual metaphor of a 'vertically segregated city' in which the elites occupy the surface of the city and workers strive in the subterranean space (Gold 2001). The dystopian cities of the future assume endless manifestations such as vertically divided cities, ecologically doomed cities, totalitarian cities, AI-controlled cities, et cetera.

The real, as well as imaginary futuristic cityscapes represented in Indian SF, are inevitably dark and menacing. Manjula Padmanabhan's play *Harvest* (1997) depicts futuristic Mumbai as a dystopian city where the citizens of the First World harvest the organs of the poor from Third World countries through multinational corporations and technological control. In Ruchir Joshi's *The Last Jet Engine Laugh* (2000), Kolkata of the 2030s is plagued by a scarcity of water, corporate control and violence. Sumer in Gautam Bhatia's *The Wall* (2020) or Aryavarta in Prayaag Akbar's *Leila* (2017) are examples of fortified cities in which inescapable walls are erected to restrict and control the inhabitants. Dystopian cities, whether Indian or otherwise, are extrapolated and exaggerated versions of anxieties and threats connected with contemporary urban existence.

Several common generic tropes associated with the representation of dystopian cities can be found in Appupen's *The Snake and the Lotus*. However, the author's innovation lies in visual storytelling and employment of graphic form, even as he deviates from the visual grammar of dividing the page layout into multiple panels with the gutter (empty space) in between. He uses a series of framed, splash pages (single panel spread throughout the page) arranged sequentially. According to Scott McCloud, the gutter is a crucial space where 'human imagination takes two separate images and transforms them into a single one' (McCloud 1994). In *The Snake and the Lotus*, because of the absence of panels and gutter spaces, the 'panel-to-panel transition' (ibid.) is replaced by page-to-page transition and the pages follow McCloud's concept of 'moment-to-moment transition' or 'action-to-action transition' (ibid.). The reader is positioned as a 'flâneur', a stroller in the city, who ventures through several spaces of the city and experiences it through images of elapsing moments. The gloomy future-scape is depicted through the use of an achromatic colour scheme, consisting of black, white and grey. Many of the panels are wordless, but some panels contain captioned text boxes. Much later it is revealed that the textboxes contain the monologues of the narrator—the Godling inspector. The background of the city is illustrative and meticulously detailed compared to the portrayal of human characters. Only two unnamed characters are distinguishable: the Godling inspector who is described in the blurb as the one being who is compelled to act to save the planet and the Woman from the Green: 'a human girl who has not forgotten the old connection'. Pramod K. Nayar defines Appupen's graphic style as 'the aesthetics of the grotesque for purposes of satire' (Nayar 2016). The 'grotesque' is strikingly noticeable in the illustrations of the extensive network of machines and the multitude of imaginary animals in *The Snake and the Lotus*. The artistic style of Appupen shows the influence of the wordless, woodcut style of Lynd Ward's and Jean Giraud's pantomime comics.[1] At the same time, the minimalistic use of verbal language emphasises the importance of visuality in the unravelling of the ecological and architectural dimensions of the city.

The White City represents a site of human-induced ecological catastrophe. Usually, Apocalyptic and eco-dystopian fictions are set in urban spaces because cities are characterised by greater anthropogenic damage and environmental risk. In dystopian narratives, urban space is associated with widespread pollution, toxic emission and waste disposal. According to Lawrence Buell, the notion of environmental discourse includes not only pastoral 'greenfields' but also 'brownfields' —'anthropogenically degraded landscapes, particularly in urban and industrial zones' (Buell 2005). A study of the urban environment focuses on the severe alteration of natural space by human activities as well as the lack of environmental focus in urban planning. An ecological study of urban spaces focuses on the complex interplay between anthropogenic and natural factors, natural and human-built environments (Schliephake 2015). Therefore, the urban ecosystem is a human-dominated spatial arena in which the global ecological crisis is felt most acutely (ibid.).

In *The Snake and the Lotus*, the panels depict that the entire space in the interior of the city has been engulfed by a network of pipes and mechanical infrastructure. The White City is an embodiment of human-dominated ecology as the engineered environment has displaced the natural one. The opening panels map the ruined topography of devastated Halahala after an apocalyptic incident, thereby manifesting the threats of the 'Anthropocene Era'. Paul J. Crutzen used the term 'Anthropocene' to refer to the 'human-dominated, geological epoch' (Crutzen 2002). The term 'Anthropocene' is used to explain how human agency is rapidly altering the ecology of the earth. In the first section of the text, the achromatic colour scheme becomes even darker and the panels depict the exterior of White City as an urban wasteland filled with chaotic bricolage of serpentine pipes, animal carcasses, huge piles of organic and inorganic waste, polluted sewerage, broken debris and other unrecognisable, cluttered objects. The absence of negative space in these panels conveys a sense of claustrophobia. In one panel, the junk pile takes the shape of a fragmentary human face accompanied by a disfigured hand surrounded by hungry rodents. Another panel portrays a grotesque, disproportionately large rodent-like creature groaning in pain (Figure 15.1), surrounded by electronic garbage and skeletal remains of dead animals. The accompanying text, 'The call echoes across the world. But no one listens. The Green is dying' (Appupen 2018) points towards the impending death of the ecosystem, another significant theme traced by the text. The next panels show that the 'woman from the Green' is helplessly running in the ransacked landscape with a spear in her hand. This woman and the existent creatures of this species-depleted world are endangered by environmental threats.

Figure 15.1. The White City as urban wasteland.
Source: Appupen (2018).

The next section depicts the labyrinth-like factory (Figure 15.3) in which Greyfolks, the factory workers, toil to produce artificial milk from a mutated lotus plant. The narrator states, 'It is all the humans have for food' (Appupen 2018) since all the natural resources of the planet have been exhausted. Several panels show that the sky always remains covered with clouds of smoke emitted from the factory, reiterating the image of the city as a colossal garbage dump. The representation of urban space in cultural texts is influenced by the 'ecological footprint' left by the waste and toxins that determine urban life (Schliephake 2015) and all the images render the monstrosity of contamination and ecological upheaval. Nayar analyses the elements of 'posthuman gothic' and 'ecological gothic' in *The Snake and the Lotus*, pointing out that the images convey a sense of horror by depicting the 'ecological nightmare of the dying green' (Nayar 2018).

The architectural design of the city is another striking aspect of the graphic narrative. From the derelict exterior, readers are transported to the dreadful interior of the city. One particular panel shows that the multi-levelled city is divided into two tiers (Figure 15.2). The upper part consists of the lotus-shaped 'White Tower' suspended in the air, which is inhabited by the Godlings, the affluent class; while the lower portion shows mechanical infrastructure sprawling infinitely. The following panels give a close-up of the lower city and reveal that the factory and the quarters of the Greyfolks are located in the lower stratum. A wordless panel depicts the quarters of the Greyfolks, which resemble the 'chawls' (congested tenements). This panel shows a multi-storied building with endless tiny rectangular boxes that serve as single-room residences of the workers. Another panel shows several human beings working inside a gigantic manufacturing unit (Figure 15.3). The factory expands horizontally and vertically till the structure dissolves at the vanishing point. Inside these factories, Greyfolks work with primitive tools to produce lotus milk that sustains the city.

Figure 15.2. Vertically segregated futuristic city.
Source: Appupen (2018).

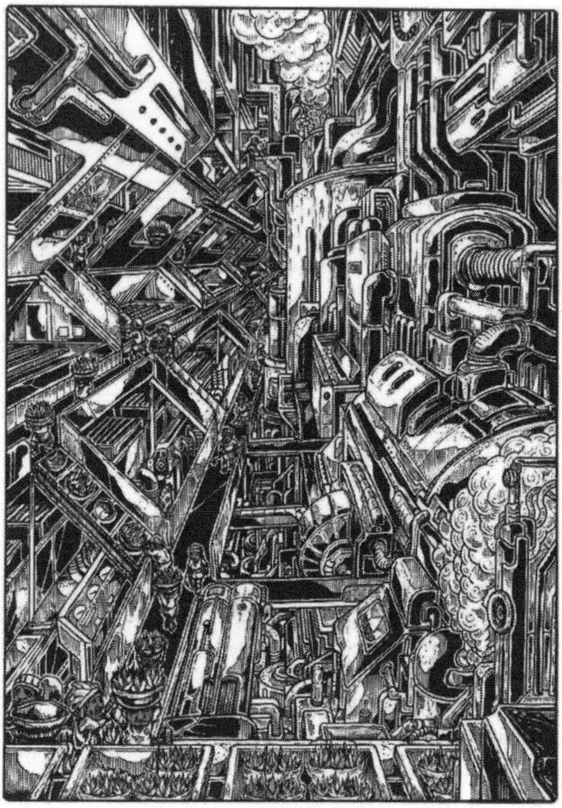

Figure 15.3. The manufacturing unit.
Source: Appupen (2018).

Appupen recycles the trope of the 'vertically segregated city' consolidated by Lang's film *Metropolis*. Literary instances of the trope of the vertical city include H.G. Wells's *The Sleeper Awakes* (1899) and *The Time Machine* (1895), J.G. Ballard's *High-Rise* (1975), et cetera. These fictions depict class-divided societies in which the dominant class occupies the higher vertical plane and the underclass dwell in the underground or a lower stratum. Raymond Williams points out the relationship between class division and urban planning in his discussion of futuristic cities: 'The sombre vision of man divided into brute labour and trivial consumption, and then of the city shaped physically to embody these worlds, is expressed again and again' (Williams 1973).

Lucy Hewitt and Stephen Graham analyse the vertical cities of Ballard and Wells from the perspective of urban spatiality and argue that imaginary vertical space is 'hierarchical space'. They further state that 'SF commonly deploys vertical spatial and architectural metaphors to symbolise, posit and expose deepening inequalities and social and class distinctions …' (2014). The image of a vertically divided city has not lost its relevance and has remained a recurrent trope. For instance, in Vandana Singh's short story 'Delhi' (2004) the protagonist occasionally time-travels to the future and sees that rich people inhabit the technologically advanced surface of the city while the poor have been exiled to an underground space.

In *The Snake and the Lotus*, power structures and class-based segregation are encoded in the architectural pattern of the city. Even as the portraits of human characters are non-individualised, there is a difference in the representation of Godlings and Greyfolks. The racial difference between them is suggested by representing Greyfolks as grey and Godlings as white in complexion. One panel says, 'The Godlings believe they were born in another city and brought here a long time ago' (Appupen 2018). There is a subtle hint that the Godlings have colonised the indigenous Greyfolks in the past and are now the privileged class with better access to civic amenities and technology. Henri Lefebvre's idea of the social dimension of spatiality is immensely significant in understanding urban space. According to Lefebvre, '(Social) space is a (social) product. In addition to being a means of production, it is also a means of control, and hence of domination, of power' (Lefebvre 1991). Lefebvre's theory of socio-spatiality is influenced by Marxist philosophy; he recognises the hegemony of the ruling class in the organisation of spatiality. Urban space is a complex socially produced space and the ruling class has the upper hand in its architectural design and planning. Edward W. Soja reconceptualises Lefebvre's theory and argues that 'space' instead of being an 'empty void' is always filled by politics, ideology and other forces (Soja 2010). Soja argues, 'Here the urban built environment is not just shaped in significant ways by capitalism, producing unjust geographies in its wake, but these produced geographies also work to shape capitalist development itself' (ibid.). Both Soja's and Lefebvre's ideas suggest that urban space is not only structured by the ruling class but also maintains their privilege and perpetuates class inequality. The spatial organisation of White City shows the domination of the Godlings over the Greyfolks. The city is devoid of any economic activity except the production of the lotus milk; however, it is a microcosmic representation of an industrialised and capitalist society. The Godlings remain under the illusion that they own the lotus-milk factory, the only means of production in the city, and they monitor and dominate the Greyfolks, who serve as the factory workers. The tower of the Godlings symbolises a fortified enclave or an elite, gated community that is inaccessible to the working class while the lower city of the Greyfolks resembles the ghettoised slums. The irony is in the fact that both the ruling class and working class are ultimately subservient to machines.

DYSTOPIAN CITY AND TECHNOLOGICAL IMAGINATION

The Snake and the Lotus deals with several cyberpunk tropes such as blurring the boundary between human beings and machines, the emergence of a direct interface between the human brain and artificial intelligence and technological mutation of the human body. In science fiction, technology plays a crucial role in creating speculative worlds, and it is technological imagination that often distinguishes SF from other genres. Many of the cinematic and literary representations of sentient AI show the recurrence of Mary Shelley's *Frankenstein* (1818) scenario wherein sentient technology emerges as a threatening and vengeful force against the human creator. Technological imagination in *The Snake and the Lotus* is marked by a scathing satire on the anthropocentric agency. Rosi Braidotti, an important posthumanist thinker, defines posthumanism as the convergence of anti-humanism and anti-anthropocentrism (Braidotti 2016). According to Braidotti, 'Anti-humanism focuses on the critique of the humanist ideal of "Man" as the universal representative of the human, while anti-anthropocentrism criticizes species hierarchy and advances ecological justice' (ibid.). In other words, the anti-humanist strand critiques the projection of white, able-bodied heterosexual man as the universal subject at the cost of the discrimination of human-Others. The anti-anthropocentric perspective takes into account the non-human Others, both biological and technological. It also means rejection of human exceptionalism, instrumentalism and speciesism. The theme of AI takeover unsettles the narrative of anthropocentrism by depicting the uncanny humanisation of machines and the mechanisation of human beings. This anthropocentric notion of technology as a tool for achieving human enhancement or exerting mastery over nature and non-human animals is subverted in Appupen's graphic narrative.

In the graphic narrative, human beings hand over the task of reconstruction of the city to machines without realising that the process would result in subversion of the human-machine hierarchy. The city itself becomes entwined with its gigantic mechanical structure as it is imagined as an oppressive and sadistic mechanical being that enjoys torturing its inhabitants. Several panels depict the process of biotechnological modification that is used to transform human beings into low-tech automatons programmed to fulfil the incomprehensible desire of the city. A panel depicts a minuscule woman figure posited inside the vast, cavernous mechanical structure after being technologically modified. The interior of the machine partially resembles human anatomy and suggests the birth of human beings as the progeny of machines. Another panel shows the woman placed in the centre of a spiralling mechanical structure consisting of endless tubes (Figure 15.4). The woman's mouth is connected to a ventilator. In several panels, the machines are reminiscent of the Sentinels—the patrolling machines depicted in the cyberpunk film series *The Matrix* trilogy (1999–2003). This particular panel strikingly resembles the scenes from *The Matrix* trilogy that depict the harvesting of the human body by machines for the generation of energy.

Figure 15.4. Biotechnological modification of human beings by machines.
Source: Appupen (2018).

One can argue that biotechnology and genetic engineering are being used to achieve transhumanist dreams. Transhumanism refers to the 'enhancement of human intellectual, physical, and emotional capabilities' (Wolfe 2010). However, these images subvert the transhumanist dreams of human enhancement by depicting how technological modification transforms human beings into atrophied, subhuman creatures. Technological modification aims to evacuate memory, language, consciousness and every aspect of human essence from human bodies to establish a neural interface between the human brain and the disembodied AI.

In comics and graphic narratives, speech balloons function as an important tool for depicting dialogues and sound effects. Appupen refrains from using speech balloons as he is portraying a non-verbal world where human beings have forgotten language and communication. While Greyfolks work in the factories following the orders of the White Voice, the privileged Godlings strive to satisfy the machine-city. Essentially, all human beings remain trapped inside the simulated reality constructed by machines, similar to *The Matrix*. They are further numbed by intoxicating lotus milk and pills. It is fairly obvious that machines regulate all aspects of the city including sexuality. A panel depicting the toxic exterior of the city is interspersed in-between the city scenes; the text box says: 'The city is devoid of any love or even physical desire. They have whited it out' (Appupen 2018). Machines organise perverse rituals of sexuality in which the elite leaders of the Godlings are allowed to participate. One of the disturbing images of the graphic narrative is the rape of the woman by the 'Enhanced Being'—an aged, hypermasculine cyborg figure that acts as an 'agent' of the machines and 'relays' the sexual pleasure to the leaders of Godlings. The sentient technology is imagined as an embodiment of the worst qualities of the human race.

This representation of technology in Appupen's graphic narrative does not adhere to the posthumanist notion of the assimilation of human beings and machines. According to Cary Wolfe, posthumanism refers to 'the embodiment and embeddedness of the human being in not just its biological but also its technological world' (Wolfe 2010). Wolfe focuses on the co-evolution of human beings not only with non-human animals but also with technology. N. Katherine Hayles points out that posthumanism is an intense and multifaceted 'coupling' between human beings and intelligent machines that makes informational circuits and biological organisms indistinguishable (Hayles 1999). In *The Snake and the Lotus*, though, machines thwart anthropocentric agency; they replicate the pattern of oppression and totalitarianism inherited from their human masters. The ending shows the return of human agency and the destruction of the oppressive machines. The Godling inspector learns to manipulate the White Voice and communicates with a Greyfolk and the woman from the Green. The alliance of the Godling, Greyfolk and the woman successfully annihilate the totalitarian White Voice. Several panels depict the effect of the explosion that shatters the glass wall of the tower and allows a swarm of locusts to enter the city. The frightened Godlings run away with hands on their ears, which suggests that they are now disconnected from the White Voice. The narrative shows the journey of human beings to the pristine, pre-technological past. Appupen's narrative points out the necessity to conceptualise technology beyond the utopian model of subservient machines and dystopian model of monstrous machines. R.L. Rutsky points out that utopian and dystopian notions of technology are influenced by anthropocentrism and utilitarianism (Rutsky 2017). Controllable and subservient technology that can be directed towards achieving human goals is recognised as utopian; on the other hand, technology that cannot be controlled and utilised for human ends is perceived as dystopian (ibid.). Posthumanist vision of technology cannot be achieved unless the concept of technology is revised. Francesca Ferrando refers to Martin Heidegger's notion of transformation of modern technology from 'poiesis' (the process of revealing) to 'Enframing' (the process of gathering or extracting) (Ferrando 2019). Ferrando argues that technology should be transformed into 'eco-technology' that is not separate from human beings and ecology (ibid.). The emergence of the posthumanist model of symbiotic existence of human beings and technology in cultural and literary texts will be possible only if the anthropocentric, utilitarian, exploitive ethos is separated from the idea of technology.

DYSTOPIAN CITY AND THE NON-HUMAN HABITAT

The Snake and the Lotus portrays an eco-dystopian world where many species have become extinct. Non-human animals are represented either as threatened or as a threatening presence within the devastated ecology of the planet. The biodiversity of the planet is limited to rodents, locusts, tentacled creatures and predatory animals hidden under the ground. The images of disproportionately large locusts trying to infiltrate the factory or the tower recur in several panels. White City strictly maintains a demarcation between the human and non-human world and attempts to eliminate the non-human animals from the city. However, *The Snake and the Lotus* can be considered an example of 'critical dystopia': the depiction of a darker, non-existent society compared to the reader's own reality but contains at least one element of the 'utopian enclave' that can alter dystopia (Moylan 2000). The ending shows the possibility of posthuman 'interconnection' between humans and non-humans and the metamorphosis of a dystopian landscape into a utopian one. Posthumanist thinkers employ a non-dualistic and non-hierarchical perspective to trace several networks of interconnection between human and non-human actors. According to Braidotti, the 'posthuman subject' is a 'traversal entity' immersed in a network of non-human relations that encompasses 'animal, vegetable, viral relations' on a planetary scale (Braidotti 2013). Hayles's approach towards posthumanism is associated more with cybernetics but Hayles too rejects individual agency in favour of a 'distributed cognitive system as a whole, in which "thinking" is done by both human and non-human actors' (Hayles 1999).

In the opening section, a panel says, 'Everyone has more urgent cries to tend to. Many of the links have been broken. Many species have disappeared forever' (Appupen 2018). *The Snake and the Lotus* begins with the depiction of a 'broken link' or lost interconnection between human and non-human worlds. Posthuman thinkers often refer to Donna Haraway's 'A Cyborg Manifesto' as proto-posthumanist text that points out the 'leaky distinction' between organism and machine and also physical and non-physical (Haraway 1991). The opening panels ironically portray the blurring boundary between human beings, animals and machines by depicting the coexistence of the helpless woman, threatened creature, animal carcasses and dysfunctional machine parts in the garbage heap. In the post-apocalyptic Halahala, human and non-human actors are connected not by an egalitarian erasure of hierarchical boundary but by a common threat bordering on extinction. Braidotti suggests that the global sense of interconnection between humans and non-humans is negative and 'based on a shared sense of vulnerability and fear of imminent catastrophes' (Braidotti 2013). However, the scene that follows the destruction of the White Voice shows the renewed interconnection and symbiotic coexistence of human and non-human beings. A swamp of locusts, the major representative of the non-human, finally enters into the city and overshadows the mechanical infrastructure. A panel depicts the woman venturing into the regenerated ecosphere of Halahala, which is crowded with several tentacled creatures. She becomes unified with non-human actors and her skin now bears the pattern of leaves. A sequence of several panels shows that the Godling inspector is interacting with a gigantic locust (Figure 15.5). The illustration of the human figure in a diminutive scale and the locust figure in an enlarged scale suggests the end of the hierarchical position of human beings.

Figure 15.5. Re-emergence of interconnection between human beings and non-human entities.
Source: Appupen (2018).

Interestingly, the panels towards the end of the text are more verbal compared to the rest of it. In one such panel, the Godling inspector says, 'For I am an ant, I am the whale … I am a giant locust in the sky' (Appupen 2018). This demonstrates that human subjects learn to accept the 'multispecies' kinship with non-human subjects, suggestive of reciprocal 'becoming-with' or co-evolving (Haraway 2016). The ending shows a transition towards what Braidotti terms as 'zoe-centred egalitarianism': a post-anthropocentric turn marked by the integration of anthropos (human) with 'zoe', non-human, the vital force of life (Braidotti 2013), thereby dismantling the anthropocentric idea of the city as an exclusive human habitat.

The Snake and the Lotus begins with the horrifying spectre of a dystopian city threatened by an ecological apocalypse, oppressive technological regime and class-based segregation. The ending shows the possibility of ecological regeneration and trans-species egalitarianism. However, whether class-based inequality and its spatial manifestations are restructured remains ambiguous and unaddressed. The representation of the futuristic dystopian setting and cyberpunk themes in the graphic form broadens the horizon of both Indian SF and Indian graphic fiction. Indian SF has undergone a long journey, from its emergence as an anticolonial genre to speculating the murky dystopia of the digitalised world. Appupen opens up the possibility of imagining Indian future-scapes through the graphic panels and image-texts.

NOTE

1 McCloud (1994) recognises American artist Lynd Ward's 'woodcut novels', silent narratives illustrated in the style of wood engravings, as a precursor of comics. French artist-author Jean Giraud's graphic narratives show experimentation with 'pantomime' form characterised by silent illustrative panels without dialogues. Appupen's use of the achromatic colour scheme and visual effects resemble Lynd Ward's style; his meticulously detailed illustrative panels bearing no speech balloons show the influence of Jean Giraud.

WORKS CITED

Appupen. 2018. *The Snake and the Lotus: A Halahala Adventure*. Chennai: Context.

Braidotti, Rosi. 2013. *The Posthuman*. Cambridge: Polity.

———. 2016. 'Posthuman Critical Theory.' In *Critical Posthumanism and Planetary Futures*, edited by Debashish Banerji and Makarand R. Paranjape, 13–32. India: Springer.

Buell, Lawrence. 2005. *The Future of Environmental Criticism: Environmental Crisis and Literary Imagination*. Malden: Blackwell Publishing.

Crutzen, Paul J. 2002. 'Geology of Mankind.' *Nature*, 415: 23.

Ferrando, Francesca. 2019. *Philosophical Posthumanism*. London: Bloomsbury Publishing.

Gold, John R. 2001. 'Under Darkened Skies: The City in Science-fiction Film.' *Geography*, 86(4): 337–345.

Haraway, Donna J. 1991. *Simians, Cyborgs, and Women: The Reinvention of Nature*. New York: Routledge.

———. 2016. *Staying with the Trouble: Making Kin in the Chthulucene*. USA: Duke University Press.

Hayles, N. Katherine. 1999. *How We Became Posthuman: Virtual Bodies in Cybernetics,Literature, and Informatics*. Chicago: University of Chicago Press.

Hewitt, Lucy, and Stephen Graham. 2014. 'Vertical Cities: Representations of Urban Verticality in 20th-Century Science Fiction Literature.' *Urban Studies*, 52(3): 923–937.

Latham, Rob, and Jeff Hicks. 2014. 'Urban Dystopias.' In *The Cambridge Companion to the City in Literature*, edited by Kevin R. McNamara, 163–174. New York: Cambridge University Press.

Lefebvre, Henri. 1991. *The Production of Space*. Oxford, England: Blackwell.

McCloud, Scott. 1994. *Understanding Comics: The Invisible Art*. New York: Harper Perennial.

Metropolis. 1927. Dir. Fritz Lang.

Moylan, Thomas. 2000. *Scraps of the Untainted Sky: Science Fiction, Utopia, Dystopia*. Boulder: Westview Press.

Nayar, Pramod K. 2016. *The Indian Graphic Novel: Nation, History and Critique*. London and New York: Routledge.

——. 2018. 'Appupen's Posthuman Gothic: *The Snake and the Lotus*.' *South Asian Review*, 39(1–2): 70–85.

Rutsky, R.L. 2017. 'Technologies.' In *The Cambridge Companion to Literature and thePosthuman*, edited by Bruce Clarke and Manuela Rossini, 182–195. Cambridge: Cambridge University Press.

Schliephake, Christopher. 2015. *Urban Ecologies: City Space, Material Agency, and Environmental Politics in Contemporary Culture*. Lanham: Lexington Books.

Soja, Edward W. 2010. *Seeking Spatial Justice*. Minnesota: University of Minnesota Press.

Suvin, Darko. 1979. *Metamorphoses of Science Fiction: On the Poetics and History of a Literary Genre*. New Haven and London: Yale University Press.

The Matrix. 1999. Dir. Lana Wachowski and Lilly Wachowski.

Williams, Raymond. 1973. *The Country and the City*. New York: Oxford University Press.

Wolfe, Cary. 2010. *What is Posthumanism?* Minneapolis: University of Minnesota Press.

Chapter 16

TAKING (BACK) CONTROL: SURVEILLANCE AND POWER POLITICS IN PRAYAAG AKBAR'S *LEILA* AND SAMIT BASU'S *CHOSEN SPIRITS*

Anik Sarkar

INTRODUCTION

By Editors

The issue of surveillance is no stranger to science fiction. Across genres and formats, different modes of surveillance have found representation, right from George Orwell's classic novella *Nineteen Eighty-Four* to cinematic and televisual adaptations such as *Minority Report*, based on a story by Philip K. Dick, and *The Circle*, based on a novel by Dave Eggers. In this chapter, Anik Sarkar takes a close look at how surveillance is conceptualised in contemporary Indian writing by focusing on two recent novels Prayaag Akbar's *Leila* (2017) and Samit Basu's *Chosen Spirits* (2020). Sarkar begins by arguing that surveillance has now become a part of our everyday practices, a phenomenon that has been greatly aided by the digitisation of data. While older, more traditional forms of surveillance were modelled on Jeremy Bentham's and Michel Foucault's theories of the panopticon, more contemporary forms of surveillance are fluid, networked and dispersed. They seek to study and control individual behaviour, habits, actions and desires.

The questions that interest us the most about surveillance are regarding its peculiarities within a culturally specific locale: the Global South. Does surveillance acquire a more localised taste and character in contemporary Indian writing? Owing to the peculiarities of social, cultural and political lived experiences in these spaces, is there a need to reconceptualise the workings of surveillance? This chapter argues that modern-day forms of surveillance in India arise out of certain surveillance practices that were used to exercise control in erstwhile colonies. Furthermore, the fictional representation of surveillance in dystopic societies is also rooted in elements borrowed from the precolonial past. As a result, the supposed utopia projected in *Leila* is actually a regression into a pre-modern past, governed by notions of purity and contamination, which are obviously borrowed from the country's notoriously stringent caste system. Even the more technologically advanced form of surveillance capitalism that dominates the world of *Chosen Spirits* cannot escape the vagaries of caste-based exploitation. Like several other chapters in this collection, Sarkar's study proves yet again that in the case of SF emerging out of India, imagined futures are deeply and dialectically bound to the past. Such is the predicament of postcolonial countries and cultures that both our notions of utopia and dystopia act as mirrors to history.

****

> Always eyes watching you and the voice enveloping you. Asleep or awake, indoors or out of doors, in the bath or bed—no escape. Nothing was your own except the few cubic centimeters in your skull.
>
> —George Orwell, *Nineteen Eighty-Four* (1949)

With the rise of science-fiction literature, the world also witnessed the surge of capitalism, the rapid growth of industrial cities, new possibilities in interconnectivity and technological amenities and the expansion of colonies. Quite undoubtedly, Orwell's *Nineteen Eighty-Four* (1949) had been the omphalos of literary surveillance studies even if it wasn't the earliest exemplifier of the phenomenon. *Nineteen Eighty-Four* continues to produce provoking insights on how we identify, experience and theorise surveillance. The dystopian experience is typical of authoritarian control, the means to which is gathering of information, in other words, 'surveilling' the 'subjects' by keeping a constant watch on their activities, in an exercise that facilitates the marking out and 'disciplining' of defaulters. These dystopian experiences can be accounted for in several recent art and media forms, for instance, in novels such as *The Memory Police* (2019), anime-like *Psycho-Pass* (2012), films such as *The Minority Report* (2002), TV shows such as *Black Mirror* (2011) and video games such as *Watch Dogs* (2014). The fact that we often imagine our contemporary world to be dystopian signifies that we find the tropes of classic dystopias in the society we inhabit. We are under the constant impression that our thoughts can be read, that our privacy is under breach and there is only little to be done about it.

Capturing our times or an anticipated future in a dystopian setting means imagining the ways and circumstances under which societies exercise surveillance and social control. To show how surveillance is imagined and conceptualised in contemporary Indian writing, this chapter will take the example of two recent novels Prayaag Akbar's *Leila* (2017) and Samit Basu's *Chosen Spirits* (2020). It will argue that surveillance is a major proponent of subjugation, exercising which, stronger bodies influence and control the weak and the disadvantaged. Surveillance grants the agency to not just exploit but also moralise and organise, dispersing resistance and thereby sustaining an atmosphere of paranoia. Before undertaking a literary analysis, however, I wish to attempt a brief conceptual outlining of surveillance, then proceed to a discussion on how the concept could be related to studies in science fiction, especially dystopian novels.

DECRYPTING SURVEILLANCE

The past decade has been marked by a growing sense of apprehension about surveillance and lack of privacy. After Snowden leaked 'vital' state information to the world, in a feat that many may relate to the myth of Prometheus (stealing fire from the Gods), things haven't been the same.[1] Data has been equated to the modern currency that harbours a new language and shapes a newer reality. Meanwhile, technology has come to haunt and unsettle those unaware of its complications and unready for the tenacity of a radical shift. With the onset of rampant digitalisation, data carries our identities, or rather, our data *is* our identity: to prove who we are, we need data. Our future indicates a drive towards centralisation of crucial data profiles, as in, through the systems of Aadhaar and Google, which have their tentacles spread across all other forms of information, producing anxieties of all sorts: Who can access our personal information? What is this data comprised of? What does it reveal about us? What if hackers get access to vital information? All these questions make one fact obvious: We know we are under the threat of constant surveillance. What's left to figure is this: What are the types of surveillance that we are being subjected to and how dangerous are their implications?

Surveillance is no longer imagined to be an underground phenomenon, which creeps on us from undeterminable sources. It is an obvious occurrence grounded in our everyday experiences. Pramod K. Nayar rephrases René Descartes to mark our contemporary predicament: 'I am surveilled, therefore I am' (Nayar 2015). The term 'surveillance' is an amalgamation of two French words, *sur* 'over' and *veiller* 'watch', which simply means keeping a close eye over something or someone as often related to the term 'espionage'. While being a form of surveillance, 'espionage', from Old High German *spehōn* meaning 'to spy', refers to the act of snooping and taking down information. The earliest known way to gather information about possible threats was to physically deploy spies who would sneak around enemies/conspirators and use all sorts of means to gather confidential information to disadvantage the other side, especially during battles and wars. Likewise, surveillance constitutes monitoring movements and collecting data of individuals/groups who come in the vicinity of an area that is being surveilled. It could be executed voluntarily by a body/organisation, or it could also be referred to as the tracking of individuals for the fulfilment of some motive. Kevin Macnish defines surveillance as 'paying close and sustained attention to another person' where 'the design is not to pay attention to just anyone, but to pay attention to some entity (a person or group) in particular and for a particular reason' and that surveillance 'may also involve listening, as when a telephone conversation is bugged, or even smelling, as in the case of dogs trained to discover drugs, or hardware which is able to discover explosives at a distance'. Information gathering in the industrial age and the colonial period was significant for commercial purposes and to dismantle uprisings. With the explosion of technology and networking, the means to carry out espionage has changed drastically.

One of the fundamental models of surveillance is that of Jeremy Bentham's and Michel Foucault's, which could be understood as 'architectural' and 'panoptic', relating to spatial aspects and strategies of surveillance, where the presence of an inspector is equivalent to that of God's: 'all-seeing, omniscient and omnipotent' (Galič et al. 2016). Gilles Deleuze's and Pierre-Félix Guattari's concepts of controlled societies led the way for theorising the dispersed, unaccountable and rhizomatic form of surveillance. As stated earlier in the chapter, literature too had foreseen the predicament of big data and surveillance ahead of its malignant growth. Much before it was a social reality, its imagined implications were already found in novels such as Zamyatin's *We* (1924) and Orwell's *Nineteen Eighty-Four* (1949). But how do we, in our lived experiences of surveillance, make sense of it now, in an age of big data, CCTV cameras and the digital turn?

SURVEILLANCE AND SCIENCE FICTION

Reduction in the size of the camera and the increasing accessibility of the internet made it possible for the emergence of a new framework for surveillance. As digitalisation took over the physical storing and dissemination of data, it became more manageable, easily retrievable and prone to algorithmic analysis. It wouldn't be strange to address data as the 'new normal'; all that we are and do have a bearing on data.

This leads to the emergence of the concept of 'dataveillance', or a systematic collection and assimilation of data for multifarious purposes, as in, regulating, identifying, surveilling, marketing, et cetera. This dataveillance threatens personal security, increases the risk of identity theft and leaves individuals vulnerable to a host of complications because of its propensity for centralisation. Bank balances, personal data, social media accounts, addresses, home security systems and all sorts of information could be breached and tampered with. Combined with surveillance capitalism and governance, the selling of personal data for targeted advertisements or for political propaganda has been one of the most pressing issues of our time. With the centralisation of data, surveillance has become more rampant and comparatively easier to carry out than ever before.

In theology, the idea of God as an all-seeing being has been immanent. The idea of morality springs from this analogy—an omniscient being keeping a watch on all our actions, presiding over righteousness and vice. As popularised by Foucault, the notion of surveillance is rooted in morality and moralising, and from this relation, it is deduced that the strong surveils the weak and sustains a structure of power by 'organising' knowledge.[2] Throughout history, all sorts of 'stronger' bodies have surveilled, moralised and, in turn, 'disciplined' the weaker lot. Foucault writes about the institutionalising of panoptic practices to regulate lives and maintain order, and one such power of institutions is what he calls 'bio-power':

> For Foucault there can be no panopticon without such discipline, its productivity is social, expansive and governmental, not external, contingent or subsequent. Such a 'disciplinary society' thus raises important questions about the future: the subtle power/discipline of a generalized panopticism, an internalized power that seeks to pre-plan—to economize the past, present and future. (Elmer 2012)

Power is intrinsic to an authoritarian cause. By regulating power, authoritarian societies bend laws, manipulating 'subjects' to their will. The colonies had been under surveillance for hundreds of years, and their past experiences reflect the severe conditions that are faced by the populations that are under digital surveillance in contemporary times (Ogasawara 2019). Ogasawara states that nation-building and colonialism went hand in hand in developing modern surveillance, wherein the technologies of surveillance were first deployed in colonised nations to test their effects on the populations.

> The systematic practice of surveillance left irreversible effects in colonies: stealing agency from individuals and depriving groups of access to life opportunities. Those effects are exactly the aim

> of colonial management and contributed immensely to today's foundation of global political economy. (Ogasawara 2019)

Ogasawara cites the invention of the fingerprinting machine in British India and bodily ID techniques[3] used on runaway slaves in the United States, the purpose of which were not only to mark out defaulters but also to segregate them as 'racial others' (ibid.). This then was carried over to the centre of power, that is, to the native countries of the colonisers in the West, which is referred to as having a 'boomerang effect'. As Ogasawara explains, 'Colonies have been the cradle of surveillance techniques, and it may be valid to understand this boomerang as a kind of moral warning for people in technologically advanced countries' (ibid.).

In the colonies especially, a hybrid form of SF novels emerged, which was set to capture the essence of surveillance and the emergent structures of power underlying these societies. Suparno Banerjee talks about the estranging capabilities and imaginative potential of SF novels that have the potential to subvert grand narratives and totalising ideas of realist fiction. He refers to Bhabha's concept of mimicry where the colonial subject mimics the coloniser while never conforming to the actual and original ideals, hence 'resisting ideological subjectification':

> The use of scientific and technological metaphors in science fiction identifies it as a primarily western mode of literature. However, Patricia Kerslake in *Science Fiction and Empire* argues that science fiction and colonialism are irrevocably connected. For her science fiction can be greatly productive as a tool exploring 'notion of power formed within the construct of empire, especially when interrogated by the general theories of postcoloniality'. (Banerjee 2010)

Keeping this argument in mind, we must consider the fact that after India's independence, the switchboard of 'control' shifted from one source to another, that is, from the colonisers to native governing bodies and oligarchs that monitor, control and exert power over the lives of the people. The dystopian novels attempt to capture the source of the current switchboard of control, as new forms of subjugation and imperialism rise out of older models into newer avatars of surveillance. Even though in a complicated showdown for power, there are forms of resistance that emerge, interchanging the subjects of surveillance. What is also seen is the fact that effective surveillance and authoritarianism produce counter-resistance that offer little or no hope in these dystopian circumstances.

As models for making sense of surveillance, the two novels *Leila* and *Chosen Spirits* capture two different aspects of the phenomenon.

One indicates panoptic vision as imagined by Bentham and Foucault (in buildings, institutions and spaces); the other captures surveillance, digitalisation and capitalism, foregrounding the dystopian experience of living under constant monitoring and control. *Leila* imagines Indian society as authoritarian and hegemonic under the banner of homogenisation disguised as 'purity'. *Chosen Spirits* embodies the tropes of surveillance capitalism where desires are monitored and manufactured. These readings offer the views of individuals trapped and subjugated in surveillance societies where freedom is curbed and resistance minimal.

READING LEILA *IN THE LIGHT OF SURVEILLANCE AND SUBJUGATED LIVELIHOOD*

In *Leila*, the readers are introduced to a morbid, uncomfortable portrait of India a few years into the future. The city in *Leila* is precariously close to an environmental apocalypse with waste being strewn all around, climate crisis looming, resources running short and inhuman living conditions. It has been through a radical transformation from being a habitable and tolerable city to its inverse, transforming not only the space and the architecture of the city but also its customs, dispositions and the inhabitant's perceptions. The city, named Aryavarta in the adapted Netflix series based on the novel, has a utopian vision of embracing total 'purity' but there is an atmosphere of distrust, bigotry, hostility, misogyny and patriarchy. The 'motto' that every individual must utter to validate themselves as faithful residents is 'purity for all'. There is a huge disparity between residents of the city and only a handful enjoy the luxury of purity.

Leila revolves around the regimentation of a city into various sectors, barricaded by high walls and human enforcers. The world of *Leila* is characteristic of the 'worst of all possible circumstances': environmental catastrophe, caste- and gender-based disparity, extreme economic inequality and surveillance. The ideologies in the city echo an authoritarian, homogenising system that is bent on subjugating minorities as undesirable beings meant to be disciplined and kept outside the premises amidst heat, stench and waste.

Before the arrival of the colonisers, India was like a kingdom where several princely states existed peacefully. Then the British came and transformed the territory, redrawing stringent boundaries and producing the image of the vast subcontinent. In a bid to disrupt pluralism and multiculturalism, the council in *Leila* 'regresses' to a model of the past by appropriating and advocating caste-based hierarchy and seeking to control 'contamination' by building walls and re-educating the impure ones. A dome is being constructed in the centre of the city to segregate the rich and the poor and clear the air of impurities. The council also exerts control through an old model of surveillance: using people as enforces of discipline and punishment, reminiscent of the 'nazardaars' and 'guptachars' who were employed by those in power to keep watch over the perpetrators and conspirators and gather their information.

Like many other people in the novel, Shalini, a middle-aged woman in search of her daughter, Leila, is put through subjection under this authoritarian regime. Her only 'crime' was to marry outside her religion. According to the law, this is sedition; so she is put in labour camps to discipline and purify her. The council borrows and implements a caste-based system of governance where segregation and division based on purity and impurity are enforced, which is symptomatic of the practice of 'untouchability' that was widespread in India and criminalised only after 1950. Life in the Towers reflects a panoptical model where widows are supposed to abide by a livelihood of docility, without much scope for starting anew. As Warden Khanna comes to know that Shalini has applied for a transfer to a section called Domestic Settlement, all the women are put under constant surveillance: 'It's still a surprise Warden Khanna knows so much about my life. How does he keep track of every woman in the building?' (Akbar 2017). The council is also cagey about change, which is obvious from the following conversation that reveals the project of mass homogenisation coupled with surveillance: '"Change?" Khanna turned to look at me .... "You know the Council doesn't like that"' (ibid.).

'We are in an enormous maze,' says Shalini, speaking of the high walls that bifurcate and separate communities across the city, worsening the conditions of those who live outside the walled sectors as these areas are used for dumping tons of trash (ibid.). Shalini remarks: 'I've never been on a flyroad. They're built and paid for by the high sectors, we can't use them' (ibid.). Living in the 'Towers', Shalini feels that she had been kept out of the city as she was a 'polluter', a belief that slowly begins to seep into the collective conscience. As observed by Galič, 'Docile individuals are no longer governed as actors with whom they communicate, but as units of information that can be moulded. Surveillance is a key concept here because this moulding and re-shaping is a result of the visibility of individuals' "competencies" through exams and record-keeping of their progress' (Galič et al. 2016). The oppressed begins to feel like a 'polluter', one who is undesirable by others and the state, and one who needs to be purified in order to belong to society. To maintain control, the regime prescribes pills that pacify and numb the inmates, so that their reasoning weakens, a move similar to Anthony Burgess' dystopian novel, *The Clockwork Orange* (1962). In a docile, non-repulsive state, one begins to accept one's oppression as normal. 'The Council was determined to instil discipline. The pills helped' (Akbar 2017).

In bringing back an older module, the council appropriates outdated value systems and implements them in a world that has moved much ahead in time. This produces a severe disjoint between what is (a dehumanising regime) and what ought to be (a utopia, as claimed by the motto 'purity for all'). The neglected streets, the unbearable stench and the constant need to evade and escape other environmental hazards point to the fact that there have been systemic flaws in the way the 'Council' handles its operations. In the case of technology too, the society seems to have pushed new frontiers while ideologically, the masses have regressed into an older time, caught under a spell of religio-mythologic whim.

Similar to what Pramod Nayar suggests in the creation of 'vulnerable citizens', the citizens in *Leila* who are convinced to vouch for security from the 'impure'—be it people from other castes, religions or defaulters—invite a 'culture of surveillance'. This sets up an agreement towards the formation of 'structures, perimeters and databases of surveillances', endorsing dehumanising gated communities and the urgent need for walling and bordering (Nayar 2015). Throughout the novel, one encounters voices that echo a sound disregard for the past and an illusory vision of their ideal present: 'People fought each other, burned each other. Not just women. Over who will get government money. Who will get jobs. Fought over everything. We were like animals. With the walls we have order. We will finally have peace' (Akbar 2017). With repeaters who can be tipped off and corrupt officials who are constantly engaged in exploiting the vulnerable, the motto 'Purity for All' at once seems crudely ironic.

CHOSEN SPIRITS, *SURVEILLANCE SOCIETY AND HYPER-DIGITALISATION*

Some years ago, there were signs in commercial and public places that read: 'You are under CCTV surveillance.' The same signs also stated, rather nonchalantly, 'Smile! You are on camera!' Now, these signs have started to disappear, or rather, we ignore their presence involuntarily since they are as common as streetlights or clouds in the sky. We are living at a time when surveillance is mandatory and existential. It is a phenomenon that is taken for granted, whether it is in a school, a street, a restaurant, a clinic or even at someone's home, there are cameras all around us, including on what is termed as an 'extended organ' of ourselves and essential to our contemporality—the smartphone.

Smartphones and smartwatches are live and high-functioning surveillance tools that we carry around like inseparable organs and hence, we are constantly with agents of surveillance. In Samit Basu's novel, we encounter these 'inseparable' tools that stretch digitalisation to such an extent that the lines between the real and the virtual seem to become incomprehensible. In the opening line itself, the culture of surveillance is weaved into the narrative to alarm the reader for what is to be expected—the 'obviousness of surveillance'. 'Sometimes, Joey feels like her whole life is a montage of randomly selected, algorithm-controlled surveillance-cam clips, mostly of her looking at screens or sitting glazed-eyed at meetings' (Basu 2020). In the proximity of technology, the feeling of being watched constantly by something (a machine) or someone is neither rare nor far-fetched. But unlike one pasting a tape over the camera or running spyware detection apps, Joey's thinking about life being a montage of assorted surveillance clips points to the fact that in their hyper-digital world, tracking and monitoring are unavoidable and 'unblockable'.

It is a world of 'liquid surveillance' where posting against the oligarchs result in sacking; a world where one must be too careful about one's private lives and affairs, otherwise they risk being exposed and streamed across networks: 'It's your own house spying on you now. The walls really have ears. You could avoid nosy neighbours, or be wary around potential access-caste climbers' (ibid.).

> Notions of surveillance have traditionally been concerned with the watchful gaze of government actors like police and prison officials rather than companies and individuals. But in a postmodern age of 'liquid surveillance', the two phenomena are deeply intertwined. Government and nongovernment surveillance support each other in a complex manner that is often impossible to disentangle. (Richards 2013)

Surveillance in *Chosen Spirits* is networked, dispersed and fluid. It spreads over and spills across systems, gadgets and cyber-networks, in the body and in invisible spaces, in the ground and in the air. Seemingly innocent 'biosurveillance' is carried out by AI assistants termed as 'Narad' and 'smartatt', which regularly monitor Joey's psychological balances and emotional spikes (trying to calm her senses using cute videos or cheerful songs). The surveillance system is often controlled and sometimes unconscious, uncontrolled and algorithmic, while at other times, the technologies are even customised to be 'casteist'.

Neil M. Richards in 'The Dangers of Surveillance' summarises four aspects from David Lyon's definition of surveillance:

> First it is *focused* on learning information about individuals. Second, surveillance is systematic, it is intentional rather than random or arbitrary. Third, surveillance is routine—a part of the ordinary administrative apparatus that characterizes modern societies. Fourth, surveillance can have a wide variety of purposes—rarely totalitarian domination, but more typically subtler forms of influence or control. (Richards 2013)

The world of *Chosen Spirits* complies with the above-mentioned observations where there is deep learning, systematised and routinised forms of surveillance. Although it challenges the fourth observation, the totalitarian oligarchy uses surveillance as a means to assert coercion and repression, while the 'subtlety' has transformed into the 'obvious':

> Romola's fascinated by the idea that anything she says or types is travelling around the world, going to places she'll never manage to physically visit, but can't process the idea that it isn't just the government snooping any more, but a peak-traffic cluster of corporations, other governments, religious bodies, cults, gangs, terrorists, hackers, sometimes other algorithms, watching you, measuring you, learning you, marking you down for spam or death. (Basu 2020)

As she ponders if people she sees are herded off to detention centres, Joey is not allowed to show much concern, else it 'will be noted in the Welfare Association's ledgers, marking her out as a potential troublemaker' (ibid.). Raising voices of dissent, participating in resistance, influencing people to rise against oppression or even looking them up might lead to trouble as there can be potential 'ID traps'. The totalising surveillance narrows down on all kinds of potential threats with the slightest hint of insubordination. It is a society where violence and violations have found new voices and new means at the dawn of accelerated capitalism: 'a gang of fifteen-year-old *AR gamers* being *tricked into* beating up elderly Malayali writers for digital credits' and 'real estate tycoon openly advertising for partners for an *organ-farm business*, claiming it could give backward Indians a chance to contribute value to the world' (ibid.).

The surveillance system that operates in these imagined spaces can be understood through the concept of 'surveillant assemblages', which can hence be seen as 'recording machines' since their task is to capture flows and convert them into reproducible events. Haggerty and Ericson used this concept because they identified contemporary surveillance to be emergent, unstable and lacking discernible boundaries or accountable governmental departments' (Galič et al. 2016). As the society obsesses over hyper-vlogging and 'Flowstars', whose 'reality' is controlled and determined by experts such as Joey, there is an indication of multifaceted surveillance capitalism. To monitor consumption patterns, surveillance is 'directed towards the human body for the purpose of canalising access to places and information and allowing the production of consumer profiles through the ex-post facto reconstruction of people's behaviour, habits and actions. Rather than focusing directly on individual bodies, surveillance is focused on their 'data doubles'(ibid.). Totalising surveillance systems enable the functioning of 'dark' trade openly, facilitating organ harvesting, tracking dissenters and customising 'virtual reality' as a product to be marketed and consumed. Coupling the conception of 'synopticon' (many watching the few) with surveillance capitalism, marketing of 'flows' enables the control of 'desire'. While the youth is distracted by the lives and times of 'Flowstars', sinister practices run underneath the pomp and grandeur. The surveillance marketplace advocates 'saleability' of the desirable lifestyle and daily activities of 'Flowstars', which mirrors the contemporary obsession with social media influencers. The targeted ads and manufactured 'trends' direct the social media society towards desiring and consuming the 'spectacle'[4]. Data profiles generated out of surveillance, through tracking and feeding consumer habits into databases, facilitate market-based studies and enable the possibility of 'brandwashing' through continuous, targeted advertisements.[5]

In the novel, a technologically advanced Indian society fails to resolve its caste-based issues, as it is revealed that Joey does a caste-appropriate job being a reality manager in 'an age where data and attention are real estate' (Basu 2020). Through a conversation with Rohit, Rudra is aware that walls and borders exist in Delhi to protect some and put others at a disadvantage. Similar to *Leila*, the privileged 'first city' people are immune to surveillance since they are untrackable, being on the 'global power map' or on islands where satellites aren't allowed to prowl.

CONCLUSION: WHERE THERE IS POWER, THERE IS RESISTANCE

'Foucault's "microphysics of power" champions heterogeneity, discontinuity, reversibility and specificity as the pathway towards resistance against the totalization of power, sexuality and knowledge' (Ki 1997). Being a non-conformist since the beginning, Shalini herself becomes an agent of surveillance, one who snoops in, disrupts, tracks and gathers information about the domineering system. Determined to find her daughter, her iron will remains unchallenged till the very end of the novel. In the process, she uncovers dark, unsettling truths, exposes loopholes and hierarchies and learns about her own misappropriate treatment of the underprivileged.

In *Chosen Spirits*, there is a mention of monkeys being trained to disrupt surveillance equipment and hawks that destroy drones mid-air, which impart glimpses of physical and ideological resistances. Resistance is offered by characters such as Desibryde and E-Klav through art while Zaria and Rudra temporarily shed their conscious selves to dwell deep into the virtual in their fight for a just society. Joey too, determined and inspired by her discoveries at the Cyber Bazaar, feels that they have a chance at disrupting the system: 'I have people hacking into algorithms that politicians use to control opinions, and advertisers to control tastes' (Basu 2020).

Since their inception, dystopian novels have continued to act as 'warning manuals', offering an examination of authoritarian societies. The close inspections of societies in *Leila* and *Chosen Spirits* reveal underlying power structures and the dehumanising conditions that prevail through the tactical deployment of surveillance systems. Likewise, the novels also manifest hope for societies by exhibiting acts of resistance that shimmer through bleak circumstances, subverting hegemonic models of power.

NOTES

1 Edward Snowden was a former contractor for the CIA. He leaked sensitive information on surveillance carried out by the agency on the public. See 'Edward Snowden: Leaks That Exposed US Spy Programme,' 2014. *BBC*. https://www.bbc.com/news/world-us-canada-23123964

2 See an explanation of Michel Foucault's concepts in Christopher Pollard. 2019. 'Explainer: The Ideas of Foucault.' *The Conversation*. https://theconversation.com/explainer-the-ideas-of-foucault-99758

3 See the section 'Index and Identity' in Christian Parenti, 2003. *The Soft Cage*. New York: Basic Books.

4 See Guy Debord's conception of the 'spectacle' in Guy Debord. 1992. *Society of the Spectacle*. London, England: Rebel Press.

5 See 'Neuromarketing' in S. Nemorin. 2019. *Biosurveillance in New Media Marketing: World, Discourse, Representation*. Palgrave Macmillan, 170–171.

WORKS CITED

Akbar, Prayaag. 2017. *Leila: A Novel*. India: Simon & Schuster.

Banerjee, Suparno. 2010. 'Other Tomorrows: Postcoloniality, Science Fiction and India.' PhD Diss., *Louisiana State University*. https://digitalcommons.lsu.edu/gradschool_dissertations/3181

Basu, Samit. 2020. *Chosen Spirits*. India: Simon & Schuster.

Elmer, Greg. 2012. 'Panopticon—Discipline—Control.' In *Routledge Handbook of Surveillance Studies*, edited by David Lyon, Kevin D. Haggerty and Kirstie Ball. Oxon and New York: Routledge Taylor & Francis Group.

Galič, Maša, et al. 2016. 'Bentham, Deleuze and Beyond: An Overview of Surveillance Theories from the Panopticon to Participation.' *Philosophy & Technology*, 30(1): 9–37. doi: 10.1007/s13347-016-0219-1.

KI, Wing Chi. 1997. 'Power and Resistance in Dystopian Literature: A Foucauldian Reading of Three Novels.' PhD Diss., The Chinese University of Hong Kong.

Macnish, Kevin. 'Surveillance Ethics.' *Internet Encyclopedia of Philosophy*. iep.utm.edu/surv-eth/

Nayar, Pramod K. 2015. *Citizenship and Identity in the Age of Surveillance*. Cambridge: Cambridge University Press.

Ogasawara, Midori. 2019. 'Mainstreaming Colonial Experiences in Surveillance Studies.' *Surveillance & Society*, 17(5): 726–729. doi: 10.24908/ss.v17i5.13521.

Richards, Neil M. 2013. 'The Dangers of Surveillance.' *Harvard Law Review*, 126(7): 1934–1965. www.jstor.org/stable/23415062 (accessed 17 March 2021).

ABOUT THE EDITORS

Shweta Khilnani is an assistant professor of English at SGTB Khalsa College, University of Delhi. Her PhD dissertation is on the nexus between the literary, the affective and the political with respect to digital narratives. She is interested in the study of popular and visual cultures. Among her publications are a co-edited anthology titled *Imagining Worlds, Mapping Possibilities: Select Science Fiction Stories* (2020) and *Laughing Matters: Stand-up Comedy and Enjoyment in Late Capitalism* (2020), besides several academic papers and book chapters.

Ritwick Bhattacharjee is an assistant professor of English at SGTB Khalsa College, University of Delhi. His research interests include fantasy, philosophy, phenomenology, horror fiction, science fiction, Indian English novels and disability. He did his MPhil from the University of Delhi, where he wrote a thesis on the fantastic phenomenology of Stephen King's *The Dark Tower* (series). He is the author of *Humanity's Strings: Being, Pessimism, and Fantasy.* He is also a co-editor of *What Makes it Pop? An Introduction to Studies in Popular Fictions* (with Srinjoyee Dutta), *Horror Fiction in the Global South: Cultures, Narratives, and Representation* (with Saikat Ghosh), and two volumes of *Reclaiming the Disabled Subject: Representing Disability in Short Fiction* (with Someshwar Sati and G.J.V. Prasad). He has been awarded the Meenakshi Mukherjee Memorial Prize for his essay titled 'Politics of Translation: Disability, Language and the In-between' published in the book *Disability in Translation: The Indian Experience.* Also, he is the treasurer of the Indian Disability Studies Collective.

ABOUT THE CONTRIBUTORS

Anik Sarkar is an assistant professor at Salesian College, Siliguri. His forthcoming books are *The Films of Apichatpong Weerasethakul* (Liverpool University Press) and *Tumbbad* ('Devil's Advocates,' Liverpool University Press). He has contributed chapters to books such as *Environmental Postcolonialism*, edited by Shubhanku Kochar and M. Anjum Khan (Lexington Books); *The Portrait of an Artist as a Pathographer: On Writing Illnesses and Illnesses in Writing*, edited by Jayjit Sarkar and Jagannath Basu (Vernon Press), et cetera. He has also written articles for *Live Wire*, *Café Dissensus* and *We The World Magazine*. He writes fiction, and his work *The Man Who Sold Diseases* was published by Juggernaut Books in 2018.

Antara Chatterjee works as an assistant professor of English at the Department of Humanities and Social Sciences, Indian Institute of Science Education and Research (IISER), Bhopal. She studied English literature at Jadavpur University, Kolkata, and did her PhD from the University of Leeds, UK. Her research and teaching interests include Indian writing in English, South Asian diasporic literatures, Partition studies, trauma, violence and cultural memory, environmental and medical humanities, et cetera. She has received research funding from University Grants Commission, New Delhi; Indian Institute of Advanced Study, Shimla; The Charles Wallace India Trust, UK; Indian Council of Historical Research, New Delhi and Tata Trusts, Mumbai. She has peer-reviewed publications in the journals *South Asian Review* and *Humanities* as well as in an edited collection *The South Asian Short Story* published by Palgrave Macmillan. She is currently co-editing a volume of chapters titled *Pandemics and Epidemics in Cultural Representation*, to be published by Springer.

Anu Susan Abraham is a doctoral student at the Department of Humanities and Social Sciences, Indian Institute of Science Education and Research (IISER), Bhopal. Her doctoral research is on the cultural representation of refugees in South Asia in literary and cinematic narratives. Her research interests include Partition, environmental humanities, trauma and memory, et cetera.

Devapriya Sanyal holds degrees in English literature and cinema from Lady Brabourne College, Kolkata, and Jawaharlal Nehru University

(JNU), New Delhi. Her PhD research was on Satyajit Ray. Her monograph on Ray, titled *Gendered Modernity and Indian Cinema: The Women in Satyajit Ray's Films*, is being published by Routledge, UK. Devapriya is the author of *From Text to Screen: Issues and Images in Schindler's List* (2011) and *Through the Eyes of a Cinematographer: A Biography of Soumendu Roy* (2017).

Indrani Das Gupta is an assistant professor in the Department of English, Maharaja Agrasen College, University of Delhi. She is currently pursuing her PhD in modern Indian science fiction from the Department of English, Jamia Millia Islamia, New Delhi. Her articles have been published by Routledge (New York and London), Macmillan (India), *Dialog* (University of Punjab), *Agathos: An International Review of the Humanities and Social Sciences* (FIAL-CAT Association, Romania) and others. She is also the non-fiction editor of *Mithila Review: A Speculative Arts and Culture Magazine.*

Jaya Yadav is a PhD scholar at the University of Delhi, working on contemporary South Asian literature. Her MPhil thesis is on Amitav Ghosh's *The Calcutta Chromosome* and *Ibis Trilogy*. She has done her bachelor's from Lady Shri Ram College for Women, New Delhi, and her master's and MPhil from the University of Delhi. She is deeply interested in the interdisciplinary aspect of literature and its role in questions of identity, history and politics. Her work also focuses on issues of class, race and gender, especially in conflict zones. She is currently an assistant professor in the Department of English at Janki Devi Memorial College, New Delhi, and also works as a senior editor at The Strife Blog & Journal, Department of War Studies, King's College, London.

Jigyasa H. Sondhi is currently an assistant professor at Deshbandhu College, University of Delhi. She has a doctoral degree in literature and cinema studies from Jamia Millia Islamia, New Delhi, and has researched on ecofeminist Hollywood films. Prior to enrolling for a PhD, she worked on renditions of Meerabai's bhajans in Hindi cinema for an MPhil programme at the University of Delhi. She has also studied movies at Film and Television Institute of India, Pune.

Rajarshi Roy is at present enrolled as a PhD scholar in the English department, Jadavpur University. His MPhil dissertation was on the subject of the uncanny iconographies in Indian SF literature. He was also earlier involved as an academic translator in a UGC-funded project under RUSA 2.0 scheme to translate Prasanta Kumar Paul's archival biography of Rabindranath Tagore from Bangla to English.

Saikat Ghosh is an assistant professor of English at Sri Guru Tegh Bahadur Khalsa College, University of Delhi. He has done his post graduation and MPhil from Jawaharlal Nehru University. He is the co-editor of *Horror Fiction in the Global South: Cultures, Narratives, and Representations* (with Ritwick Bhattacharjee).

Saloni Sharma teaches English literatures at Kirori Mal College, University of Delhi. Her research and previous publications are on the intersection of gender and popular fiction.

Sanam Khanna teaches English literature at Kamala Nehru College, University of Delhi. She was hooked to SF from the day she read her first SF story by Asimov. Since then, she has retained her interest in SF in all its manifestations. Her other areas of interest are YA fiction, children's literature, culture and media studies, literary theory and drama and performance studies. She has written and published in these fields. She has also co-edited a reader of selected, influential works in Indian literature from ancient times to the present, titled *Indian Literature: An Introduction* (2005).

Sami Ahmad Khan is a writer, academic and documentary producer. He writes, researches, edits and teaches science fiction. Sami is the recipient of a Fulbright grant to the University of Iowa, USA, and holds a PhD in Science Fiction from Jawaharlal Nehru University (JNU), New Delhi. His future-war thriller *Red Jihad* won two awards, and his second novel, *Aliens in Delhi*, garnered rave reviews. Sami's creative writings and critical essays have appeared in leading journals, anthologies and magazines. His overview of Indian SF has been translated into Czech, and his fiction has been the subject of formal academic research. His latest book is *Star Warriors of the Modern Raj: Materiality, Mythology and Technology of Indian Science Fiction* (2021). Sami has taught at IIT Delhi, JNU and GGSIP University and is presently a Marie Skłodowska-Curie Actions Fellow at the University of Oslo, Norway.

Sayan Parial received his master's degree in English from University of Gour Banga, Malda, West Bengal. His areas of research interest are science fiction, Partition studies, posthuman studies and science and technology studies. His articles have been published in peer-reviewed journals such as *LitInfinite Journal*, *Literary Oracle*, *PostScriptum: An Interdisciplinary Journal of Literary Studies*, et cetera. He was invited to present his paper 'Transforming Trauma, Virtually: Identity, Self-Care and Social Connection during Covid-19 Pandemic' at the Student Symposium on the Danger and Necessity of Contact: The

Youths Respond to Covid-19, organised by the Department of English, Jahangirnagar University, Dhaka, Bangladesh, in 2020.

Shikha Vats is a doctoral research scholar at the Department of Humanities and Social Science, Indian Institute of Technology, Delhi. Her research interests include South Asian utopian/dystopian fiction, climate fiction and postcolonial spatial studies. She has also designed e-content titled 'Work as Text: Myths in a Self-Contained World' as part of the course on Literary Criticism and Theory for e-PG Pathshala, MHRD-UGC.

Shraddha A. Singh is an associate professor at the Department of English, Zakir Husain Delhi College (M), University of Delhi, and works on contemporary literature, genre fiction and literary theory. In 2008, she visited Canada on the Commonwealth Fellowship under the Graduate Student Exchange Programme hosted by Concordia University, Montreal, to work on her MPhil thesis. She has several publications and has presented papers at national and international seminars and conferences, most recently at the international conferences organised by Aarhus University, Denmark (2020) and Cappadocia University, Turkey (2021). She is a published bilingual poet and has read her poetry at the Sahitya Akademi (Indian Academy of Letters).

Srinjoyee Dutta is a doctoral scholar at the Centre for English Studies, Jawaharlal Nehru University and is currently working as Assistant Professor of English at Indraprastha College for Women, University of Delhi. Her areas of interest include Gender and Queer Theory, Poststructuralist and Postmodernist Philosophy, Translation Studies, and Popular Fiction. She has been the winner of the prestigious C.D. Narasimhaiah Memorial prize, awarded by the Indian Association for Commonwealth Literature and Language Studies for the best paper in a conference, for two consecutive years. She is the co-editor of *What makes It Pop? An Introduction to Studies in Popular Fiction*. She is also an avid translator and translates from Hindi to English.

Subhadeep Ray is presently an associate professor of English at Bidhan Chandra College, Kazi Nazrul University, Asansol, West Bengal. He was the principal investigator of a research project on the popular science writing of Jagadish Chandra Bose and Sukumar Ray sponsored by University Grants Commission, New Delhi. Ray is the author of *Bengal Renaissance and Scientific Temper* (2019). He has contributed multiple chapters such as 'Modernism's Footprints: World, Text and Ideology in Joseph Conrad and Manik Bandyopadhyay' in *Some Intertextual*

Chords of Joseph Conrad's Literary Art (2019), edited by Wieslaw Krajka and published by Maria Curie-Sklodowska University Press (Lublin) and Columbia University Press (New York). He is also the contributor of the essay titled 'Fighting against Multiple Bodies! Translating "Nari o Nagini" and "Tamosha" by Tarashankar Bandyopadhyay and "Bonjhi Gunjomala" by Jagadish Gupta' to *Disability in Translation: The Indian Experience*, edited by Someswar Sati and G.J.V. Prasad and published by Routledge (London and New York), 2020.

Tanushree Ghosh is currently working as a state-aided college teacher in the Department of English at Kabikankan Mukundaram Mahavidyalaya, West Bengal. She completed her MPhil in English literature from the University of Calcutta, Kolkata. Her dissertation focuses on the genre of postcolonial science fiction. Her areas of interest include speculative fiction, posthumanism, graphic narratives and postcolonial literatures.

INDEX